THE

RELIGIOUS INSTRUCTION

OF THE

NEGROES.

IN THE UNITED STATES

BY CHARLES C. JONES

NEGRO UNIVERSITIES PRESS
NEW YORK

Originally published in 1842
by Thomas Purse, Savannah

Reprinted 1969 by
Negro Universities Press
A DIVISION OF GREENWOOD PUBLISHING CORP.
NEW YORK

SBN 8371-1645-7

PRINTED IN UNITED STATES OF AMERICA

PREFACE.

THE preparation of the following pages has been undertaken at the suggestion of friends, seconded by the convictions of my own mind, that a small volume on the *Religious Instruction of the Negroes in the United States* would not be an unacceptable offering to the Public, and especially the Christian Public, at the present time. Whatever I have before prepared or published on the subject has been freely used, whenever it has suited my purpose, in the present composition.

I have endeavored to confine myself to the Religious Instruction of the Negroes, and have touched upon other subjects only when it has been necessary for the illustration or support of the one before me.

I commend the Book to the candid consideration of those who read it. My design has been to speak the truth plainly and in love, and to do good. May the blessing of Almighty God attend the effort.

CHARLES COLCOCK JONES.

Riceboro, Liberty County, Ga.,
July 4th, 1842.

CONTENTS

PART I.

HISTORICAL SKETCH OF THE RELIGIOUS INSTRUCTION OF THE NEGROES FROM THEIR FIRST INTRODUCTION INTO THE COUNTRY IN 1620 TO THE YEAR 1842: DIVIDED INTO THREE PERIODS.

PART II.

THE MORAL AND RELIGIOUS CONDITION OF THE NEGROES

PART III.

OBLIGATIONS OF THE CHURCH OF CHRIST TO AT-
TEMPT THE IMPROVEMENT OF THE MORAL AND
RELIGIOUS CONDITION OF THE NEGROES IN THE
UNITED STATES, BY AFFORDING THEM THE GOSPEL.

PART IV.

MEANS AND PLANS FOR PROMOTING AND SECURING THE RELIGIOUS INSTRUCTION OF THE NEGROES IN THE UNITED STATES.

PART I.

Historical Sketch of the Religious Instruction of the Negroes from their first introduction into the Country in 1620 to the year 1842.

CHAPTER I.

THE FIRST PERIOD — From their first Introduction, in 1620, to the first Census, in 1790: a period of 170 years.

SUCH is the scarcity of materials, and the difficulty of arriving at the scattered sources of information, that I have called the following Historical Notice of the Religious Instruction of the Negroes in the United States, "A SKETCH." It deserves no better name, although, perhaps, it may embody the principal facts on the subject.

FOR the sake of perspicuity, the SKETCH is divided into PERIODS OF TIME — the *First Period,* extending from the Introduction of the Negroes into the Country, in 1620, to the first Census, in 1790; a period of 170 years: the *Second Period,* from 1790 to 1820; a period of 30 years: and the *Third Period,* from 1820 to 1842; a period of 22 years.

1. *Account of the Introduction of Negroes into the the Colonies under the Government of Great Britain.*

It was in the year 1501 that Isabella of Spain granted permission for the introduction of Negro slaves into Hispaniola; but such only as had been born in Spain, or in slavery among Christians; and in the following year a few had been sent into the New World.

In 1508 the Spaniards opened a direct trade in slaves, and imported Negroes into Hispaniola from the Portugese settlements on the Coast of Guinea. Ferdinand V., by royal ordinance, enjoined a direct traffic in slaves between Guinea and Hispaniola, in 1511, and Charles V., in 1512–13.

In 1517 Charles V. granted a patent to one of his Flemish favorites, containing an exclusive right of importing slaves, four thousand annually, into Hispaniola, Cuba, Jamaica, and Puerto Rico. This favorite sold his patent to some Genoese merchants for 25,000 ducats, and they were the first who brought into regular form that commerce for slaves between Africa and America, which has since been carried on under such revolting circumstances and to such an amazing extent.

Forty-five years after, in 1562–3, the English entered the trade under Sir John Hawkins and carried Negroes from Africa to Hispaniola, and in 1567 Queen Elizabeth protected and shared the traffic. Thus the Mother Country was engaged in the traffic *forty-five years* before the first permanent settlement was made in her American Colonies, which was at Jamestown, Virginia in 1607.

The Dutch, in common with other maritime nations of Europe, engaged in the trade, and a man-of-war of that nation, from the Coast of Guinea, in August, 1620, (four months before the Plymouth Colony arrived in America,) landed *twenty Negroes* for sale, in the Colony of Virginia, on James river, which determines the epoch of their introduction into the Colonies. From this period they were gradually, and at different times, introduced into all the Colonies from Massachusetts to Georgia; and for the most part, *contrary to the wishes of the Colonists.*

The first cargo of Negro slaves was brought into *Boston* in 1645, and though their introduction was denounced and the Negroes ordered to be "returned at public charge;" yet it was afterwards permitted, and people engaged in the trade.

In *Maryland* acts were passed encouraging the importation of Negroes, in 1671; and in this same year they were first introduced into South Carolina. They were *legally* admitted into *Georgia* in 1747. The precise year of their admission into the remaining eight of the old thirteen Colonies is not accurately known.

2. *Estimated Negro Population of the Colonies at the Declaration of Independence; and Census of* 1790.

I have no references at hand by which to determine the number of Negroes in each of the Colonies, nor the aggregate in all, *before* the Declaration of Independence, as no general census was ever taken of the Colonies while they continued such. But there are statements of the number in most of the Colonies, given in different years, which I shall proceed to mention.

Virginia was settled in 1607, and in 1671 contained 2,000 Negroes; in 1763, 100,000.

Massachusetts was settled in 1620, and in 1763 contained 4,500.

Rhode Island was settled in 1636. In 1680 had imported but a few Negroes, in 1730 contained 1,648, and in 1748, 4,373.

Connecticut was settled in 1635. In 1680 had 30 Negroes, and in 1774, 6,464.

New Hampshire was settled from Massachusetts and became a separate Colony in 1741, and in 1775 contained 659 Negroes.

New York was settled by the Dutch in 1613. In 1756 contained 13,542.

New Jersey was settled 1627. In 1738 contained 3,981 Negroes and slaves, and in 1745, 4,606.

Maryland was granted to Lord Baltimore in 1632. In 1755 contained 42,764 Negroes, and for a time, 2,000 were imported annually. Mr. Burke says, in 1757 the number was upwards of 60,000.

North Carolina was permanently settled in 1650, and became distinct from Virginia in 1727. In 1701 it had 5,000 inhabitants, *besides* Negroes and Indians, and in 1702, 6,000.

South Carolina was granted to Lord Clarendon in 1662. In 1723 contained 18,000 Negroes; in 1724, 439 were imported; in 1730 contained 28,000; in 1731 1,500 were imported. In 1765 contained 90,000; in 1773 over 6,000 were imported. This Colony lost 25,000 Negroes in the Revolutionary war.

Georgia was settled in 1732–3. Slavery was legalized in 1747, and in 1772 contained 14,000 Negroes.

The probable number of Negroes in the Colonies at the Declaration of Independence in 1776, may be ascertained in the following manner. Take the known population in the different Colonies nearest the year 1776; compare that with the census of 1790; take into consideration the rate of increase from nature and from importation, and also the decrease; and then give the supposed population in round numbers.

Massachusetts. — *Last return* in 1763 to 1776, 13

years, the population decreasing; supposed
population in 1776. _____   3,500

Rhode Island.—1748 to 1776, 28 years,
stationary._____   4,373

Connecticut.—1774 to 1776, 2 years, decreasing. _____   6,000

New Hampshire.—1775 to 1776, 1 year,
stationary._____   659

New York.—1756 to 1776, 20 years in-
creasing._____   15,000

New Jersey.—1745 to 1776, 31 years in-
creasing._____   7,600

Delaware.—Estimated in 1776 compared
with 1790._____   9,000

Pennsylvania.—Estimated in 1775 compared with 1790, the act of Abolition in 1780
taken into the account._____   10,000

In 1757, Mr. Burke says, "not the fortieth
part of the inhabitants were Negroes."

Maryland.—1755 to 1776, 21 years, in-
creasing._____   80,000

Virginia—1763 to 1776, 13 years, increas-
ing._____   165,000

North Carolina.—Estimated in same way
as Delaware._____   75,000

South Carolina.—1765 to 1776, 11 years,
increasing, and loss in Revolution considered.   110,000

Georgia.—1772 to 1776, 4 years, increasing.   16,000

Total,_____   502,132.

Making a total, in round numbers, of 500,000 Negroes
who had, in the course of 156 years, from 1620 to 1776,
accumulated on our shores, by importation and natural
increase.

The proportion of *free* Negroes, in this estimate, at

the Declaration of Independence, must have been inconsiderable ; as it was not until *after* the Revolution that manumissions by owners, and manumissions in the progress of acts of Abolition, multiplied.

The Census of the United States for 1790, gives 697,697 Slaves and 59,481 Free Persons of Color ; a total of 757,178.

3. *Efforts for their Religious Instruction, both in Great Britain and America, year by year, during this Period.*

Having brought distinctly to view this multitude of people introduced amongst us in the inscrutable providence of God, the *original stock* being in a state of absolute *Heathenism*, we may inquire into the efforts made for their Religious Instruction.

1673.   Mr. Baxter published his "*Christian Directory*," in which he has a chapter of "Directions to those Masters in Foreign Plantations who have Negroes and other slaves ; being a solution of several cases about them."

The first Direction calls upon masters to "understand well how far your power over your slaves extendeth and what limits God hath set thereto."

"Remember that they have immortal souls, and are equally capable of salvation with yourselves : and therefore you have no power to do any thing which shall hinder their salvation. Remember that God is their absolute owner, and that you have none but a derived and limited propriety in them ; — that they and you are equally under the government and laws of God ; — that God is their reconciled tender Father, and if they be as good, doth love them as well as you ; — and that they are the redeemed ones of Christ : — Therefore, so use them as to preserve Christ's right and interest in them."

The 2d. *Direction.* — " Remember that you are Christ's trustees, or the guardians of their souls; and that the greater your power is over them, the greater your charge is of them and your duty for them. So must you exercise both your power and love to bring them to the knowledge and the faith of Christ, and to the just obedience of God's commands."

The 3d. — " So serve your necessities by your slaves as to prefer God's interest and their spiritual and everlasting happiness. Teach them the way to heaven, and do all for their souls which I have before directed you to do for all your other servants. Tho' you may make some difference in their labor and diet and clothing, yet none as to the furthering of their salvation. If they be infidels use them so as tendeth to win them to Christ and the love of religion, by shewing them that Christians are less worldly, less cruel and passionate, and more wise and charitable and holy and meek, than any other persons are. Wo to them that by their cruelty and covetousness do scandalize even slaves and hinder their conversion and salvation."

The 7th *and last Direction.* — "Make it your chief end in buying and using slaves to win them to Christ and save their souls. Do not only endeavor it on the by when you have first consulted your own commodity, but make this more of your end than your commodity itself; and let their salvation be far more valued by you than their service; and carry yourself to them as those that are sensible that they are redeemed with them by Christ from the slavery of Satan and may live with them in the liberty of the saints in glory."

The works of this eminent servant of God had an extensive circulation, and these Directions may have been productive of much good on the Plantations of those owners into whose hands they fell.

1680. Forty-four years after the settlement of Connecticut, the Assembly forwarded answers to the Inquiries of the Lords of the Committee of Colonies, wherein they say : " There are but few servants and fewer slaves; not above 30 in the colony. There come sometimes three or four blacks from the Barbadoes, which are sold for 22*l* each. Great care is taken of the instruction of the people in the Christian religion, by ministers catechising and preaching twice every Sabbath and sometimes on lecture days; and also by masters of families instructing their children and servants, which the law commands them to do."

1701. " *The Society for the Propagation of the Gospel in Foreign Parts,*" was incorporated under William III. on the 16th day of of June 1701, and the first meeting of the society under its charter was the 27th of June of the same year. Thomas Lord Bishop of Canterbury, Primate and Metropolitan of all England was appointed by his Majesty the first President.

This society was formed with the view, *primarily*, of supplying the destitution of religious institutions and privileges among the inhabitants of the North American Colonies, members of the established church of England ; and *secondarily*, of extending the Gospel to the Indians and Negroes.

It had been preceded by a company incorporated by Charles II. in 1661, for " *the Propagation of the Gospel amongst Heathen Nations of New England and the parts adjacent in America ;*" which, however, did not accomplish much ; the design, for the times then present and the necessities of the Colonies, being too narrow. The Honorable Robert Boyle, was first President of this company, and it was his connection with this society which led him to a deeper interest in the defence and propagation of the Christian religion, and he therefore left in his will an annual salary, forever, for the support of eight sermons in the year, for proving the Christian religion against notorious Infidels; and he requires that the preachers employed, " shall be assisting to all companies and encouraging them in any undertaking for propagating the Christian religion in Foreign Parts."

The Society for the Propagation of the Gospel in Foreign Parts entered upon its duties with zeal, being patronized by the King and all the dignitaries of the Church of England.

They instituted inquiries into the religious condition of the Colonies, responded to " by the Governors and persons of the best note;" (with special reference to Episcopacy,) and they perceived that their work " consisted of three great branches: *the care and instruction of our people* settled in the Colonies; *the conversion of the Indian Savages;* and *the conversion of the Negroes.*" Before appointing Missionaries, they sent out a traveling preacher, the *Rev. George Keith,* (an itinerant missionary,) who associated with himself the *Rev. John Talbot.* Mr. Keith preached between North Carolina and Piscataquay river in New England, a tract above 800 miles in length, and completed his mission in two years, and returned and reported his labors to the society.

The annual meetings of this society were regularly held from 1702 to 1819 and 118 sermons preached before it by Bishops of the Church of England, a large number of them distinguished for piety, learning, and zeal. The society still exists.

The efforts of the society *for the Religious Instruction of the Negroes,* are briefly as follows.

In June 1702 the Rev. Samuel Thomas, the first missionary, was sent to the Colony of *South Carolina*. The society designed he should attempt the conversion of the Yammosee Indians; but the Governor, Sir Nathaniel Johnson, appointed him to the care of the people settled on the three branches of Cooper river, making Goose creek his residence. He reported his labors to the society, and said " that he had taken much pains also in instructing the Negroes, and learned 20 of them to read. He died in October 1706.

Dr. LeJeau succeeded him in 1706, and found " parents and masters indued with much good will and a ready disposition to have their children and servants taught the Christian religion." " He instructed and baptised many Negroes and Indian slaves." His communicants in 1714 arose to 70 English and 8 Negroes. Dr. LeJeau died in 1717, and was succeeded permanently by Rev. Mr. Ludlam, who began his mission with great dilligence. " There were in his parish a large number of Negroes, natives of the place, who understood English well; he took good pains to instruct several of them in the principles of the Christian religion and afterwards admitted them to baptism. He said if the masters of them would heartily concur to forward so good a work, all those who have been born in the country might without much difficulty be instructed and received into the church. Mr. Ludlam continued his labors among the Negroes and every year taught and baptised several of them; in one year eleven, besides some *mulattoes*."

The Indian war checked the progress of the society's missions for several years. The Parishes of St. Paul's, (1705,) St. John's, (1707,) St. Andrew's and St. Bartholomew's, (1713,) St. Helen's, (1712,) received missionaries. Mr. Hasell was settled in the last named parish, and the inhabitants were "565 whites, 950 Negroes, 60 Indian slaves, and 20 free Negroes."

Rev. Gilbert Jones was appointed missionary of Christ Church Parish, 1711. He used great pains to persuade the masters and mistresses to assist in having their slaves instructed in the Christian faith ; but found this good work lay under difficulties as yet insuperable. He wrote thus concerning this matter : "Though laboring in vain be very discouraging, yet (by the help of God,) I will not cease my labors ; and if I shall gain but one proselyte, shall not think much of all my pains." He was succeded in 1722 by Rev. Mr. Pownal. Two years after he reported in his parish 470 free born, and "above 700 slaves, some of which understand the English tongue ; but very few know any thing of God or religion."

In the parish of St. George, taken out of St. Andrew's, the church stands 28 miles from Charleston, (1719,) Mr. Peter Tustian was sent missionary, but soon removed to Maryland. The Rev. Mr. Varnod succeeded him in 1723. A year after his arrival, at Christmas, he had near 50 communicants, and what was remarkable, 17 Negroes.

He baptised several grown persons, besides children and Negroes, belonging to Alexander Skeene, Esquire. The Rev. Mr. Taylor, missionary at St. Andrew's parish in South Carolina, reported to the society "the great interest taken in the religious instruction of their Negroes by Mrs. Haige and Mrs. Edwards, and their remarkable success ; 14 of whom on examination he baptised." The clergy of South Carolina, in a joint letter, acquainted the society with the fact " that Mr. Skeene, his lady, and Mrs. Haige, his sister, did use great care to have their Negroes instructed and baptised." And the Rev.

Mr. Varnod, missionary, had baptised 8 Negro children belonging to Mr. Skeene and Mrs. Haige, and he writes to the society that "at once he had 19 Negro communicants."

Mr. Neuman was sent as a missionary to *North Carolina* in 1722. He reported some time after "that he had baptised 269 children, 1 woman, and 3 men, and 2 Negroes, who could say the creed, the Lord's prayer, and ten commandments, and had good sureties for their further information."

The Rev. Mr. Beekett, missionary in *Pennsylvania*, in 1723, reported that he had baptised "two Negro slaves."

In 1709 Mr. Huddlestone was appointed school master in *New York City.* He taught 40 poor children out of the societies funds, and publicly catechised in the steeple of Trinity Church every Sunday in the afternoon, "not only his own scholars, but also the children, servants, and slaves of the inhabitants, and above 100 persons usually attended him."

The society established, also, a catechising school in New York city in 1704, in which city there were computed to be about 1,500 Negro and Indian slaves. The society hoped their example would be generally followed in the Colonics. Mr. Elias Neau, a French protestant was appointed catechist; who was very zeallous in his duty and many Negroes were instructed and baptised. In 1712 the Negroes in New York conspired to destroy all the English, which greatly discouraged the work of their instruction. The conspiracy was defeated, and many negroes taken and executed. Mr. Neau's school was blamed as the main occasion of the barbarous plot; two of Mr. Neau's school were charged with the plot; one was cleared and the other was proved to have been in the conspiracy, but guiltless of his master's murder. "Upon full trial the guilty Negroes were found to be such as never came to Mr. Neau's school; and what is very observable, the persons whose Negroes were found most guilty were such as were the declared opposers of making them Christians." In a short time the cry against the instruction of the Negroes subsided: the Governor visited and recommended the school. Mr. Neau died in 1722, much regretted by all who knew his labors. He was succeeded by Rev. Mr. Wetmore, who afterwards was appointed missionary to Rye in New York. After his removal "the rector, church wardens, and vestry of Trinity Church, in New York City," requested another catechist, "there being about 1,400 Negro and Indian slaves, a considerable number of them had been instructed in the principles of Christianity by the late Mr. Neau, and had received baptism and were communicants in their church. The society complied with this request and sent over Rev. Mr. Colgan in 1726, who conducted the school with success."

Mr. Honeyman, missionary in 1724, in *Providence*, Rhode Island, had baptized, in two years, 80 persons, of which 19 were grown, 3 Negroes, and 2 Indians, and 2 Mulattoes.

In *Naragansett*, the congregation was reported to be 160, (1720) with 12 Indian and black servants.

At *Marblehead*, the missionary reported (1725) having baptized 2 Negroes; "a man about 25 years old and a girl 12, and that a whole family in Salem had conformed to the church."

The society looked upon the instruction and conversion of the Negroes as a principal branch of their care; esteeming it a great reproach to the Christian name, that so many thousands of persons should continue in the same state of Pagan darkness under a Christian government and living in Christian families, as they lay before under in their own heathen countries. The society immediately from their first institution strove to promote their conversion, and in as much as their income would not enable them to send numbers of catechists sufficient to instruct the Negroes; yet they resolved to do their utmost, and at least to give this work the mark of their highest approbation. They wrote, therefore, to all their missionaries, that they should use their best endeavors, at proper times, to instruct the Negroes, and should especially take occasion to recommend it zealously to the masters to order their slaves at convenient times, to come to them that they might be instructed. These directions had a good effect, and some hundreds of Negroes had been instructed, received baptism, and been admitted to the communion, and lived very orderly lives."

The History of the Society goes on to say: "It is a matter of commendation to the clergy that they have done thus much in so great and difficult a work. But, alas! what is the instruction of a few hundreds in several years, with respect to the many thousands uninstructed, unconverted; living, dying, utter pagans! It must be confessed, what hath been done is as nothing with regard to what a true Christian would hope to see effected." After stating several difficulties in respect to the religious instruction of the Negroes, (which do not exist at the present time, but in a very limited degree,) it is said: "But the greatest obstruction is the masters themselves do not consider enough the obligation which lies upon them to have their slaves instructed." And in another place, "the society have always been sensible the most effectual way to convert the Negroes was by engaging their masters to countenance and promote their conversion." The Bishop of St. Asaph, Dr. Fleetwood, preached a sermon before the society in the year 1711, setting forth the duty of instructing the Negroes in the Christian religion. The society thought this so useful a discourse that they printed and dispersed abroad in the Plantations great numbers of that sermon, in the same year; and in the year 1725, reprinted the same and dispersed again large numbers. The Bishop of London, Dr. Gibson, (to whom the care of the Plantations abroad, as to religious affairs, was committed,) became a second advocate for the conversion of the Negroes, and wrote two letters on this subject. The first in 1727, "addressed to masters and mistresses of families, in the English Plantations abroad, exhorting them to encourage and promote the instruction of their Negroes in the Christian faith. The second, in the same year, addressed to the missionaries there; directing them to distribute the said letter, and exhorting them to give their assistance towards the instruction of the Negroes within their several parishes."

The society were persuaded this was the true method to remove the great obstruction to their conversion, and hoping so particular an application to the masters and mistresses from the See of London would have the strongest influence, they printed 10,000 copies of the letter to masters and mistresses, which were sent to all the Colonies on the continent, and to all the British Islands in the West Indies, to be distributed among the masters of families, and all other inhabitants. The society received accounts that these letters influenced many masters of families to have their servants instructed. The Bishop of London soon after wrote "an address to serious Christians *among ourselves*, to assist the Society for Propagating the Gospel in carrying on this work." •

The letters of Dr. Gibson referred to, for their intrinsic excellence, and as an indication of the state of feeling on the subject, 'at the time they were written, render it proper that they should be inserted in this Sketch. I have not been able to obtain a copy of Dr. Fleetwood's sermon.

"*The Bishop of London's Letter to the Masters and Mistresses of Families in the English Plantations abroad; exhorting them to encourage and promote the Instruction of their Negroes in the Christian Faith. London*, 1727.

The care of the Plantations abroad being committed to the Bishop of London, as to religious affairs, I have thought it my duty to make particular inquiries into the state of religion in those parts; and to learn, among other things, what number of slaves are employed within the several governments, and what means are used for their instruction in the Christian faith. I find the numbers are prodigiously great; and am not a little troubled to observe how small a progress has been made in a Christian country towards the delivering those poor creatures from the pagan darkness and superstition in which they were bred, and the making them partakers of the light of the Gospel, and of the blessings and benefits belonging to it. And, which is yet more to be lamented, I find there has not only been very little progress made in the work, but that all *attempts* towards it, have been by too many industriously discouraged and hindered; partly by magnifying the *difficulties* of the work beyond what they really are; and partly by mistaken suggestions of the change which baptism would make in the condition of the Negroes, to the loss and disadvantage of their masters.

I. *As to the Difficulties:* it may be pleaded that the Negroes are *grown persons* when they come over, and that having been accustomed to the pagan rites and idolatries of their own country, they are prejudiced against all other religions, and more particularly against the Christian, as forbidding all that licentiousness which is usually practised among the heathens.

But if this were a good argument against attempting the conversion of Negroes, it would follow that the Gospel is never further to be propagated than it is at present, and that no endeavors are to be used for the conversion of heathens at any time, or in any country, whatsoever : because all heathens have been accustomed to pagan rites and idolatries, and to such vicious and licentious living as the Christian religion forbids. But yet, God be thanked, heathens have been converted and Christianity propagated in all ages, and almost all countries, through the zeal and diligence of pious and good men; and this without the help of miracles. And if the present age be as zealous and diligent in pursuing the proper *means* of conversion, we have no reason to doubt, but that the divine assistance is, and will be, the same in all ages.

But a further difficulty is, that they are *utter strangers to our language* and *we to theirs;* and the gift of tongues being now ceased, there is no means left of instructing them in the doctrines of the Christian religion. And this, I own, is a real difficulty, as long as it continues, and as far as it reaches. But if I am rightly informed, many of the Negroes who are grown persons when they come over, do of themselves attain so much of our language as enables them to understand and to be understood, in things which concern the ordinary business of life; and they who can go so far, of their own accord, might doubtless be carried much further, if proper methods and endeavors were used to bring them to a complete knowledge of our language, with a pious view to the instructing them in the doctrines of our religion. At least some of them, who are more capable and more serious than the rest, might be easily instructed both in our language and religion, and then be made use of to convey instruction to the rest in their own language. And this, one would hope, may be done with great ease, wherever there is a hearty and sincere zeal for the work.

But whatever difficulties there may be in instructing those who are *grown up* before they are brought over, there are not the like difficulties in the case of *their children*, who are born and bred in our own Plantations, who have never been accustomed to pagan rites and superstitions, and who may easily be trained up, like all other children, to any language whatsoever, and particularly to our own; if the making them good Christians be sincerely the desire and intention of those who have the property in them and the government over them.

But supposing the difficulties to be much greater than I imagine, they are not such as render the work *impossible*, so as to leave no hope of *any degree* of success; and nothing less than an *impossibility* of doing any good at all, can warrant our giving over and laying aside all means and endeavors, where the propagation of the Gospel and the saving of souls are immediately concerned.

Many undertakings look far more impracticable before

trial, than they are afterwards found to be in experience ; especially where there is not a good heart to go about them. And it is frequently observed that small beginnings, when pursued with resolution, are attended with great and surprising success. But in no case is the success more great and surprising than when good men engage in the cause of God and religion, out of a just sense of the inestimable value of a soul, and in full and well grounded assurance that their honest designs and endeavors for the promoting religion, will be supported by a special blessing from God.

I am loth to think so hardly of any *Christian* master, as to suppose that he can *deliberately hinder* his Negroes from being instructed in the Christian faith ; or which is the same thing, that he can, upon sober and mature consideration of the case, finally resolve to deny them the *means and opportunities* of instruction. Much less may I believe that he can, after he has seriously weighed this matter, permit them to labor on the Lord's day : and least of all, that he can put them under a kind of *necessity* of laboring on that day, to provide themselves with the conveniences of life ; since our religion so plainly teaches us that God has given one day in seven, to be a day of rest ; not only to man, but to the beasts. That it is a day appointed by him for the improvement of the soul, as well as the refreshment of the body ; and that it is a duty incumbent upon masters, to take care that all persons who are under their government, keep this day holy, and employ it to the pious and wise purposes for which God, — our great Lord and Master — intended it. Nor can I think so hardly of any missionary, who shall be desired by the master to direct and assist in the instruction of his Negroes, (either on that day or on any other, when he shall be more at leisure,) as to suppose that he will not embrace such invitations with the utmost readiness and cheerfulness, and give all the help that is fairly consistent with the necessary duties of his function, as a parochial minister.

If it be said that no time can be spared from the daily labor and employment of the Negroes, to instruct them in the Christian religion; this is in effect to say that no consideration of propagating the Gospel of God, or saving the souls of men, is to make the *least abatement* from the temporal profit of the masters; and that God cannot or will not make up the little they may lose in that way, by blessing and prospering their undertakings by sea and land, as a just reward of their zeal for his glory and the salvation of men's souls. In this case, I may well reason as St. Paul does in a case not unlike it, that if they make you partakers of their temporal things, (of their strength and spirits, and even of their offspring,) you ought to make them partakers of your spiritual things, though it should abate somewhat from the profit which you might otherwise receive from their labors. And considering the *greatness* of the profit that is received from their labors, it might be hoped that all Christian masters, those especially who are possessed of considerable numbers, should also be at some small *expense* in providing for the instruction of these poor creatures, and that others, whose numbers are less, and who dwell in the same neighborhood, should join in the expense of a common teacher for the Negroes belonging to them. The Society for Propagating the Gospel in Foreign Parts, are sufficiently sensible of the great importance and necessity of such an established and regular provision for the instruction of the Negroes, and

earnestly wish and pray, that it may please God to put
it into the hearts of good Christians, to enable them to
assist in the work, by seasonable contributions for that
end: but at present their fund does scarce enable them
to answer the many demands of missionaries, for the
performance of divine service in the poorer settlements,
which are not in a condition to maintain them at their
own charge.

II. But it is further pleaded, that the instruction of
heathens in the Christian faith, is in order to their baptism: and that not only the *time* to be allowed for
instructing them, would be an abatement from the profits
of their labour, but also, that the *baptizing* them when
instructed would destroy both the property which the
masters have in them as slaves bought with their money
and the right of selling them again at pleasure, and that
the making them Christians, only makes them less
diligent and more ungovernable.

To which it may be very truly replied, that Christianity and the embracing of the Gospel does not make
the least alteration in civil property, or in any of the
duties which belong to civil relations; but in all these
respects, it continues persons just in the same state as it
found them. The freedom which Christianity gives is a
freedom from the bondage of sin and satan, and from
the dominion of men's lusts and passions and inordinate
desires; but as to their *outward* condition, whatever
that was before, whether bond or free, their being baptized and becoming Christians, makes no manner of
change in it. As St. Paul has expressly told us, 1 *Cor.*
7 : 20, where he is speaking directly to this point, "Let
every man abide in the same calling wherein he was
called:" and at the 24th verse, "Let every man where-

in he is called therein abide with God " And so far is Christianity from discharging men from the duties of the station or condition in which it found them, that it lays them under stronger obligations to perform those duties with the greatest diligence and fidelity, not only from the fear of man but from a sense of duty to God, and the belief and expectation of a future account. So that to say that Christianity tends to make men less observant of their duty in any respect, is a reproach that it is very far from deserving : and a reproach that is confuted *by the whole tenor of the Gospel precepts*, which inculcate upon all, and particularly upon servants (many of whom were then in the condition of slaves,) a faithful and diligent discharge of the duties belonging to their several stations out of conscience towards God. And it is also confuted by *our own reason*, which tells us how much more forcible and constant the restraint of *conscience* is, than the restraint of *fear ;* and last of all, it is confuted *by experience*, which teaches us the great value of those servants who are truly religious, compared with those who have no sense of religion.

As to their being more ungovernable after baptism than before, it is certain that the Gospel every where enjoins not only diligence and fidelity, but also *obedience* for conscience sake : and does not deprive masters of any proper methods of enforcing obedience, where they appear to be necessary. Humanity forbids all cruel and barbarous treatment of our fellow-creatures, and will not suffer us to consider a being that is endowed with reason on a level with brutes: and Christianity takes not out of the hands of superiors any degrees of strictness and severity that fairly appear to be necessary for the preserving subjection and government.

The general law both of humanity and of Christianity, is kindness, gentleness and compassion towards all mankind, of what nation or condition soever they be; and therefore we are to make the exercise of those amiable virtues our *choice* and *desire*, and to have recourse to severe and vigorous methods unwillingly and only out of necessity. And of this *necessity*, you yourselves remain the judges, as much *after* they receive baptism as *before;* so that you can be in no danger of suffering by the change; and as to *them*, the greatest hardships that the most severe master can inflict upon them is not to be compared to the cruelty of keeping them in the state of heathenism and depriving them of the means of salvation as reached forth to *all mankind* in the Gospel of Christ. And in truth one great reason why severity is at all necessary to maintain government, is the *want* of religion in those who are to be governed, and who therefore are not to be kept to their duty by any thing but *fear and terror;* than which there cannot be a more uneasy state, either to those who govern or those who are governed.

III. That these things may make the greater impression upon you, let me beseech you to consider yourselves not only as masters, but as *Christian* masters, who stand obliged by your profession to do all that your station and condition enable you to do, towards breaking the power of satan and enlarging the kingdom of Christ, and as having a great opportunity put into your hands of helping on this work, by the influence which God has given you over such a number of heathen idolaters, who still continue under the dominion of satan. In the next place let me beseech you to consider *them* not barely as slaves, and upon the same level with laboring beasts, but as *men*-slaves and *women*-slaves, who have the same frame and faculties with yourselves and have souls capable of being made eternally happy, and reason and understanding to receive instruction in order to it. If they came from abroad, let it not be said that they are as far from the knowledge of Christ in a Christian country as when they dwelt among pagan idolaters. If they have been born among you and have never breathed any air but that of a Christian country,. let them not be as much strangers to Christ as if they had been transplanted, as soon as born, into a country of pagan idolaters.

Hoping that these and the like considerations will move you to lay this matter seriously to heart, and excite you to use the best means in your power towards so good and pious a work ; I cannot omit to suggest to you one of the best motives that can be used for disposing the heathens to embrace Christianity, and that is *the good lives of Christians.* Let them see in you and in your families, examples of sobriety, temperance and chastity, and of all the other virtues and graces of the Christian life. Let them observe how strictly you oblige yourselves and all that belong to you to abstain from cursing and swearing, and to keep the Lord's day and the ordinances which Christ hath appointed in the Gospel. Make them sensible, by the general tenor of your behaviour and conversation, that your inward temper and disposition is such as the Gospel requires, that is to say, mild, gentle and merciful, and that as oft as you exercise vigor and severity, it is wholly owing to their idleness or obstinacy.

By these means you will open their hearts to instruction, and *prepare* them to receive the truths of the

Gospel; to which if you add a pious *endeavor and concern* to see them duly instructed, you may become the instrument of saving many souls, and will not only secure a blessing from God upon all your undertakings in this world, but entitle yourselves to that distinguishing reward in the next which will be given to all those who have been zealous in their endeavors to promote the salvation of men and enlarge the kingdom of Christ. And that you may be found in that number, at the great day of accounts, is the sincere desire and earnest prayer of your faithful friend. **EDM. LONDON.**"

May 19, 1727.

" *The Bishop of London's Letter to the Missionaries in the English Plantations : exhorting them to give their assistance towards the Instruction of the Negroes of their several Parishes in the Christian Faith.*

GOOD BROTHER :

Having understood by many letters from the Plantations, and by the accounts of persons who have come from thence, that very little progress hath hitherto been made in the conversion of the Negroes to the Christian faith ; I have thought it proper for me to lay before the masters and mistresses the obligations they are under to promote and encourage that pious and necessary work. This I have done in a letter directed to them, of which you will receive several copies in order to be distributed to those who have Negroes in your parish ; and I must entreat you, when you put the letter into their hands, to enforce the design of it by any arguments that you shall think proper to be used ; and also, to assure them of your own assistance in carrying on the work.

I am aware that in the Plantations where the parishes are of so large extent, the care and labor of the parochial ministers must be great; but yet I persuade myself that many vacant hours may be spared from the other pastoral duties, to be bestowed on this ; and I cannot doubt of the readiness of every missionary, in his own parish, to promote and further a work so charitable to the souls of men, and so agreeable to the great end and design of his mission.

As to those ministers who have Negroes of their own, I cannot but esteem it their indispensable duty to use their best endeavors to instruct them in the Christian religion in order to their being baptized ; both because such Negroes are their proper and immediate care, and because it is in vain to hope that other masters and mistresses will exert themselves in this work, if they see it wholly neglected or but coldly pursued in the families of the clergy ; so that any degree of neglect on your part, in the instruction of your own Negroes, would not only be withholding from *them* the inestimable benefits of Christianity, but would evidently tend to the obstructing and defeating the *whole design* in every other family.

I would also hope that the school masters in the several parishes, part of whose business it is to instruct youth in the principles of Christianity, might contribute somewhat towards the carrying on this work, by being ready to bestow upon it some of their leisure time; and especially upon the Lord's day, when both they and the Negroes are most at liberty, and the clergy are taken up with the public duties of their function.

And though the assistance they give to this pious design, should not meet with any reward from men, yet their comfort may be that it is the work of God and will assuredly be rewarded by him ; and the less they are *obliged* to this on account of any reward they receive from *men*, the greater will their reward be from the *hands of God.* I must therefore entreat you to recommend it to them in my name, and to dispose them by all proper arguments and persuasions, to turn their thoughts seriously to it, and to be always ready to offer and lend their assistance at their leisure hours.

And so, not doubting your ready and zealous concurrence in promoting this important work and earnestly begging a blessing from God upon this and all your other pastoral labors, I remain, your affectionate friend and brother.   **EDM. LONDON.**"

May 19, 1727.

Dean Stanhope (of Canterbury)' states in his sermon, 1714, that success had attended the efforts of the society, and speaks of " children, servants, and slaves catechised."

Bishop Berkley was in the Colony of Rhode Island from 1728 till late in 1730, and he also preached a sermon before the society, February 18, 1731, in which he thus speaks of the Negroes : " the Negroes in the government of Rhode Island, are about half as many more than the Indians, and both together scarce amount to a seventh part of the whole Colony. The religion of these people, as is natural to suppose, takes after that of their masters. Some few are baptized : several frequent the different assemblies ; and far the greater part, none at all.

An ancient antipathy to the Indians, whom, it seems,
our first planters (therein as in certain other particulars,
affecting to imitate Jews rather than Christians) imagine
they had a right to treat on the foot of Canaanites or
Amalekites, together with an irrational contempt of the
Blacks, as creatures of another species, who had no
right to be instructed or admitted to the sacraments;
have proved a main obstacle to the conversion of these
poor people. To this may be added an erroneous notion
that the being baptized is inconsistent with a state of
slavery. To undeceive them in this particular, which
had too much weight, it seemed a proper step, if the
opinion of his Majesty's Attorney and Solicitor General
could be procured. This opinion they charitably sent
over, signed with their own hands: which was accordingly printed in Rhode Island, and dispersed through
the Plantations. I heartily wish it may produce the
intended effect. It must be owned our reformed planters
with respect to the natives and the slaves, might learn
from the Church of Rome how it is their interest and
duty to behave. Both French and Spaniards, take care
to instruct both them and their Negroes in the Popish
religion, to the reproach of those who profess a better."

From a " proposal to establish a college in Bermuda,"
first published in 1725, the Bishop remarks: " Now the
clergy sent over to America have proved, too many of
them, very meanly qualified, both in learning and morals,
for the discharge of their office. And indeed, little can
be expected from the example or instruction of those,
who quit their native country on no other motive than
that they are not able to procure a livelihood in it,
which is known to be often the case. To this may be

imputed the small care that hath been taken to convert the Negroes of our Plantations, who, to the infamy of England, and scandal of the world, continue heathen under Christian masters, and in Christian countries; which would never be if our planters were rightly instructed and made sensible that they disappointed their own baptism by denying it to those who belong to them: that it would be of advantage to their affairs to have slaves who should "obey in all things their masters according to the flesh, not with eye-service as men pleasers, but in singleness of heart, as fearing God:" that Gospel liberty consists with temporal servitude: and that their slaves would only become better slaves by being Christians."—[*Berkley's Works:* copied by Rev. W. W. Eells.]

In 1741, Archbishop Secker, after enumerating other successes, adds: "in less than 40 years great multitudes on the whole, of Negroes and Indians, brought over to the Christian faith."

Bishop Drummond, in 1754, notices the Negroes in his sermon before the society, and insists upon the duty and safety of giving them the Gospel.

The amiable Porteus, 1783, when Bishop of Chester, (afterwards Bishop of London,) took a lively interest in this work, and preached a sermon before the society in support of it which may be found in his works.

In the year, 1783, and the following, soon after the separation of our Colonies from the Mother Country, the society's operations ceased, leaving in all the Colonies, 43 missionaries; two of whom were in the Southern States, one in North, and one in South Carolina. The affectionate valediction of the society to them was issued in 1785. Thus terminated the connection of this noble society with our country, which, from the foregoing notices of its efforts, must have accomplished a great deal for the religious instruction of the Negro population.

Thus, it is perceived, that the Negroes were not forgotten by the Church of Christ *in England*. Were they remembered by the Church of Christ *in the Colonies themselves?* We have no record of missions or of missionary stations established *by or in any of the Colonies*, in behalf, exclusively, of the Negroes, up to the year 1738.

1738. *The Moravian or United Brethren were the first who formally attempted the establishment of Missions, exclusively to the Negroes.*

A succinct account of their several efforts down to the year 1790, is given in the report of the Society for the Propagation of the Gospel among the Heathen, at Salem N. C., October 5th 1837; by Rev. J. Renatus Schmidt, and is as follows:

"A hundred years have now elapsed since the Renewed Church of the Brethren first attempted to communicate the Gospel to the many thousand Negroes of our land. In 1737 Count Zinzendorf paid a visit to London, and formed an acquaintance with General Oglethorpe and the Trustees of Georgia, with whom he conferred on the subject of the mission to the Indians, which the Brethren had already established in that Colony, (in 1735.) Some of these gentlemen were associates under the will of Dr. Bray, who had left funds to be devoted to the conversion of the Negro slaves in South Carolina; and they solicited the Count to procure them some missionaries for this purpose. On his objecting that the Church of England might hesitate to recognize the ordination of the Brethren's missionaries, they referred the question to the Archbishop of Canterbury, Dr. Potter, who gave it as his opinion, 'that the Brethren being members of an Episcopal Church whose doctrines contained nothing repugnant to the Thirty-nine Articles, ought not to be denied free access to the heathen.' This declaration not only removed all hesitation from the minds of the trustees as to the present application; but opened the way for the labors of the Brethren amongst the slave population of the West Indies; — a great and blessed work, which has, by the gracious help of God, gone on increasing even to the present day.

The same year Brother Peter Boehler was deputed to commence the desired mission, with Brother George Schulius as his assistant. They set out by way of London, in February 1738, and repaired, in the first instance, to Georgia, hoping to be provided with means for the prosecution of their journey by the colony of the Brethren already established there. Obstacles however being interposed, through the interested views of certain individuals, this mission failed and our Brethren, settling at Purisburg, took charge of the Swiss Colonists and their children in that town; Georgia not being at that period a slave-holding Colony. In 1739, Schulius departed this life. Peter Boehler emigrated in 1740, to Pennsylvania, with the whole Georgia Colony, of which he was minister; because they were required to bear arms, in the war against the Spaniards, which had recently broken out. In 1747 and 1748 some Brethren belonging to Bethlehem, undertook several long and difficult journies through Maryland, Virginia, and the borders of North Carolina, in order to preach the Gospel to the Negroes, who, generally speaking, received it with eagerness.

Various proprietors, however, avowing their determination not to suffer strangers to instruct their Negroes, as they had their own ministers, whom they paid for that purpose, our brethren ceased from their efforts. It appears from the letters of brother Spangenberg, who spent the greater part of the year 1749 at Philadelphia, and preached the Gospel to the Negroes in that city, that the labours of the brethren amongst them were not entirely fruitless. Thus he writes in 1751 — 'on my arrival in Philadelphia, I saw numbers of Negroes still buried in all their native ignorance and darkness, and my soul was grieved for them. Soon after some of them came to me, requesting instruction, at the same time acknowledging their ignorance in the most affecting manner. They begged that a weekly sermon might be delivered expressly for their benefit. I complied with their request and confined myself to the most essential truths of scripture. Upwards of 70 Negroes attended on these occasions, seve al of whom were powerfully awakened ap l ed fo further instruction and expressed a desire to be united to Christ and his Church by the sacrament of Baptism whi h was accordingly administered to them.'

At the Provincial Synod which was held in Pennsylvania in 1747, brother Christian Frohlich was commissioned to take charge of the Negroes of New-York, who had evinced a great desire for the gospel, and of whom several had been already won for the Redeemer, by means of their attendance on the ministry of the word. In 1751 he visited the scattered Negroes in New-Jersey, by whom he was every where received with joy, and preached Christ crucified to a hundred of them at once with considerable effect, besides conversing with them at their work.

A *painting* is preserved at Bethlehem in which the eighteen first-fruits from the heathen who had been brought to Christ by the instrumentality of the brethren, and had departed in the faith, prior to the year 1747, are represented, dressed in their native costume and standing before the throne of Christ with palms in their hands, with the inscription beneath : ' These are redeemed from among men, being the first fruits unto God and to the Lamb.' — (*Rev.* 14 : 4.) Amongst the number are Johannes, a Negro of South Carolina, and Jupiter, a Negro from New York. The graves of colored christians, who have died in the Lord, are also met with in several of our burial grounds in the North American congregations.

At the request of Mr. Knox, the English Secretary of State, an attempt was made to evangelise the Negroes of Georgia. In 1774 the brethren, Lewis Muller, of the Academy at Nesky, and George Wagner, were called to North America, and in the year following, having been joined by brother Andrew Broesing of North Carolina, they took up their abode at Knoxborough, a Plantation so called from its proprietor, the gentleman above mentioned. They were however almost constant sufferers from the feyers which prevailed in those parts, and Muller finished his course in the October of the same year. He had preached the Gospel with acceptance to both whites and blacks, yet without any abiding results. The two remaining brethren being called upon to bear arms on the breaking out of the war of independence, Broesing repaired to Wachovia, in North Carolina, and Wagner set out in 1779 for England."

In the great Northampton revival, under the preaching of Dr. Edwards in 1735 and 6, when for the space of five or six weeks together the conversions averaged at least "four a day :" Dr. Edwards remarks, " There are several Negroes who, from what was seen in them then and what is discernible in them since, appear to have been truly born again in the late remarkable season."

At a meeting of the General Association of the Colony of Connecticut, 1738, "It was inquired — whether the infant slaves of Christian masters may be baptized in the right of their masters — they solemnly promising to train them in the nurture and admonition of the Lord : and whether it is the *duty* of such masters to offer such children and thus religiously to promise. Both questions were affirmatively answered." *Records as reported by Rev. C. Chapin, D. D.*

Of the condition of the Negroes about this time in New England, it has been said, "Their lot was far from being severe. They were often bought by conscientious persons, for the purpose of being well instructed in the Christian religion. They had universally the enjoyment of the Sabbath as a day of rest: or of devotion."

Looking over the old record of "Entryes for Publications" (i. e. for marriages) " within the town of Boston," I observed the following, among others :

1707. *Negro.*—Essex, a Negro man of Mr. William Clarke, Esqre.; Gueno, a R. Wo. of Walle Winthrop, Esqre.

Negro. Will, reg. serv't of Wm. Webster; Betty, reg'r serv't of Wm. Keen, March 9th.

1710. *Negroes.*—Charles and Peggy, Negro serv'ts of Mr. James Barnes, July 19.

Negro.—Jack, Negro serv't of Sam'l Bill; Esther, Negro serv't of Robert Gutridge, Oct'r 27.

By which it would appear that the community was not indifferent to their condition in as much as their marriages were public and legalized.

1747. Direct efforts for the religious instruction of Negroes, continued through a series of years, were made by *Presbyterians in Virginia.* They commenced with the Rev. Samuel Davies, afterwards President of Nassau Hall, and the Rev. John Todd of Hanover Presbytery.

Mr. Davies began his ministry in Hanover in 1747 and left Virginia about 1773 or 4. Mr. Davies, four or five years after his settlement in Hanover, "found it impossible to afford even a monthly supply of preaching to the congregations organized by him. Accordingly he sought an assistant in Mr. John Todd, a young preacher from Pennsylvania, who was installed in the upper part of Hanover, November 12, 1752."

In a letter addressed to a friend and member of the "Society in London for promoting Christian knowledge among the poor," in the year 1755, he thus expresses himself: "The poor neglected Negroes, who are so far from having money to purchase books, that they themselves are the property of others: who were originally

African savages, and never heard of the name of Jesus
or his Gospel until they arrived at the land of their
slavery in America: whom their masters generally
neglect, and whose souls none care for, as though
immortality were not a privilege common to them, as
with their masters; these poor unhappy Africans are
objects of my compassion, and I think the most proper
objects of the Society's charity. The inhabitants of
Virginia are computed to be about 300,000 men, the
one-half of which number are supposed to be Negroes.
The number of those who attend my ministry at particular times, is uncertain, but generally about 300, who
give a stated attendance; and never have I been so
struck with the appearance of an assembly, as when I
have glanced my eye to that part of the meeting-house
where they usually sit, *adorned* (for so it has appeared
to me) with so many black countenances, eagerly attentive to every word they hear and frequently bathed in
tears. A considerable number of them (about a hundred) have been baptised, after a proper time for instruction, having given credible evidence, not. only of their
acquaintance with the important doctrines of the Christian religion, but also a deep sense of them in their
minds, attested by a life of strict piety and holiness.
As they are not sufficiently polished to dissemble with
a good grace, they express the sentiments of their souls
so much in the language of simple nature and with such
genuine indications of sincerity, that it is impossible to
suspect their professions, especially when attended with
a truly Christian life and exemplary conduct. There
are multitudes of them in different places, who are willing and eagerly desirous to be instructed and embrace

every opportunity of acquainting themselves with the
doctrines of the Gospel; and though they have generally
very little help to learn to read, yet to my agreea
ble surprise, many of them, by dint of application in
their leisure hours, have made such progress that they
can intelligibly read a plain author, and especially their
bibles; and pity it is that any of them, should be without them." Mr. Davies furnished the Negroes with
what books he could procure for them, and requested a
supply from the society of bibles and Watt's psalms and
hymns. Having received a supply he distributed them
to the great joy of the Negroes. "The books were all
very acceptable, but none more so than the psalms and
hymns, which enable them to gratify their peculiar taste
for psalmody. Sundry of them have lodged all night
in my kitchen, and sometimes when I have awaked about
two or three o'clock in the morning, a torrent of sacred
harmony has poured into my chamber and carried
my mind away to heaven. In this seraphic exercise
some of them spend almost the whole night. I wish,
Sir, you and other benefactors could hear some of these
sacred concerts. I am persuaded it would surprise and
please you more than an Oratorio or a St. Cecelia's day."
He observes: "The Negroes, above all the human
species that ever I knew, have an ear for music and a
kind of extatic delight in psalmody, and there are no
books they learn so soon, or take so much pleasure in as
those used in that heavenly part of divine worship."

On one sacramental occasion "he had the pleasure of
seeing 40 of them around the table of the Lord, all of
whom made a credible profession of Christianity, and
several of them gave unusual evidence of sincerity, and
he believed that more than 1,000 Negroes attended on

his ministry at the different places where he alternately officiated."

Mr Davies writes Dr. Bellamy, in 1757, " what little success I have lately had, has been chiefly among the extremes of Gentlemen and Negroes. Indeed, God has been remarkably working among the latter. I have baptized about 150 adults ; and at the last sacramental solemnity, I had the pleasure of seeing the table *graced* with about 60 black faces. They generally behave well as far as I can hear, though there are some instances of apostacy among them." The counties in which Mr. Davies labored were Hanover, Henrico, Goochland, Caroline, and Louisa.

" The Society for Propagating the Gospel in Foreign Parts," already noticed, in 1745 established a school in Charleston, S. C., under the direction of Commissary Garden. It flourished greatly and seemed to answer their utmost wishes. It had at one time 60 scholars and sent forth annually about 20 young Negroes well instructed in the English language and the Christian faith. This school was established in St. Phillip's church and some of its scholars were living in 1822, of orderly and decent characters. — *Bp. Meade and Dr. Dalcho.*

The year 1747 was marked in the Colony of Georgia by the authorized introduction of slaves. Twenty three representatives from the different districts met in Savannah, and after appointing Major Horton president, they entered into sundry resolutions the substance of which was " that *the owners of slaves, should educate the young and use every possible means of making religious impressions upon the minds of the aged,* and that all acts of inhumanity should be punished by the civil authority."

1764. The Rev. Ezra Stiles, D. D., afterwards president of Yale College, and Dr. Samuel Hopkins, undertook the education of two apparently promising Negroes with a view to the ministry ; but it was finally a failure. *Dr. Plumer's Report.*

1770. While Dr. Stiles was pastor in Newport, R. I., there were many African slaves in that town. "Of 80 communicants in his church in that town, 7 were Negroes. These occasionally met, by his direction, for religious improvement in his study."

Methodism was introduced into this country in New York, 1766 and the first missionaries were sent out by Mr. Wesley in 1769. One of these, Mr. Pillmore, in a letter to Mr. Wesley, from New York, in 1770, says, "the number of blacks that attend the preaching affects me much." The first regular conference was held in Philadelphia, 1773. Number of ministers 10 and of members 1,160. From this year to 1776 there was a great revival of religion in Virginia under the preaching of the Methodists, in connection with Rev. Mr. Jarratt of the Episcopal Church, which spread through 14 counties in Virginia and 2 in North Carolina. One letter states, " the chapel was full of white and black ;" another " hundreds of Negroes were among them with tears streaming down their faces." At Roanoke another remarks, "in general the white people were within the chapel and the black people without."

1780. At the 8th conference in Baltimore the following question appeared in the minutes. " *Ques.* 25.— Ought not the assistant to meet the colored people himself and appoint as helpers in his absence proper *white* persons, and not suffer them to stay late and meet by themselves? *Ans.*—Yes." Under the preaching of Mr.

Garretson in Maryland, "hundreds both white and black expressed their love of Jesus."

1786. The *first* return of *colored* members distinct from *white* occurs in the minutes of this year, and then yearly afterwards, white 18,791, *colored* 1,890. "It will be perceived from the above," says Dr. Bangs in his history of the Methodist Episcopal Church, "that a considerable number of colored persons had been received into the church, and were so returned in the minutes of conference. Hence it appears that at an early period of the Methodist ministry in this country it had turned its attention to this part of the population."

Mr. Rankin writing on the general state of Methodism in the Colonies at the the commencement of hostilities, observes, "in May 1777 we had 40 preachers in the different circuits and about 7000 members in the society, besides many hundreds of Negroes, who were convinced of sin, and many of them happy in the love of God." *Life of Coke, p.* 53.

In the year 1786 the following case of conscience was overtured from Donegal Presbytery, in the Synod of New York and Philadelphia ; namely,

"Whether Christian masters or mistresses ought in duty to have such children baptized, as are under their care though born of parents not in the communion of any Christian church?"

Upon this overture "the synod are of opinion that Christian masters and mistresses whose religious professions and conduct are such as to give them a right to the ordinance of baptism for their own children, may and ought to dedicate the children of their household to God, in that ordinance, when they have no scruple of conscience to the contrary,"—*Min. p.* 413, *and Min, of Gen'l Assem. p,* 97.

And on the next page (414) it was overtured " whether Christian slaves having children at the entire direction
of unchristian masters, and not having it in their power
to instruct them in religion, are bound to have them
baptized; and whether a Gospel minister in this predica-
ment ought to baptize them?" The synod determined
the question in the *affirmative.*

1787. The minutes of the Methodist conference for
this year, furnish the following question and answer,
indicative of continued interest in the colored population.
" *Ques.* 17. — What directions shall we give for the
promotion of the spiritual welfare of the colored people? *Ans.* — We conjure all our ministers and preachers
by the love of God and the salvation of souls, and do
require them by all the authority that is invested in us
to leave nothing undone for the spiritual benefit and
salvation of them, within their respective circuits or
districts; and for this purpose to embrace every opportunity of inquiring into the state of their souls, and to
unite in society those who appear to have a real desire
of fleeing from the wrath to come ; to meet such in
class, and to exercise the whole Methodist discipline
among them." Number of colored members 3,893.

1790. Again : " *Ques.* — What can be done in order to
instruct poor children, white and black, to read? *Ans.*
Let us labor as the heart and soul of one man to establish Sunday schools in or near the place of public worship. Let persons be appointed by the bishops, elders,
deacons, or preachers, to teach gratis all that will attend
and have a capacity to learn, from 6 o'clock in the
morning till 10, and from 2 P. M. till 6, where it does
not interfere with public worship. The council shall
compile a proper school-book to teach them learning and

piety." The experiment was made, but it proved unsuccessful and was discontinued. Number of colored members this year 11,682.

The Methodist is the only denomination which has preserved returns of the number of colored members in its connection. I find it impossible to make any estimate of the number in connection with the other denominations. The Methodists met with more success during this period in the Middle and Southern States than in the Northern, and as they paid particular atten tion to the Negroes large numbers were brought under their influence.

The first *Baptist* church in this country was founded in Providence, R. I., by Roger Williams, in 1639. Nearly one hundred years after the settlement of America, " only 17 Baptist churches had arisen in it." The Baptist church in Charleston S. C., was founded in 1690. The denomination advanced slowly through the Middle and Southern States and in 1790 it had churches in them all. Revivals of religion were enjoyed, particularly one in Virginia which commenced in 1785 and continued until 1791 or 1792. "Thousands were converted and baptized, besides many who joined the Methodists and Presbyterians." A large number of Negroes were admitted to the Baptist churches during the seasons of revival, as well as on ordinary occasions; they were however, not gathered into churches *distinct* from the whites south of Pennsylvania except in Georgia. Brief notices of churches composed exclusively of Negroes will be given in the second period of this Sketch. Before the Revolution the Negroes in Virginia attended in crowds the Episcopal church, there being no other denomination of Christians of consequence in the State ;

but upon the introduction of other denominations they went off to them. Old Robert Carter, or *Counsellor* or *King* Carter, as he was commonly called, among the richest men in the State, owning some 700 or 800 slaves and large tracts of land; built *Christ's Church* in Lancaster county, Va., and reserved *one-fourth* for his servants and tenants. He was himself baptized, and afterwards emancipated a large number of his Negroes and living fourteen or fifteen years a Baptist, embraced and died in the faith of *Swedenborg*.

The independence of the American Colonies was acknowledged and peace establish d in 1783. The articles of confederation of 1778 were superseded by our present Constitution in 1787, from the ratification of which to the present time our country has been rapidly advancing in prosperity.

From the beginning of our controversies with the mother country to the breaking out of the revolutionary war; throughout the period of that arduous struggle; and from its close, throughout the period of national exhaustion, loss of public credit, derangement in trade, political excitements, and conflicting opinions, to the ratification of the constitution, a period of near 20 years, the colonies suffered immeasurably in a moral and religious point of view; and the notices during this period of the state of the churches and of the progress of the Gospel, are gloomy, and some of them of the gloomiest character. Of course the Negroes suffered in common with the rest of the population.

A few remarks suggested by the facts embraced in this *first period* of our Sketch, shall bring it to a conclusion.

The religious condition of the colonies up to the

period of the revolution, taken on the whole, was not one remarkable for its prosperity, notwithstanding there had been some revivals of religion. The New England Colonies were in respect to a supply of ministers and religious privileges and improvement beyond all the rest. But the whole country was in a *forming* state: but recently settled; every year receiving fresh colonists from abroad, and the older settlers pushing their way into new and unexplored regions ; while repeated wars with the Indians, and wars with the French, the Dutch, and the Spaniards, threw different portions into protracted, distressing, and injurious commotions. Agriculture, commerce, manufactures, and the arts, were but in their infancy ; and the general conduct of the mother country in regard to the government of the colonies and the policy to be pursued towards them, was wretched ; sometimes contradictory, frequently oppressive and injurious, and contrary to the wishes of the colonists.

Such being the state of affairs, we ought not to anticipate any remarkable degree of attention, to the religious instruction of the Negroes, within the Colonies, as an *independent* class of population. Especially too, as the effect of the slave trade, during its existence, was to harden the feelings against the unfortunate subjects of it, while their degraded and miserable appearance and character, their stupidity, their uncouth languages and gross superstitions, and their constant occupation, operated as so many checks to benevolent efforts for their conversion to Christianity. And thus, those who advocated the slave-trade on the ground that it introduced the Negroes to the blessings of civilization and the Gospel, saw their favorite argument losing its force, in great measure, from year to year.

The fact, however, is worthy of remembrance, that while the *Indians* — some of whom received us as guests and sold us their lands at almost no compensation at all, and others were driven back to make us room ; and with whom we had frequent and bloody wars, and we became from time to time, mutual scourges — received some eminent missionaries from the colonists, and had no inconsiderable interest awakened for their conversion ; the *African* who were brought over and bought by us for servants, and who wore out their lives as such, enriching thousands, from Massachusetts to Georgia and were members of our households, never received *from the colonists themselves a solitary missionary* exclusively devoted to their good ; nor was there *ever a single society established within the Colonies*, that we know of, with the express design of promoting their religious instruction !

The conclusion, however, would be unwarrantable, that they were *wholly neglected*. The language of President Davies, "that no man cared for their souls," must be received with abatement. For they had attracted the serious attention of societies in Europe, and of men eminent for wisdom, learning, and piety ; and able appeals were written to promote their religious instruction : and some attempts were made to send over missionaries and also to engage the services of the settled clergy in their behalf, the Church of England in this good work taking the lead.

We are certified also, that efforts were made for their instruction, especially in the Southern Colonies, where their numbers were greater ; and that owners did to some small extent desire and attempt the instruction of their households ; and that the settled as well as itinerant ministers did not wholly neglect them. Many Negroes were received into the churches from one end of the Colonies to the other, and the rest and privileges of the Lord's day were secured to them either by custom or law. We see them occasionally noticed in the proceedings of ecclesiastical associations. There were catechetical schools and schools for teaching them to read, in a few places. The Negroes were allowed to read, and books were, upon occasions, distributed to them; but the privileges of education were gradually discouraged and withheld, more particularly in those Colonies and States containing a large population of them, and whose policy it was to perpetuate the system of slavery.

Were it possible for us to obtain from all the ministers of various denominations throughout the Colonies, who flourished during these 170 years, a report of their regular pastoral labors, such as have been furnished by a few, it might possibly appear that the Negroes received a larger share of religious instruction than, upon a consideration of the facts now before us, many would be led to imagine.

CHAPTER II.

1790. The interest awakened in Virginia, by the labors of President Davies, continued throughout this period, as appears by the following letter from the venerable Dr. Alexander of Princeton.

"In addition to the efforts made by the Rev. Mr. Davies of Hanover, I would mention the name of a faithful coadjutor in this field, the effects of whose labors are still apparent in Cub-creek congregation, in Charlotte county, Va. The minister to whom I allude was the Rev. Robert Henry, a native of Scotland, who was for many years the pastor of Cub-creek and Briery congregations united, although their distance apart was not less than twenty miles. This gentleman possessed very humble talents as a preacher; blundered much, and sometimes lost himself, so that he had to conclude abruptly. He was so *absent* that on one occasion after preaching, finding the horse of another person hitched where he commonly left his own beast, he mounted and rode him without noticing the mistake. He was *notoriously* a man of prayer; for when he turned out of the public road to go to the house where he usually lodged

the evening before he preached at Briery, he could be
heard praying aloud long before he was in sight, and
sometimes he became so much engaged that his old bald
horse would come up and stop at the gate whilst he
was still in earnest supplication.

This man judiciously turned much of his attention to
the Negroes; and to them his ministry was attended
with abundant success. Many were converted and
gathered into the church at Cub-creek. As this congregation was situated on the northern bank of Staunton
river, where the land is very fertile, there were several
large estates, possessing many slaves, within reach of
the house of worship where he preached."

The Rev. Henry Lacy succeeded Mr. Henry; during
whose ministrations at Cub-creek about 200 were added
to the church. There were 60 belonging to the church
under the care of Mr. Cob. — *Rev. W. S. Plumer's
Report.*

Dr. Alexander proceeds: "Many years after Mr.
Henry's death, I was settled for several years in this
county, and preached at the same places where Mr.
Henry had labored. At Cub-creek I found about 70
black communicants, twenty-four of whom belonged to
one estate. They were, in general, as orderly and as
constant in their attendance on the word preached as the
whites. Some of them had been received in Mr. Henry's time, but others afterwards. The session of the
church appointed two or three leading men among them
to be a sort of overseers or superintendents of the rest,
and we found that they performed their duties faithfully.

It was in this same county and very much to the
large colored congregation at Cub-creek, that Dr. Rice

labored after I left the place. He was when first settled pastor of Cub-creek and Bethesda, a new congregation which grew out of the former. As he was willing to bestow a part of his time entirely to the blacks, *the Committee on Missions of the general Assembly*, appointed him for about three months in the year to labor among them, and I know that he was much encouraged in his work ; had some very promising young converts ; and the number of communicants was not diminished in his time. The present pastor (1840) is the Rev. Clement Read, a native of the county. He has labored there and at Bethesda for many years past. *In general the Negroes were followers of the Baptists* in Virginia, and after a while, as they permitted many colored men to preach, the great majority of them went to hear preachers of their own color, which was attended with many evils. In some parts of the state the *Methodists* also paid much attention to the Negroes and received many of them into their society : but still professors among the Baptists were far more numerous. In many instances those who had been brought into the Presbyterian church were swept off by one or the other of these sects. But as long as I was acquainted with the congregation at Cub-creek, I never knew one of them to leave their own communion for another. We had the testimony of their masters and mistresses, to their conscientiousness, fidelity, and diligence. The lady who owned 25 of the communicants, selected all her house servants from the number, though not herself a communicant in the Presbyterian church. And on several estates instead of overseers, some of these pious men were appointed to superintend the labor of the other field servants."

The Rev. Henry Patillo, pastor of the Grassy Creek and Nutbush churches in Greenville county, North Carolina, labored successfully among the Negroes about this time; the good effects of whose efforts continued to be felt for many years after.— *Dr. Plumer's Report to Synods of N. Carolina and Virginia.*

1792. Towards the close of this year the first colored Baptist church in the city of Savannah, began to build a place of worship. The corporation of the city gave them a lot for the purpose. The origin of this church —the parent of several others—is briefly as follows:

George Leile, sometimes called George Sharp, was born in Virginia about 1750. His master sometime before the American war, removed and settled in Burke county Georgia. Mr. Sharp was a Baptist and a deacon in a Baptist church, of which Rev. Matthew Moore was pastor. George was converted and baptized under Mr. Moore's ministry. The church gave him liberty to preach. He began to labor with good success at different plantations. Mr. Sharp gave him his freedom not long after he began to preach: for about three years he preached at Brampton and Yamacraw in the neighborhood of Savannah. On the evacuation of the country, (1782 and 1783,) he went to Jamaica. Previous to his departure he came up from the vessel lying below the city in the river, and baptized an African woman by the name of *Kate*, belonging to Mrs. Eunice Hogg, and *Andrew*, his wife *Hannah*, and *Hagar*, belonging to the venerable Mr. Jonathan Bryan.

The Baptist cause among the Negroes in Jamaica, owes its origin to the indefatigable and pious labors of this worthy man, George Leile. It does not come within my design to introduce an account of his efforts in that island; I shall add only that in 1784 he commenced preaching in Kingston, and formed a church, and in 1791 had gathered a company of 450 communicants and commenced the erection of a commodious meeting house. It finally cost with steeple and bell 4,000*l.* He was alive in 1810 and about *sixty* years of age.

About nine months after George Leile left Georgia. Andrew, surnamed Bryan, a man of good sense, great zeal, and some natural elocution, began to exhort his black brethren and friends. He and his followers were reprimanded and forbidden to engage further in religious exercises. He would however pray, sing, and encourage his fellow worshippers to seek the Lord. Their persecution was carried to an inhuman extent. Their evening assemblies were broken up and those found present were punished with stripes! Andrew Bryan and Sampson his brother, converted about a year after him, were twice imprisoned, and they with about fifty others were whipped. When publicly whipped, and bleeding under his wounds, Andrew declared that he rejoiced not only to be whipped, but would freely suffer death for the cause of Jesus Christ: and that while he had life and opportunity, he would continue to preach Christ. He was faithful to his vow, and by patient continuance in *well-doing*, he put to silence and shamed his adversaries; and influential advocates and patrons were raised up for him. Liberty was given Andrew by the civil authority to continue his religious meetings under certain regulations. His master gave him the use of his barn at Brampton, three miles from Savannah, where he preached for two years, with little interruption.

Not long after Andrew began his ministry he was visited by the Rev. Thomas Barton, who baptized *eigh-*

teen of his followers on profession of their faith. The next visit was from the Rev. Abraham Marshall of Kioka, who was accompanied by a young colored preacher, by the name of Jesse Peter, from the vicinity of Augusta. On the 20th of January 1788, Mr. Marshall ordained Andrew Bryan, baptized forty of his hearers, and constituted them with others, 69 in number, a church, of which Andrew was the pastor. Such was the origin of the first colored Baptist church in Savannah. — *Holcombe's Letters; Analytical Repository; and Benedict's Hist. of Baptists:* from which the preceding account has been taken.

Before dismissing this notice, I cannot forbear introducing the remarks of Dr. Holcombe on Andrew Bryan, written in 1812.

" Andrew Bryan has, long ago, not only honorably obtained liberty, but a handsome estate. His fleecy and well-set locks have been bleached by eighty winters: and dressed like a bishop of London, he rides, moderately corpulent, in his chair, and with manly features, of a jetty hue, fills every person to whom he gracefully bows, with pleasure and veneration, by displaying in smiles even rows of natural teeth, white as ivory, and a pair of fine black eyes, sparkling with intelligence, benevolence, and joy. In giving daily thanks to God for his mercies my aged friend seldom forgets to mention the favorable change that has of late years appeared through the lower parts of Georgia, as well as of South Carolina, in the treatment of servants." — *Let.* 17.

1793. The African church in Augusta, Ga., was gathered by the labors of Jesse Peter, and was constituted this year by Rev. Abraham Marshall and David Tinsley. Jesse Peter was also called Jesse Golfin on account of his master's name — living twelve miles below Augusta.

The number of Baptists in the United States this year was 73,471, allowing *one-fourth to be Negroes* the denomination would embrace between *eighteen and nineteen thousand*

1795. The returns of colored members in the Methodist denomination from 1791 to 1795, inclusive, were 12,884, 13,871, 16,227, 13,814, 12,170.

Several annual conferences recommended a *general fast*, to be held March 1796, and in the enumeration of blessings to be invoked the last mentioned was "that *Africans* and Indians may help to fill the pure church of God." And in the matters recommended as subjects of grateful remembrance in the day of thanksgiving for the last Thursday in October 1796, the last mentioned is — "And for African liberty ; we feel grateful that many thousands of these poor people are free and pious."

1797. The Methodists reported in 1796, 11,280 colored members. The recapitulation of the numbers for 1797 is given by States, and as it is a most interesting document I insert it entire, so far as it relates to the Negroes.

Mass.	8	Penn.	198	S. C.	890
R. I.	2	Del.	823	Ga.	148
Conn.	15	Md.	5 106	Tenn.	42
N. Y.	238	Va.	2 490	Ky.	57
N. J.	127	N. C.	2 071		

Making a total of 12,215; nearly *one-fourth* of the whole number of members, were colored. There were *three* only in Canada.

Dr. Bangs adds: "It will be seen by the above enumeration that there were upward of 12,000 people of color attached to the Methodist Episcopal Church. These were chiefly in the Southern States, and had been gathered principally from the slave population.

At an early period of the Methodist ministry in this country it had turned its attention and directed its efforts towards these people, with a view to bring them to the enjoyment of Gospel blessings. The preachers deplored with the deepest sympathy their unhappy condition, especially their enslavement to sin and satan; and while they labored unsuccessfully by all prudent means to effect their disenthralment from their civil bondage, they were amply rewarded for their evangelical efforts to raise them from their moral degradation, by seeing thousands of them happily converted to God. These efforts added much to the labor of the preachers, for such was the condition of the slaves that they were not permitted, on working days, to attend the public administration of the word in company with their masters; and hence the preachers devoted the evenings to their instruction after the customary labors of the day were closed. And although at first there was much aversion manifested by the masters, towards these benevolent efforts to elevate the condition of the slaves; yet, witnessing the beneficial effects of the Gospel upon their hearts and lives, they gradually yielded their prejudices and encouraged the preachers in their labors, assisted in providing houses to accommodate them in their worship and otherwise protected them in their religious privileges. While, therefore, the voice of the preachers was not heard in favor of emancipation from their civil bondage, nor their remonstrances against the evils of slavery heeded, the voice of truth addressed to the understandings and consciences of the slaves themselves, was often heard with believing and obedient hearts and made instrumental in their deliverance from the shackles of sin and the bondage of satan. Those who were thus redeemed were enroled among the people of God and were consequently entitled to the privileges of the church of Christ. In some of the northern cities houses of worship were erected for their special and separate accommodation, and they were put under the pastoral charge of a white preacher, who was generally assisted by such colored local preachers as may have been raised up among themselves; for many such, from time to time, possessing gifts for edification, were licensed to preach the Gospel to their colored brethren, and some of these have been eminently useful. In the more Southern States, where the municipal regulations in respect to slaves are more severe, some portion of the churches where the white population assemble is usually set apart for the blacks. Their behaviour has generally been such as to insure the confidence of their masters and the protection of their civil rulers, though they labored under the disabilities incident to a state of servitude."

1799 This year is memorable for the commencement of that extraordinary awakening which, taking its rise in Kentucky and spreading in various directions and with different degrees of intensity, was denominated, "the great Kentucky revival." It continued for above four years, and its influence was felt over a large portion of the Southern States. Presbyterians, Methodists, and Baptists participated in this work. In this revival originated *Camp-Meetings*, which gave a new impulse to Methodism. From the best estimates the number of Negroes received into the different communions, during this season, must have been between *four* and *five thousand.*

1800. Number of members in connection with the Methodists 13,452. The bishops of the M. E. church were authorized to ordain African preachers, in places where there were houses of worship for their use, who might be chosen by a majority of the male members of the society to which they belonged and could procure a recommendation from the preacher in charge and his colleagues on the circuit, to the office of local deacons. *Richard Allen* of Philadelphia was the *first* colored man who received orders under this rule.

1803. The *second* African church in Savannah formed out of the first, 26th Dec'r, 1802 ; and Henry Cunningham elected pastor and ordained to the work of the ministry, January 1st, 1803. On the 2d of January 1803, another church was formed out of the *first*, called the *Ogechee Colored Baptist Church*, and Henry Francis appointed to supply it. Henry Cunningham was a slave, but obtained his fredom. He is still the pastor of the 2d African church, far advanced in life, and from age unable to attend to his sacred duties, except to a very limited extent. He still enjoys, (as he has always enjoyed,) the confidence and esteem of all classes of the community in which he has lived so long, so virtuously, and so usefully. The Methodist conferences reported 22,453 colored members — an increase over the last year of 3,794.

In the report of the congregation of the *Moravian Brethren* at Graceham, Maryland, for 1801, the Rev. Frederick Schlegel under date of April 19th, writes : " As a number of Negroes had for several Sundays successively attended our divine worship, I collected thirteen of them and after a suitable address, prayed with them. They were very devout, and declared it to be their sincere desire to be truly converted. A few Sundays after brother Browne (who preached the Gospel to the Negroes on Staten Island) being here on a visit, preached to thirty Negroes, and after the sermon baptized two children. The transaction made such an impression on two of the adult Negroes that they requested this rite might be immediately performed on them. They were however satisfied with the reasons I assigned for defering it till they had received further instruction in Christianity. A very affecting scene took place at the close of the meeting. A Negro overseer who was present, kneeled down with his people and in an impressive prayer thanked God for what their souls had enjoyed that day. The number of Negroes that attended increased almost every week. At their request a regulation was made according to which separate meetings will be held with them at stated times. Opportunities will also be offered them for private conversation on religious subjects." Some children and a few adults were in the sequel baptized. — *Hist. of the Church of the Brethren, vol.* 2, *pp.* 292 293.

1805. An African church formed in Boston under the ministry of Thomas Paul a colored man. Their house of worship was finished in 1806; the lower story fitted up for a school room.

1806. The Baptist churches in South Carolina were 130, the number of ministers 100, and communicants 10,500, of which perhaps 3,500 were Negroes.

1807. Hanover Presbytery, Va., addressed a circular to the churches under their care, solemnly exhorting them not to neglect their duty to their servants. — *Va. Mag., vol.* 3, *p.* 159.

1809. The Abyssinian or African church formed in the *City of New York*. House of worship in Anthony street. Also an African church *in Philadelphia;* supplied for a time by Henry Cunningham of Savannah, Ga. The estimate of colored communicants in the Baptist churches in *Virginia* this year, I set down at 9,000.

1810. By the reports of the state of the congregations of the Protestant Episcopal Church in South Carolina, made in the convention, there were 199 colored communicants in 3 churches, viz: St. Philips' and St. Michaels', Charleston, 120 and 73, and Prince George's, Winyaw, 6. The other reports do not distinguish between white and colored communicants.

1813. There were 40,000 Negroes connected with the Baptist denomination in the States of Pennsylvania, Delaware, Virginia, North Carolina, South Carolina and Georgia. The historian remarks, " that among the African Baptists in the Southern States, there are a multitude of preachers and exhorters whose names do not appear on the minutes of associations. They preach principally on the plantations to those of their own color, and their preaching, though broken and illiterate, is in many cases highly useful."

1816. There was a report adopted by the General Assembly of the Presbyterian church in the United States, on the question, " ought baptism on the promise of the master to be administered to the children of slaves?" as follows: 1. that it is the duty of masters who are members of the church, to present the children of parents in servitude, to the ordinance of Baptism, provided they are in a situation to train them up in the nurture and admonition of the Lord; thus securing to them the rich advantages which the Gospel promises.

2. That it is the duty of Christian ministers to inculcate
this doctrine and to baptize all children when presented
to them by their masters." — *Minutes of the Assembly.*

The subject of *Missions to the Negroes* occupied the
attention of the General Assembly, but no plan of missions was carried into effect.   Dr. Rice of Virginia was
employed by the committee on missions in the assembly
for a part of the year, and his labors were encouraging,
as already stated by Dr. Alexander in his letter, and as
appears also from the *Minutes of the Assembly, p.* 372.

The Colonization Society was formed this year, and I
notice it. as furnishing an index to the feelings of
many in relation to the improvement of the Negro race.

The Methodists reported this year 42,304 colored
members, and a decrease of 883 since 1815.   Dr. Bangs
says, "this was owing to a defection among the colored
people in the city of Philadelphia, by which upwards of
1,000 in that city withdrew from our church and set up
for themselves, with *Richard Allen*, a colored local
preacher, an elder in the Methodist Episcopal Church
at their head.—By habits of industry and economy,
though born a slave in one of the Southern States, he
had not only procured his freedom, but acquired considerable wealth, and since he had exercised the office
of a preacher and an elder, obtained great influence
over his brethren in the church   At the secession they
organized themselves into an independent body, under
the title of the "African Methodist Episcopal Church."
At their first general conference in April, 1816, Richard
Allen was elected Bishop.—At the conference in 1828,
Morris Brown was elected joint superintendent with
Allen : and on the death of Allen, in 1836, Edward Wat-
ters was elected joint superintendent with Brown.   The

colored congregations in New York city follo wed te example. — They adopted the itinerant mode of preaching and have spread themselves in different parts of Pennsylvania, New York, New Jersey, Maryland and Delaware. There are also some in the Western States and a few in Upper Canada. In the more Southern States the Allenites could make no favorable impression, as their preachers were not recognized by the laws of the States, and the Slave population who were members of our church had the character of our white ministry pledged as a guarantee for their good behaviour."

1818. Under the report of colored members for this year, the same writer remarks, " that while there was an increase of white members, amounting to 9,035, there was a decrease of 4,261 of the colored members." He states that this was owing to the Allenite secession : although not all who through its influence declared themselves independent, attached themselves to the Allenites.

1819. The increase of colored members this year was but 24: 1819, 39,174, and 1818, 39,150. The smallness of the increase accounted for by the secession of the Negroes in New York city, amounting to " 14 local preachers and 929 private members, including class-leaders, exhorters and stewards."

A report dated June 14th, 1819, of a committee of the board of managers of the Bible society of Charleston, S. C., respecting the progress and present state of religion in South Carolina, will cast some light on the subject before us. " From the best information the committee have been able to obtain, they find that the Gospel is now preached to about 613 congregations of Protestant Christians; that there are about 292 ordained clergymen who labor amongst them, besides a a considerable number of domestic missionaries, devoted and supported by each denomination, who dispense their labors to such of the people as remain destitute of an established ministry. From actual returns and cautious estimates where such returns have not been obtained, it appears that in the state there are about 46,000 Protestants who receive the holy communion of the Lord's Supper. In the city of Charleston *upwards of one-fourth* of the communicants *are slaves or free persons of color;* and it is supposed that in the other parts of the state the proportion of such communicants may be estimated at about *one-eighth.* In every church they are freely admitted to attend on divine service : in most of the churches *distinct accommodations* are provided for them, and the clergy in general make it a part of their pastoral care to devote *frequent and stated* seasons for the religious instruction of catechumen from amongst the black population."

It may be proper to state in connection with this report, that from the beginning, with scarcely an exception, the Negroes applying for admission into the churches have been under the instruction of white ministers or members : have been examined and approved as candidates for baptism : have been baptized and have partaken of the Lord's Supper at the same time with white candidates and members, and been subject to the same care and discipline ; no distinction being made between the two classes of members in respect to the privileges and discipline of the churches.

The Episcopal church reported in part the number of colored members from 1812 to 1818, the majority in

Charleston. The highest number reported was in 1817
328. In 1818 there were 289.

1820. Bishop McKendree presented an address to
the general conference at Baltimore, in which he took
notice of " the condition of the slaves." The number
of colored members, by the minutes of conference, was
40,558.

The census of 1800 gave us 893,041 Negro slaves and
110,555 free, making a total of 1.003,596. That of
1810 was 1,191,364 slave and 195,643 free; total Negro
population, 1,387,007. That of 1820, 1,538,064 slave
and 244,020 free; total 1,782,084.

The importation of Africans into our country ceased,
by law, on the 1st of January 1808. The traffic was
abolished by Virginia in 1778, and by Pennsylvania,
Massachusetts, Connecticut, and Rhode Island, in 1780,
1787, 1788. And before the year 1820 measures were
taken by all the present free states, in which slavery had
existed, for bringing the system to a close. What
special efforts, if any, were made in these states by the
churches, or by societies, for the religious instruction of
the Negroes thus attaining their freedom, I have no
means of ascertaining with accuracy. From the best
information in my possession *special* efforts were very
few and very limited.

As a nation we were scarcely reviving from the Revolution and the excitement of the formation and establishment of our Constitution, when we were involved in a
war with France, which, with its influences, and what
was worse, the infidelity and skepticism which our previous connection with that nation introduced among us,
most seriously affected the interests of religion, and the
decline was perceptible in a greater or less degree over

the whole Union. Not long after, our troubles with England began, which resulted in a four years war. Notwithstanding these interruptions, the Spirit of God was poured out largely in different parts of the country. Indeed, the first quarter of the nineteenth century witnessed a remarkable revival of the missionary spirit in the American as well as English churches. Many societies were organized on a large and liberal scale, (in whose existence the world has reason to rejoice,) for the spreading of the Gospel, both at home and abroad, as well by the circulation of the scriptures and auxiliary publications, as by the living teacher.

This spirit wrought in the hearts of ministers and people generally, and a new and mighty impulse was given to religion. In the South it awakened many to see the spiritual necessities of the Negroes. Many ministers began to preach particularly and more faithfully to them and to attempt a regular division of their time on the Sabbath, between the whites and blacks. Attempts were also made in some parts of the South, to teach the Negroes letters, so as to enable them to read the word of God for themselves. These schools were short-lived but the fact of their existence, evidences that there was considerable interest felt in their religious instruction. Houses of public worship, exclusively for the use of the Negroes, were erected in many of the chief towns, and they worshipped in them, under the care of white or colored teachers. In numbers of white churches space was allowed for the accommodation of the Negroes, in the galeries or in the body of the house below; and within sight and hearing of country churches, in some pleasant grove fitted up with booths, with a stand or pulpit for preaching, the Negroes would oft times be seen assembling for worship between services, or in the afternoon. There were planters also, who undertook to read and explain the scriptures, and pray with their people.

It is not to much to say that the religious and physical condition of the Negroes were both improved during this period. Their increase was natural and regular, ranging, every ten years, between 34 and 36 *per cent.* As the old stock from Africa died out of the country the grosser customs, the ignorance and paganism of Africa, died with them. Their descendants, *the country-born,* were better looking, more intelligent, more civilized, more susceptible of religious impressions. Growing up under the eyes and in the families of owners, they became more attached to them, were identified in their households and accompanied them to church. The Gospel was preached to masters and servants; servants having no religion to renounce grew up in the belief of that of their masters. On the whole, however, but a minority of the Negroes, and that a small one, attended regularly the house of God, and taking them as a class, their religious instruction was extensively and most seriously neglected.

CHAPTER III.

THE THIRD PERIOD — From 1820 to 1842 — a Period of 22 years.

1821. The Methodist Episcopal Church reported this year 42,059 colored members in the United States; and their numbers gradually increasing.

1822. The account of the labors of the Moravian Brethren by Mr. Schmidt, already referred to, brings down their labors to 1837, and is as follows:

"In January 1822, a Female Auxiliary to the Missionary Society was formed at Salem and at their special request an attempt was made to collect the Negroes into a separate congregation of their own — a plan which had, indeed, long been an object of desire. Brother Abraham Steiner was commissioned to make a commencement of the work by holding a monthly preaching on a plantation about three miles distant from Salem, where the Negro communicants resided. At his first sermon there, March 24th, 1822, more than fifty black and colored people were present. After a fervent prayer he discoursed on the words of our Saviour, "the Son of Man is come to seek and to save that which was lost." With this monthly preaching, which was well attended by the Negroes, catechetical instruction in the great truths of our religion was combined. May 19th the Lord's Supper was celebrated with the three persons who were already communicants as the first fruits of this infant Negro flock. Great stillness and devotio:. continued to mark the attendance of the Negroes on divine worship, yet few sought for closer fellowship, so that this little flock has never to the present day numbered more than twenty members.

A Negro chapel was built in 1823, at the expense of the Female Auxiliary and consecrated by brother Benade, the resident Bishop, December 28th, in the presence of near a hundred Negroes and colored people, and many members of the congregation at S lem. This was followed by the baptism of a married Negro woman, and the solemnities of the day were closed by a cheerful love feast, at which the object of our covenant was explained and two Negroes were received into the congregation. It was a day of blessing for the Negroes, many of whom seemed to be deeply affected. Having now a place of worship of their own, the meetings could be better adapted to their circumstances. Several sisters offered themselves, to keep a Sunday school for their benefit, and it was diligently frequented, not only by children, but also by adults. This hopeful project was soon, however, painfully interrupted by a law which passed the legislature of North Carolina, forbidding any school instruction to be imparted to the Negroes; — a prohibition which likewise operated very injuriously on their attendance at the meetings. May 22d, 1833, the Negroes were called to mourn over the loss of their faithful and much loved pastor, brother Abraham Steiner, and his place was supplied by brother John Renatus Schmidt. For the last year or two, they have manifested a greater desire for the word of life and visited the house of God more diligently, and our testimony to the sufferings and death of Jesus appears to find more entrance into their hearts. In the private meetings of the little Negro flock, and particularly at the holy communion, the peace of God is powerfully perceptible. The company of emancipated Negroes, upwards of twenty in number, who sailed last year for Liberia, on the western coast of Africa, had all been diligent attendants on our meetings and former Sunday school, and one of them was a communicant member of our flock. At parting they declared with tears that nothing grieved them so much as the loss of these privileges. They promised to devote themselves to the Lord Jesus and to remain faithful to him.

In the fourteen years which have elapsed since their church was dedicated 10 adults and 73 children have been baptized and 8 received into the congregation. The little flock consists at present (1837,) of 17 adult members, 10 of whom are communicants.

On the settling of the Brethren in Wachovia, (N. C.,) it was their most cherished object to communicate the Gospel both to the Indians on the borders of the Southern States and to the Negro population of those States, amounting to several thousands, especially to such as resided in the neighborhood of our congregations, hoping that they might be favored to gather from among them a reward for the travail of the Redeemer's soul. Special meetings were accordingly commenced at Hope and Bethany, and elsewhere in the neighborhood of Salem, and the Negroes who were numerous in these districts, were in general diligent in attending them. The various ministers stationed at Salem, the late breth-

ren Fritz, Kramsch, Wohfahrt, Abraham Steiner, and
their wives, interested themselves with particular affection for the spiritual welfare of the Negroes in their
vicinity, and the Lord so blessed their labors to the
hearts of many that they could be admitted to a partici-
pation of the Lord's supper. A thankful remembrance
of their faithful services is still retained by the Negroes.

In the prosecution of the mission amongst the Chero-
kees, and in the attempt to establish one amongst the
Creek Indians, the Negroes dispersed among them were
not forgotten. Our brethren at Springplace had the
gratification of baptizing the firstling of these Negroes
July 29th 1827. He was a native African of the Tjamba
tribe, and was baptized into the death of Jesus by the
name of Christian Jacob, continuing faithful to his
Christian profession till his happy end."

The Rev. John Mines, pastor of a church in Lees-
burg, Va., published, "The Evangelical Catechism, or
a plain and easy system of the principal doctrines and
duties of the Christian religion. Adapted to the use of
Sabbath schools and families : with a new method of
instructing those who cannot read. Richmond 1822."

His "new method," was what is called "oral instruction ;" the scholars repeating the answers after the
teacher until committed to memory. Mr. Mines was
much interested in the religious instruction of the Negroes. In the preface to his catechism, he states that
"he had several classes of them (taught by his friends)"
he commends the use of it to *masters and mistresses*,
as "an humble attempt" to furnish them with appropriate means for the instruction of their servants in religious
knowledge ; and he commends it also to "*his colored
friends in the United States*," as a book written "espe-

cially for them," and says, "with the help of God, I
will attend particularly to your spiritual interests while
I live."

1823. Bishop Dehon of the Diocese of South Carolina, had all his good feelings excited in behalf of the
Negroes. "In his own congregation he was the laborious and patient minister of the African; and he encouraged among the masters and mistresses in his flock, that
best kindness towards their servants — a concern for
their eternal salvation." "He endeavored to enlighten
the community on this subject." "He would gladly embrace opportunities to converse with men of influence
relating to it," etc. — *Life, by Dr. Gadsden.*

The Rev. Dr. Dalcho, of the Episcopal church,
Charleston, this year issued a valuable pamphlet entitled
"Practical Considerations, founded on the Scriptures,
Relative to the Slave Population of South Carolina."
Its design is given in the first paragraph, namely, "to
show from the Scriptures of the Old and New Testament, that slavery is not forbidden by the Divine Law:
and at the same time, to prove the necessity of giving
religious instruction to our Negroes." Dr. Dalcho
mentions that in 1822 there were 316 colored communicants in the Episcopal churches in Charleston, and 200
children in their colored Sunday schools.

A few months before this pamphlet appeared, Dr.
Richard Furman, President of the Baptist State Convention of S. C., in the name of that convention,
addressed a letter to his Excellency, Governor Wilson
giving an "Exposition of the Views of the Baptists
relative to the Colored Population in the United States:"
in which, among other observations, we find the following: "Their religious interests claim a regard from

their masters of the most serious nature, and it is indispensable."

The lamented Dr. John Holt Rice, already mentioned in this Sketch, presented the subject of the religious instruction of the Negroes in a strong light to the consideration of his fellow citizens of Virginia in the *Evanglical Magazine*, *vol.* 8 *pp.* 613–4. He printed a sermon on the duty of masters to educate and baptize the children of their servants. Through his influence many in Virginia were induced to give the duty of the religious instruction of the Negroes serious consideration, which resulted in action   One of his objects in devoting himself to the establishment of the Prince Edward Theological Seminary, was that a ministry might be educated at home and fitted for the field *composed as it is*, of masters and servants, bond and free. This was also one prominent object in the minds of many ministers, elders, and laymen, in the foundation and endowment of the Theological Seminary of the Synod of South Carolina and Georgia in Columbia, S. C.

1828. Number of colored members in Methodist E. Church, 48,096 and for 1825, 49,537; 1826, 51,334; 1827, 53,565; 1828, 58,856; showing a steady increase. In 1828, "a plain and easy Catechism, designed chiefly for the benefit of colored persons, with suitable Prayers and Hymns annexed," was published by Rev. B. M. Palmer, D. D., pastor of the Circular Church, Charleston, S. C." Six or eight years before this he had published a smaller work of the same kind and bearing nearly the same title. During all his ministry in Charleston he was a firm supporter of the religious instruction of the Negroes, both in word and deed.

1829. The Honorable Charles Cotesworth Pinckney

of the Episcopal church, delivered an address before the Agricultural Society of South Carolina, in which he ably and largely insists upon the religious instruction of the Negroes. This address went through two or more editions and was extensively circulated and with the happiest effects.

1830. The historian of the Methodist Episcopal church remarks, " this year several missions were commenced for the special benefit of the slave population in the States of South Carolina and Georgia. This class of people had been favored with the labors of the Methodist ministry from the beginning of its labors in this country, and there were at this time 62,814 of the colored population in the several states and territories in our church fellowship, most of whom were slaves. It was found, however, on a closer inspection into their condition, that there were many that could not be reached by the ordinary means, and therefore preachers were selected who might devote themselves exclusively to their service."

He alludes particularly to the "Missionary Society of the South Carolina Conference, Auxiliary to the Missionary Society of the Methodist Episcopal Church," of which, at least so far as its efforts respect the Negro population, the Rev. William Capers, D. D., of Charleston, S. C., is *the founder.* He has been superintendent of these missions to the Negroes from their commencement and has spared no exertions to extend and render them successful. The reports of the board of managers, drawn up from year to year by himself exhibit the purity and fervor of his zeal in so good a cause, as well as the remarkable progress which it has made.

In the winter of 1830 and the spring of 1831, two Associations of planteis were formed in Georgia for the special object of affording religious instruction to the Negroes, by their own efforts and by missionaries employed for the purpose. The *first* was formed by the Rev. Joseph Clay Stiles in McIntosh county, embracing the neighborhood of Harris' neck, which continued in operation for some time, until by the withdrawment of Mr. Stiles' labors from the neighborhood and the loss of some of the inhabitants by death and removals it ceased. The *second* was formed in Liberty county by the Midway Congregational church, and the Baptist church under their respective pastors the Rev. Robert Quarterman and the Rev. Samuel Spry Law; which Association, with one suspension from the absence of a missionary, has continued its operations to the present time.

One or more associations for the same purpose were formed in St. Luke's Parish, S. C., in which John David Mungin, Esquire, took an active part.

1831. An address, entitled, "the Religious Instruction of the Negroes," delivered before the Associations of McIntosh and Liberty counties, was published and circulated in newspaper and pamphlet form.

1832. Edward R. Laurens, Esquire, delivered an address before the Agricultural Association of S. C., in which this duty in the form of oral instruction, under proper arrangements is recognised.—*Southern Agriculturist*, 1832. "A short Catechism for the use of the colored members on trial of the M. E. Church in South Carolina : by W. Capers, D. D., Charleston, 1832."

This short catechism was prepared by Dr. Capers, for the use of the Methodist missions to the Negroes of the

S. C. conference, and it is used by all the missionaries.

1833 The Missionary Society of the S. C. Conference which had now fairly entered upon its work, reported that the missions were generally in flourishing circumstances; that there were 1,395 colored members, and 490 children under catechetical instruction at the mission stations. The society also recommended the establishment of four or five new stations and the appointment of three or four new missionaries for stations already occupied. — *Report pp.* 12 — 15.

The " First Annual Report, " of the Liberty County Association, was published and circulated in two editions.

Two essays were read before the presbytery of Georgia, in April, 1833, one on " The Moral and Religious condition of our coloured population, " and the other, a " Detail of a Plan for the Moral Improvement of Negroes on plantations, " by Thomas Savage Clay, Esq., of Bryan County. They were both published by order of presbytery. The " Detail, etc., " by Mr. Clay, which was indeed the result of his own experience and observation on his own plantation for many years, was extensively circulated and received with approbation, and has done, and still is doing, much good.

In December, of this year, the " Report of the Committee, to whom was referred the subject of the religious instruction of the Negroes, " of the synod of South Carolina and Georgia was published. To this report a series of resolutions were subjoined.

1. " That to impart the Gospel to the Negroes of our country is a duty which God in his providence and in his word imposes on us. 2. That in the discharge of this duty, we separate entirely the civil and religious condition of this people; and while we devote ourselves to the improvement of latter, we disclaim all interference with

the former. 3. That the plan which we shall pursue for their religious instruction shall be that permitted by the laws of the States constituting the bounds of this synod. 4. That we deem religious instruction to master and servant every way conducive to our interests for this world and for that which is to come. 5. That every member of this synod, while he endeavors to awaken others, shall set the example and begin the religious instruction of the servants of his own household, systematically and perseveringly, as God shall enable him. 6. That we cannot longer continue to neglect this duty without incurring the charge of inconsistency in our Christian character; of unfaithfulness in the discharge of our ministerial duty; and at the same time meeting the disapprobation of God and our consciences." The narrative of religion of the synod, at the same session, holds the following language: " the synod continue to feel the same responsibilities and desires on this subject which they have repeatedly expressed. They rejoice to find that increasing attention is paid to it on the part of many who are largely interested as owners in this class of our population." — *Min. pp.* 24, 34.

The project of forming a *Domestic Missionary Society,* under the care of the synod, *with special reference to the religious instruction of the Negroes,* was somewhat discussed, chiefly in private, and a committee was appointed by the synod to bring in a report at the next meeting.

The reports from the Episcopal churches in South Carolina to the convention, evidenced much attention to the Negroes. The Rev. Joseph R. Walker, of Beaufort, reported 57 communicants and 234 members of the Sunday school, which was conducted by the first and best society in the place.

Bishop Ives of North Carolina, addressed to his convention, " on the interesting subject of providing for our slave population a more adequate knowledge of the doctrines of Christ crucified." He stated in a letter to Bishop Meade, that active efforts in behalf of this people were made in five or six of the churches, and singled out the church of St. John's, Fayetteville, embracing between three and four hundred worshippers of whom forty were communicants.

There were several religious newspapers, conducted by different denominations, that advocated openly and efficiently, about this time, the religious instruction of the Negroes: the "Gospel Messenger," Episcopal, Charleston: the "Charleston Observer," Presbyterian: the "Christian Index," Baptist: the "Southern Christian Advocate," Methodist: the "Western Luminary," Kentucky: and there may be added, the "New Orleans Observer," and the "Southern Churchman," Alexandria; besides others. Through these papers, having an extensive circulation, the subject was presented to the minds of thousands of our citizens.

There was published this year. (1833,) "a Plain and Easy Catechism: designed for the benefit of colored children, with several verses and hymns, with an appendix: compiled by a missionary: Savannah." This missionary was a Methodist; the Rev. Samuel J. Bryan, who labored among the Negroes on the Savannah river

"The encouraging success which had attended the labors of our preachers among the slave and free black population of the South, stimulated our brethren in the Southwest to imitate their example by opening missions for the special benefit of this class of people. Hence at the last session of the Tennessee conference the

African Mission, embracing the colored population of Nashville and its vicinity was commenced; a regular four week's circuit was formed, and the good work was prosecuted with such success that in 1834 there were reported 819 church members." — *Bangs* 4, *p.* 143.

1834. " A meeting was held in Petersburg, Va., in March 1834, composed of representatives from the synods of North Carolina and Virginia. After disposing of the *special business* for which the meeting was called, the subject of the religious instruction of the Negroes was discussed and as a result a committee was appointed, consisting of three ministers and elders in each of the States, " to bring before the presbyteries the subject of ministers giving more religious instruction to the colored people; and to collect and publish information on the best modes of giving oral instruction to this class of our population." That committee, of which Rev. William S. Plumer, D. D., now of Richmond, was the chairman, performed its duty and presented a report to the synods of North Carolina and Virginia at their fall sessions in 1834. The same report, with some accompanying documents was forwarded to the synod of South Carolina and Georgia, and read before that body in December, 1834.

The committee of the synods of North Carolina and Virginia, reported a plan "*for forming a society* by the concurrence of two or more synods for the purpose of affording religious instruction to the Negroes in a manner consistent with the laws of the States and with the feelings and wishes of planters." The plan was laid before the synod of North Carolina, and acceded to. It was laid over by the synods of Virginia and South Carolina and Georgia, to their sessions in 1835 and then, for special reasons, indefinitely postponed. A report was presented by a committee of the synod of South Carolina and Georgia, *on this plan.* The report was *adverse* to it, on account of the *extent* of the proposed organization; the *excitement* of the times; and the belief that *each synod could of itself* conduct the work more successfully, than when united with the other two. The constitution of the proposed society, the reasons in favor of it, and Dr. Plumer's report, were all laid before the public in the columns of the Charleston Observer. The report has been several times referred to in this Sketch.

The synod of South Carolina and Georgia, December 1834, passed the following resolutions: " 1. That it be enjoined upon all the churches in the presbyteries comprising this synod, to take order at their earliest meeting to obtain full and correct statistical information of the number of colored persons in actual attendance at our several places of worship, and the number of colored members in our several churches, and make a full report to the synod at its next meeting; and for this purpose that the stated clerk of this synod furnish a copy of this resolution to the stated clerk of each presbytery. 2. That it be enjoined on all presbyteries in presenting their annual report to synod, to report the state of religion in the colored part of their congregations, and also to present a statistical report of the increase of colored members, *and that this be the standing rule of synod on this subject.*" The narative states "that increasing efforts had been made to impart religious instruction to the Negroes."— *Min. pp.* 22, 29.

The synod of Mississippi and Alabama, in their narrative, November 1, 1831, say, "another very encour-

aging circumstance in the situation of our churches is
the deep interest which is felt in behalf of our colored
population, and the efforts which are made to impart to
them religious instruction.   All our ministers feel a deep
interest in the instruction of this part of our population,
and when prudently conducted we meet with no opposition.   A few of us, owing to peculiar circumstances,
have no opportunity of preaching to them separately and
at stated times; but embrace every favorable opportunity that occurs.   Others devote a portion of every
Sabbath; others a half of every Sabbath; and *two* of
our number preach *exclusively* to them.   During the
past year the condition and wants of the colored population, have occupied more of our attention than at any
previous period, and in future we hope to be more untiring in all our efforts to promote their happiness in this
life and in that which is to come."   In their resolutions
this synod enjoined all under their care directly to make
"united efforts to provide means for the employment of
missionaries to give oral instruction to the colored population on the plantations with the permission of those
persons to whom they belong."

In this same year, (1834,) "the Kentucky Union, for
the moral and religious improvement of the colored
race," was formed, and a "circular" addressed to the
ministers of the Gospel in Kentucky, by the executive
committee of that Union; to which the constitution was
appended.   It was a "union of the several denominations of christians, in the State."   The Rev. H. H.
Cavanaugh was president; there were *ten* vice presi-
dents, selected from different quarters of the State; and
an executive committee of *seven* members located in
Danville, of which Rev. John C. Young was chairman.

President Young told me at the general assembly of 1839 that this Union had not accomplished much.

The "*second* annual report" of the Liberty County Association was published, giving some good account of their operations. "An Essay on the Management of Slaves, and especially on their religious instruction," read before the agricultural society of St. John's Colleton, S. C., by Whitemarsh B. Seabrook, president, was published by the society. Mr. Seabrook reviews some former publications on the religious instruction of the Negroes, and suggests his own plans and views on the subject. The Right Reverend William Meade, Assistant Bishop of Virginia, published an admirable "*pastoral letter*, to the ministers, members, and friends of the Protestant Episcopal Church in the diocese of Virginia, on the duty of affording religious instruction to those in bondage." The Bishop in his zeal and personal efforts on this subject, demonstrates the sincerity of his published opinions.

The missionary society of the S. C. conference reported five missionaries to the blacks, in N. C. *one*, the rest in S. C., and 2,145 members and 1,503 children under catechetical instruction.

"The Colored man's Help: or the Planters Catechism: Richmond, Va." was now published.

Also, in the "Charleston Observer," "Biographies of Servants mentioned in the Scriptures: with Questions and Answers."

These admirable sketches were prepared by Mrs. Horace S. Pratt, then of St. Mary's, Ga. and now of Tuscaloosa, Ala. The Rev. Horace S. Pratt previously to his appointment to a professorship in the Alabama College at Tuscaloosa, and while Pastor of the St. Mary's Presbyterian Church, gave much of his attention to the religious instruction of the Negroes, and prepared at his own expense a comfortable and commodious house of worship for them, and which they occupy at the present time.

Also, "A Catechism for Colored Persons. By C. C. Jones," printed in Charleston.

1835. "The Third Annual Report of the Liberty County Association," was printed and more extensively circulated than the two preceeding.

In the narrative of the state of religion in the synod of South Carolina and Georgia, it is said: "even the religious instruction of our slave population, entirely suspended in some parts of the country, through the lamentable interference of abolition, fanatics has proceeded with almost unabated diligence and steadiness of purpose through the length and breadth of our Synod." *Min.* 1835, *p.* 62.

Bishop Bowen of the diocese of S. C. prepared at the request of the convention and printed, "A Pastoral Letter on the Religious Instruction of the slaves of members of the Protestant Episcopal Church in the State of South Carolina;" to which he appended "Scripture Lessons," for the same.

The subject had been presented to the Convention by an able report from a committee and a portion of the report, was embodied in Bishop Bowen's letter.

The Missionary Society of the S. C. conference reported this year, 2,603 members, and 1,330 children under catechetical instruction.

1836. The Rev. George W. Freeman, late Rector of Christs' Church Raleigh, N. C. published two discourses on "The Rights and Duties of Slaveholders."

Mr. Freeman with pathos and energy, urges upon masters and mistresses the duty of religious instruction. — *p.* 3) — 34

The report of the L'berty County Association was prepared, but not published this year. The operations of the Association during the year had been successful.

The bishops of the M. E. Church in the United States, in their letter of reply to the letter from the Wesleyan Methodist Conference, England, held the following language : "It may be pertinent to remark that of the colored population in the Southern and South-western States, there are not less than 70,000 in our church membership ; and that in addition to those who are mingled with our white congregations, we have several prosperous missions exclusively for their spiritual benefit, which have been and are still owned of God, to the conversion of many precious souls. On the plantations of the South and South-west our devoted missionaries are laboring for the salvation of the slaves, catechising their children and bringing all within their influence, as far as possible to the saving knowledge of Jesus Christ ; and we need hardly add, that we shall most gladly avail ourselves, as we have ever done, of all the means in our power to promote their best interests. " The total number of colored members reported for 1836, was 82,661.

1837, 1838. The subject of the religious instruction of the Negroes was called up and attended to in the synod of South Carolina and Georgia both these years, and many Sunday schools for children and adults reported from the different presbyteries. It also received attention in all the southern synods. There appeared to be a growing conviction of the duty itself, and on the whole an increase of efforts.

The instruction of the Negroes in Liberty county, by the Association, was carried forward as usual during the summers of these years, but in consequence of the absence of the missionary in the winters, no reports were published.

The Missionary Society of the South Carolina conference prosecuted its work with encouraging success. In an annual meeting in the town of Columbia, S. C., they collected for their missions to the Negroes between twelve and fifteen hundred dollars.

Bishop Meade collected and published "Sermons, Dialogues and Narratives *for servants,* to be read to them in families: Richmond, 1836."

The *second* edition of "the Catechism for colored persons," by C. C. Jones: Savannah, T. Purse, 1837. Also, "a Catechism to be used by the teachers in the religious instruction of persons of color, etc.: prepared in conformity to a resolution of the Convention, under the direction of the Bishop: Charleston." The Reverend gentlemen of the diocese of South Carolina who united in preparing this catechism, were Dr. Gadsden, (now Bishop,) Mr. T. Trapier, and Mr. William H. Barnwell.

The following resolution was passed in the Episcopal convention of South Carolina in 1838: "*Resolved,* That it be respectfully recommended to the members of our church, who are proprietors of slaves individually and collectively, to take measures for the *support* of clerical missionaries and lay catechists who are members of our church, for the religious instruction of their slaves." And again, "*Resolved,* That it be urged upon the rectors and vestries of the country parishes, to exert themselves to obtain the services of such clerical missionaries and lay catechists."

1839, 1840. From the reports of the Liberty county Association for these years, it appears that a revival of religion commenced toward the close of the summer of 1838 among the Negroes, and extended very nearly over the whole county, and continued for two years. The whole number received into the Congregational and Baptist churches, on profession of their faith, was fully *two hundred and fifty.* The number of adults and children under catechetical instruction in the Sabbath schools connected with the Association and in the different churches, ranged from *five* to *seven hundred.*

The Missionary Society of South Carolina Conference reported in 1839, 13 missions, 210 plantations, 19 missionaries, 5,482 church members, and 3,769 children catechised. In 1840, 13 missions, 232 plantations, 19 missionaries, 5,482 members, and 3,811 children. — *Minutes.*

The Methodists returned in 1840, 94,532 colored persons in their connection.

The Rev. T. Archibald, (Presbyterian,) laboured as a missionary to the Negroes in Mississippi for several years, and in 1839 after leaving his charge in consequence of the Abolition excitement, he received a call to preach to the Negroes in Morengo county, Alabama.

The Rev. James Smylie and Rev. William C. Blair, (of the same denomination) were and still are (if our late information be correct) " engaged in this good work systematically and constantly " in Mississippi. The Rev, James Smylie, is characterized as " an aged and indedefatigable father : his success in enlightening the Negroes has been very great : — a large proportion of the Negroes in his old church can recite both Willison's and the Westminster catechism very accurately."

The names of many other pastors in the South might be given, who have conscientiously and for a series of years, devoted much time to the religious instruction of the Negroes connected with their churches.

The Rev. James Smylie and Rev. John L. Montgomery were appointed by the synod of Mississippi in 1839 to write or compile a catechism for the instruction of the Negroes. The manuscript was presented to synod in October 1840 and put into the hands of a committee of revision, but it has not yet been published.

The table on the state of the churches of the Sunbury Baptist Association, Georgia, gives six *African* churches with a total of members of 3,987, as returned ; one of these churches did not return the number of communicants. Of the other churches in the table, *five* have an overwhelming majority of colored members. The three African churches in Savannah are all connected with this association. In the appendix to the minutes it is said, " The committee, to whom was referred brother Sweat's letter on the subject of a mission among the African churches report — that it is highly important that such a mission should be established and recommend that the subject be turned over to the executive committee, with instructions that the brethren engaged in that work, during the past year, be compensated for their services : your committee further recommend that brother Connor be employed as a missionary by the association, *provided*, he will devote half his time to the colored people." And again : " That the table showing the state of the churches, may be more correct than the present, it is requested that at the next meeting of the association, the church clerks will distinguish in their reports, between the white and colored members, and that such churches as send no delegates will forward a statement of their condition."

"Missions to the people of color," are noticed in the annual report of the missionary society of the M. E. Church, in 1840. The report thus speaks. "And surely those who devote themselves to the self-sacrificing work of preaching the Gospel to these people on the rice and sugar plantations of the South and South-west, are no less deserving the patronage of the missionary society than those who labor for the same benevolent object in other portions of the great work. Of these there are, chiefly in the Southern conferences, 12,402 members under the patronage of this society."—*Report p.* 23.

1841. The report of the same society for this year, refers also to "*missions to the colored population.*" "In no portion of our work are our missionaries called to endure greater privations or make greater sacrifices of health and life, than in these missions among the slaves, many of which are located in sections of the Southern country which are proverbially sickly, and under the fatal influence of a climate which few white men are capable of enduring even for a single year. And yet, notwithstanding so many valuable missionaries have fallen martyrs to their toils in these missions, year after year there are found others to take their places, who fall likewise in their work, 'ceasing at once to work and live.' Nor have our superintendents any difficulty in finding missionaries ready to fill up the ranks which death has thinned in these sections of the work; for the love of Christ and the love of the souls of these poor Africans in bonds, constrain our brethren in the itinerant work of the Southern conferences to exclaim, 'here are we, send us!' The Lord be praised for the zeal and success of our brethren in this self-denying and self-sacrificing work."

The missionary society of the S. C. conference, reported this year, of missions exclusively to the Negroes, 14 ; plantations served, 301 ; members, 6,145 ; children under catechetical instruction, 3,407 ; and missionaries, 18. The report gives an animated and cheering view of the prospects of these missions. The great object of the society in them is thus expressed. " So to preach this Gospel that it may be believed ; and being believed, may prove ' the power of God unto salvation,' is the great object, and, we repeat it, the *sole* object of our ministrations among the blacks. This object attained, we find the terminus of our anxieties and toils, of our preaching and prayers." — *Report pp.* 12 — 17.

The total of colored communicants in the Methodist connection is given in the minutes of the annual conferences for the years 1840, 1841. For 1840, 94,532 ; for 1841, 102,158. The South Carolina conference is ahead of all, having 30,481 ; next comes the Baltimore conference, 13,904 ; then the Georgia conference, 9,989 ; Philadelphia, 8,778 ; Kentucky, 6,321, and so on. — *Min. p.* 156.

The Sunbury association reported this year seven African churches, with 4,430 members ; (from one no returns:) adding to this number the returns from the mixed churches of white and black, and an estimate of some from which no returns were made, a total of 5,664 colored members is obtained. Appendix B : "*Resolved,* That the committee be authorized to offer a sum not exceeding $50 per month, for one or more ordained ministers to labor among the colored people and destitute churches within the bounds of this association."

Bishop Meade of Va. made a report to the convention of his diocese "on the *best means* of promoting the religious instruction of servants," the result of his extended observation and long experience in this department of labor.

Bishop Gadsden of S. C. devotes a considerable portion of his address to the convention, to the subject of the religious instruction of the Negroes. He thus speaks. "Of that class peculiar to our social system — the colored people — many are members of our church; as are the masters of a very large number of them who as yet are not converted to the Gospel. To make these fellow creatures, who share with us the precious redemption which is by Jesus Christ, good Christians, is a purpose of which this church is not and never has been regardless. The interest and efforts in this cause have increased. But the feeling ought to be much deeper, and the efforts more extended. Consider the large number who are yet almost, if not entirely, without the restraints, the incentives, the consolations, and the hopes of the Gospel; under the bondage of satan, on the precipice of the second death! I speak more particularly of those the smoke of whose cabins is in sight of our ministers; who live on the same plantations with members of our church. Can nothing, ought not every thing that can, be done to bring such persons to the knowledge and obedience of Christ?"

There are 31 parochial reports. In twenty-two of the thirty-one churches there are colored members, amounting to 869. In fifteen there are Sabbath schools for colored children, amounting to 1,459 scholars. *Eight* of the clergy preach on plantations as well as at their respective churches and give special attention to their colored congregations ; and there are *two missions to the Negroes,* embracing 1,400 in the congregations. Children catechised on the plantations.

The practice of the Episcopal church in this diocese cannot be too highly commended to those who are of similar faith in the matter referred to, which is the *baptism of the infants and children of Negroes who are members of the church.* When God established his visible church on earth he constituted the infant seed of believers members of it, and therefore commanded that the sign and seal of his gracious covenant should be applied to them. His church has ever remained the same ; the members the same ; under the same constitution. Our practice ought to conform to our faith ; to the plain teachings of the word of God. A recurrence to this subject will be necessary when the means and plans for the religious instruction of the Negroes come under consideration in the fourth part of this work, and I therefore dismiss it in this place. There were 159 colored children baptized in the churches of the diocese, by the parochial reports.—*Journal of Fifty-second Convention, pp.* 10—13. *and pp.* 33—48.

From the seventh annual report of the Liberty County Association for the religious instruction of the Negroes, it appears that the efforts of the Association during the year had been successful. There were 450 children and youth under catechetical instruction ; and adding *four* schools not immediately under the care of the Association, but conducted by members of it, there were 265 more. Seven Sabbath schools in all were returned, and three stations for preaching. Congregations during the year full and attentive ; general order of the people commendable.

Appended to this report is the address to the Association, by the president, the Rev. Josiah Spry Law. An address which received the cordial and unanimous approbation of the Association as one which placed the religious instruction of the Negroes in a clear light, as *the great duty* of their owners; as well as of the churches. It was believed by the Association that the address was calculated to exert a favorable influence wherever it should be circulated in our country and it was therefore, with the consent of the author ordered to be printed.

Having now presented such facts and information under each year of this period, as I have been able to collect, I shall now give *a summary* (and a very brief one) *of the action of ecclesiastical bodies, and of what has been done by different denominations of christians.*

I know of no action of ecclesiastical bodies on the great subject of the religious instruction of the Negroes, in the *free States,* at least of no very prominent action; altho' efforts have been made by benevolent individuals and societies, for their physical, intellectual and moral improvement in most of the cities and chief towns of the free States, and not without success. These efforts came into notice about the beginning of the period now under consideration. Children and youth were gathered into week day and Sabbath schools: improvements were made in their houses for public worship, and some permanent supplies obtained for their pulpits. Distressed families and orphans were sought out and visited and taken care of, and persons out of employment were assisted in obtaining it. But a small part however of the entire population was reached and permanently benefited, as I had occasion to know from personal observation in 1827 and in 1829 in Massachusetts, Rhode Island, Connecticut, New York, New Jersey and Pennsylvania. For example, I found them in Providence, Rhode Island, with almost none to care for their souls. With a few respectable exceptions, they inhabited the most cast-away, decayed and debauched parts of the town, and were as deep in poverty, idleness, improvidence and immorality as can well be imagined. I saw two, three and four, and sometimes even more families occupying the different rooms and stories of one house. The Negro quarters of Boston, New York and Philadelphia presented pretty much the same features. My observations repeated again in the spring and summer of 1839 convinced me that there was abundant room for the improvement of the Negroes of the free States, and moreover, that the *practical* interest among the whites in their religious instruction was not remarkable. But to proceed, Dr. Anderson of Boston informed me while on a visit to that city in 1839 "that the present generation of Negroes who had enjoyed the advantages of education were in advance of those that had preceded them, and were getting into respectable employments; and that very considerable efforts had been made on their behalf." The Rev. Samuel S. Jocelyn has been for many years an indefatigable laborer, for the moral and religious improvement of the Negroes in New Haven. Professor Maclean showed me a neat house of worship erected by himself in conjunction with other benevolent individuals, for the Negroes in Princeton, New Jersey.

There are houses of public worship exclusively for the Negroes in all the cities of the free States, where there numbers make it an object, and the pulpits are supplied by ministers of their own color, and some of

them educated men of highly respectable talents and
standing, sometimes they are supplied by white ministers. There are Sabbath schools for the instruction of
children and youth, supported and taught chiefly by
white persons. For example, " in Portland, Maine, the
colored population is about 400. They have one Congregational church, and an educated colored pastor, and
a Sabbath school conducted by white teachers."

It is not necessary to go into an enumeration of the
houses of public worship in Boston, New York, Philadelphia and other places. In country towns and villages,
the Negroes have seats appropriated to them in the white
churches. They are of different denominations, Episcopal, Baptist, Methodist and Presbyterian.

Of late years the Negroes in the free States have manifested a strong inclination to be independent of the
influence and control of the whites, and to create and
manage their ecclesiastical establishments in their own
way; a very natural inclination, and not to be wondered
at, nor objected against, *provided*, they are capable of
taking care of themselves, which however, many of their
warmest friends not only seriously doubt but *wholly deny*.
As a specimen of this disposition I would refer to the
secession of Richard Allen and his associates in Philadelphia, from the Methodist church, which secession
extended into New York and other states. Of this secession in New York, Dr. Bangs thus writes, " it is now
(1839) twenty years since this secession took place, and
the degree of their prosperity may be estimated from
the following statement of their number of circuits and
stations, preachers and members taken from their minutes for 1839. Circuits 21, preachers 32, members 2,608.
These circuits and stations are found in the states of

New York, New Jersey, Connecticut, Rhode Island and Massachusetts. In the city of New York where the secession originated they have a membership of 1,325, making an increase of 396 in twenty years, which is by no means in a ratio with their increase while they remained under the care of their white brethren. In the city of Boston however, their success has been greater in proportion, In 1819 they had only 33, but now, in 1839 they have 126. As the M. E. Church never derived any temporal emolument from them, so we have sustained no other damage by the secession than what may arise from missing the opportunity of doing them all the good in our power as their pastors, etc."

In the *slave States* there has been action in *ecclesiastical bodies* on the religious instruction of the Negroes, and the value of such action is, that it discovers a good disposition on the part of ministers and churches to fulfil their duty to this people.

The Episcopal church, has rather taken the lead in making efforts and in keeping up an interest in its own bosom. Bishop Meade of Virginia, a long and unwearied advocate of this cause, Bishop Ives of North Carolina: Bishop Bowen of South Carolina (before his decease) and the present bishop of that State, Dr. Gadsden, have each addressed their dioceses on this subject; and commended it to the clergy and laity. The subject has been discussed in their conventions, accompanied with some able reports. Many of the clergy devote time to the instruction of the Negroes attached to their congregations; and have regular and flourishing Sabbath schools. It is stated as a fact, that in the Episcopal churches generally in South Carolina there are Sabbath schools for the Negroes, and some of them large and flourishing.

There are several Episcopal missionaries to this people in the State. The churches in Charleston have always been active in the instruction of the Negroes; and the present bishop, Dr. Gadsden, has been long known as an advocate of the work. The lately elected bishop of Georgia, Rev. Stephen Elliott, D. D., has brought the subject before his convention in his "*primary address*," (1841,) and urged attention to it with an energy and a zeal which promise great blessings to the Negroes connected with the churches of his new and interesting diocese. The Negroes connected with the Episcopal church have generally been noted for intelligence and fidelity.

The Methodists perhaps do not yield in interest and efforts to any denomination. From the commencement of their church in the United States, they have paid attention to the Negroes; of which we have had ample proof in the progress of this Sketch. In the slave States they have, next to the Baptists, the largest number of communicants. The Negroes are brought under the same church regulations as the whites, having class leaders and class-meetings and exhorters; and cases of church discipline, are carefully reported and acted upon as the discipline requires. The number of Negro communicants is reported at their conferences, as well as labors in their behalf and where it is necessary traveling preachers are directed to pay attention to them. In the South Carolina conference the missionary society already referred to, has a field of operations among the Negroes along the seaboard, from North Carolina to the southern counties of Georgia. The missionaries of this society labor chiefly on river bottoms, and in districts where the Negro population is large and the white population small ; and, it is understood, receive most of their support from the planters themselves, whose plantations they serve. We know of no other missionary society in this denomination so fully devoted to this particular field ; but there are Methodist missionaries for the Negroes, in Tennessee, Mississippi, and Alabama, and other of the slave-holding states. Without doubt as the Lord has opened wide the door of usefulness to this denomination, among the Negroes, it will not fail to exert itself to the utmost. Bishop J. O. Andrew, whose circuit is in the Southern States, has taken up the subject in good earnest and is prosecuting it with energy and success.

The Baptists have no societies in existence expressly for evangelizing the Negroes ; although their associations and conventions do from time to time call up the subject and act upon it. There are more Negro communicants, and more churches regularly constituted, exclusively of Negroes, with their own regular houses of public worship, and with ordained Negro preachers, attached to this denomination than to any other denomination in the United States.

It is difficult to collect the *direct* efforts of this denomination for the instruction of Negroes, as the reports of the associations are not easily obtained, they being printed and circulated chiefly within their respective bounds. If investigation was carefully made it might be found that in many of the associations of this denomination as much attention is paid to the instruction of the Negroes, as in the Sunbury association, Georgia, already referred to. There are missionaries in destitute settlements who devote a portion of their time to this people. Perhaps in most of the chief towns in the South there are houses of public worship erected for the Negroes alone; there are *three*, for example, in the city of Savannah. A year or two since I preached to the Baptist Negroes in Petersburg, Va., in their own house of worship, crowded to suffocation.

The Presbyterians have had ecclesiastical action within the present period, in the synods of Virginia and North Carolina; South Carolina and Georgia; Kentucky Mississippi, and Alabama; and in presbyteries in all these synods. Some presbyteries have distinguished themselves by their zeal and activity in the instruction of the Negroes.

It is unnecessary to transcribe the resolutions, reports and acts of these several bodies. Some have already met the eye of the reader. The latest and most general and satisfactory returns in our possession were gathered from the statements of members of the general assembly of 1839, from the slave-holding States, at a meeting called by themselves for the purpose of taking into consideration the religious instruction of the Negroes, and of communicating information and suggesting plans of operation. It will suffice to present the sum of the whole in a few words.

In the synods of Kentucky, Virginia, North Carolina, Tennessee, and West Tennessee, it is the practice of a number of ministers to preach to the Negroes *separately* once on the Sabbath, or during the week. There are also Sabbath schools in some of the churches for children and adults; and in all the houses of worship, with but few exceptions, a greater or less number of colored members and Negroes form a portion of every Sabbath congregation. In portions of these synods the abolition excitement checked and in others materially retarded the work of instruction.

In the synods of Alabama and Mississippi, almost all
the ministers devote a portion of the Sabbath to the
Negroes. There are two or three missionaries within
the bounds of these synods, and some flourishing Sabbath schools. Access in many parts of the two States
may be had to the Negroes, of unlimited extent. The
abolition excitement injured the cause.

In the synod of South Carolina and Georgia many
ministers preach to the Negroes separately on the Sabbath or during the week, and maintain Sabbath schools;
especially is this the fact, along the sea-board of the two
States. The presbytery of Georgia has one missionary
to the Negroes, and in the county where he labors, there
are seven Sabbath schools connected with the Congregational and Baptist churches, and upwards of 600 children
and youth in a course of catechetical instruction. There
are three stations for missionary preaching on the Sabbath, occupied in rotation, and in addition, during the
winter and spring, preaching on the plantations. There
are colored members in all the churches in this synod,
and accommodations for the Negroes in the houses of
public worship; the sessions conduct the discipline of
the colored members in the same manner that they do
the white; they are received into the churches, under
the same form and partake of the ordinances at the same
time.

The ministers in the newly formed Presbytery of Flo-
rida are devoting attention to this field of labor, dispers-
ing information and preaching as opportunity offers.

Such are the principal facts touching the religious
instruction of the Negroes during the third Period, from
1820 to 1842. And in view of them, as we close the
Period, we feel warranted in considering it *a period of*

the revival of religion in respect to this particular duty, throughout the Southern States; more especially between the years 1829 and 1835.

This revival came silently, extensively, and powerfully; affecting masters, mistresses, ministers, members of the church, and ecclesiastical bodies of all the different evangelical denominations. Some local associations of planters were formed, and societies on a large scale contemplated, and one brought to perfect organization. Sermons were preached and pamphlets published; the daily press lent its aid; and manuals of instruction were prepared aud printed. Nor was there any opposition of moment to the work, conducted by responsible individuals, identified in feeling and interest with the country. Some portions of the South were in advance of others, both in respect to the acknowledgement and performance of the great duty; but the light was gradually diffusing itself every where.

Such was the onward course of things when the excitement in the free States on the *civil* condition of the Negroes manifested itself in petitions to Congress, in the circulation of inflammatory publications, and other measures equally and as justly obnoxious to the South; all which had a disastrous influence on the success of the work we were attempting to do. The effect of the excitement was to turn off the attention of the South from the *religious* to the *civil* condition of the people in question; and from the salvation of the soul, to the defence and preservation of political rights. The very foundations of society were assailed and men went forth to the defence. A tenderness was begotten in the public mind on the whole subject, and every movement touching the improvement of the Negroes was watched

with jealousy.   Timid, ambitious, and factious men, and
men hostile to religion itself, and men desirous of ward-
ing off suspicion from themselves, agitated the public
mind within our own borders.   The result was, to
arrest in many places efforts happily begun and successfully prosecuted for the religious instruction of the Negroes.   It was considered best to disband schools and
discontinue meetings, at least for a season ; the formation
of societies and the action of ecclesiastical bodies, in
some degree ceased.

The feelings of men being excited, those who had
undertaken the religious instruction of the Negroes were
looked upon with suspicion and some of them were
obliged to quit the field.   It was not considered that a
separation might be made between the *religious* and the
civil condition and interests of a people ; and that a
minister could confine himself to the one without interfering at all with the other.   This entire effect upon the
slave States of the movements in the free States, considering all circumstances, was *natural*, but it was *wrong*
— wrong, because, let others act as they might, we
should have gone forward and done what was obviously
our duty.   We could have done it ; for the whole arrangement of the religious instruction of the Negroes, as to
teachers, times, places, matter and manner, was *in our
own power*.   And wrong again, because, admitting that
the wishes of these professed friends of the Negroes
were to be consummated, no better could be done for
the Negroes, nor for ourselves, than to teach them their
duty to God and man.   The Gospel certainly hurts no
man and no body of men. Parts of the Southern
Country took such action as was deemed necessary, (if
any at all,) calmly and decidedly, nor were any difficul-

ties thrown in the way of the regular course of religious instruction. A missionary in the heart of three or four thousand Negroes, during the period of excitement, visited plantations during the week, and met congregations on the Sabbath varying from 150 to 500 persons; yet it cannot be denied that the Northern movements did sensibly affect the feeling in favor of the religious instruction of the Negroes, throughout the whole slave-holding States, and the first and prominent cause of decline in the revival of which we speak, was unquestionably those movements; and I mention the fact because the cause of that decline is sometimes inquired into.

From information obtained by correspondence, and in other ways, there are favorable indications that a reaction has taken place within one or two years past; and that, taking the country throughout, more religious instruction is communicated to the Negroes now than ever before. The old friends of the cause for the most part retain their integrity, and labor on, while the Lord is impressing deeply the hearts and consciences of owners and is raising up many youth in the ministry and in the churches to carry forward the work more extensively.

—

The third Period is now completed, and with it this Historical Sketch of the Religious Instruction of the Negroes, since their first introduction into this country to the present time. I shall add, in the conclusion, the following general observations:

1. The Negro race has existed in our country for *two hundred and twenty-two years;* in which time the Gospel has been brought within the reach of, and been communicated to, multitudes; and tens of thousands of them have been converted, and have died in the hope

of a blessed immortality. And there are at the present time, tens of thousands connected by a credible profession, to the church of Christ ; and the Gospel is reaching them to a greater extent and in greater purity and power than ever before.

2. While there have been but few societies, and they limited in extent and influence, formed for the special object of promoting the moral and religious instruction of the Negroes ; and while there have been comparatively but few missionaries exclusively devoted to them : yet they have not been altogether overlooked by their owners, nor neglected by the regular ministers of the various leading denominations of Christians, as the facts adduced in this Sketch testify.

3. Yet it is a remarkable fact in the history of the Negroes in our Country that their regular, systematic religious instruction, has never received in the churches at any time, that general attention and effort which it demanded ; and the people have consequently been left, both in the free and in the slave states, in great numbers, in moral darkness, and destitution of the means of grace.

4. *The great and good work, therefore, of the thorough religious instruction of our Negroes remains to be performed.*

The colored population of the United States in 1830 was 2,009,043 *slave* and 319,599 *free* ; making a total of 2,328,642 : by the last census, 1840. it was 2,487,113 *slave* and 386,235 *free*, with a total of 2,873,348. This aggregate of 2,873,348, is certainly large enough to awaken our most serious attention, whether we view this people in a religious or civil point of light.

Their *actual moral and religious condition*, next claims our notice.

PART II.

THE Moral and the Religious Condition of the Negroes in the United States.

CHAPTER I.

Disadvantages to be encountered in prosecuting an inquiry into the Moral and Religious condition of the Negroes in the United States.

A knowledge of the moral and religious condition of the Negroes is essential to correct feeling and action thereto. Until we arrive at such knowledge and have it pressed upon our serious consideration, we shall have no just sense of obligation — we shall feel no criminality for past neglect — no disposition for future amendment: nor shall we be able to adopt plans for their improvement, as we must necessarily become acquainted with the nature and extent of a disease before we can hopefully prescribe for it.

That an inquiry into the moral and religious condition of the Negro population of the United States, may be prosecuted with success, admits of no question. And yet, whether we live at the North or at the South, notwithstanding we enjoy favorable advantages for the inquiry, we certainly labor under some very serious *disadvantages*, which threaten to impair the faithfulness with which it should be prosecuted and answered. Nay, these disadvantages may exert such an influence upon some, that admitting the inquiry to be prosecuted and answered *according to truth*, they may withhold assent. These disadvantages therefore demand consideration. They arise, in general, out of our intimate and long continued connection with this people.

Habits of feeling and prejudices in relation to any subject are wont to take their rise out of our education or circumstances. Every man knows their influence to be great in shaping opinions and conduct, and ofttimes how unwittingly they are formed; that while we may be unconscious of their existence they may grow with our growth and strengthen with our strength. Familiarity converts deformity into comeliness. Hence we are not always the best judges of our condition. Another may remark inconveniences and indeed real evils in it, of which we may be said to have been all our lives scarcely conscious. So also evils which upon first acquaintance revolted our whole nature and appeared intolerable, custom almost makes us forget even to see. Men passing out of one state of society into another encounter a thousand things to which they feel that they can never be reconciled; yet shortly after, their sensibilities become dulled — a change passes over them they scarcely know how — they have accommodated themselves to their new circumstances and relations — they are Romans in Rome.

That the people of the United States indulge *prejudices* in respect to the Negroes, both in favor of and adverse to them, as a distinct variety of the human family and as a subordinate class in society, is a fact not to be disguised. On the one hand their ignorance, vulgarity, idleness, improvidence, irreligion, and vice, are to be ascribed altogether to their position and circumstances; let these be changed for the better, and the African will immediately equal, if not greatly excel, the rest of the human family in majesty of intellect, elegance of manners, purity of morals and ardor of piety; yea, they will become the very *beau ideal* of character, the admiration of the world. On the other hand, the race has been from time immemorial just what it is and just what it must continue to be. It occupies the position designed for it in nature and Providence, and no changes and no efforts can ever, on the whole, alter it for the better. Prejudices, also, lie all along between these extreme oscillations of opinion. Happy is that mind which under gales of excitement and conflicting with waves of agitation, preserves its balance, and keeping its eye upon the truth, steadily advances towards it. It may be likened to the well adjusted compass, which noiselessly preserves its equilibrium, and faithfully points to the star, although the mountain waves roar and the ship is driven with the fierce winds and tossed.

The first disadvantage which I shall mention is *our intimate knowledge of the degraded moral character of the Negroes.*

From childhood we have been accustomed to their slovenly, and too frequently, their scanty dress; to their broken English, ignorance, vulgarity, and vice. What in them would disgust or grieve a stranger, or truly afflict us if seen in white persons, we pass by with little or no impression, as a matter of course; — they are *Negroes.* Their character is held in low estimation, throughout the United States; and, considering what it is, not without reason; for that character cannot be esteemed which in itself is not estimable. Whatever is idle, dissolute, criminal, and worthless, attaches to them. Unconsciously, or rather, instinctively, we determine what the fruits must be from their known character, condition, and circumstances; and when they do appear, we are not surprised. We say, "what better can be expected?"

Such a general corruption of morals as would blast the reputation of any *white* community, is known to exist among them; and yet how unaffected are we by it? Indeed, *the habit of our mind* is to consider them in a state of moral degradation; to expect little that is truly excellent and praiseworthy; and to feel lightly, and to pass over as well as we can, what is revolting in them. We are disposed not to try them as we would others by that standard which is holy, just, and good; but by a low and worldly standard, accommodated to their character and circumstances. Vice seems to lose its hideousness in proportion as it shades itself *in black;* as in painting, with *black* we obliterate the warm light and soft shades, and native hues, which gave depth and life and beauty to the picture, and the eye rests upon the dark, dead surface without emotion.

A second disadvantage is our difference of color, and our superior relations to them in society.

At the head of the varieties of the human race, stands *the fair,* or *Caucassian variety;* "which," to use the language of another, "has given birth to the most civilized nations of ancient and modern times, and has exhibited the moral and intellectual powers of human nature in their highest degree of perfection." At the foot, stands *the black or Ethiopian variety,* "which has ever remained in a rude and barbarous state; and been looked upon and treated as inferior by all the other varieties of the human race, from time immemorial."

There is superiority on the one hand and inferiority on the other. Ascribe it to whatever cause you may; whether to the immediate providence of God, or to nature itself — to a difference in original constitution, or to circumstances; the fact remains, and it can but be seen and felt. It is only with *the fact*, and its influence on us, that we have to do. We learn the fact in our elementary studies at school; a larger acquaintance with the history of the world and extensive observation in after life, impress it more deeply. A sense of this superiority is *hereditary* in the citizens of the free States; originally and not very long ago these States were *slave* States. It has been propagated from father to son, and exhibits itself in the manners and customs, and on all the face of society there. It may be wearing out, but very slowly.

What renders the superiority more palpable and influential in our case in the South, is that we still continue to maintain the relation of *master*, and all the *differences* in our standing, privileges, and circumstances in society, created by that relation, in custom and in law. There is, consequently, superiority on the one side and inferiority on the other, in almost every point of view. But as we are masters, so are we *managers*. They neither can nor will plan and execute their work by *directions* alone. We are compelled to see that they do their work. Neither will they act honestly, quietly, nor virtuously, left to themselves, we are again compelled to regulate their conduct by fixed laws: to warn, encourage, reward, and punish. Hence are we brought directly in contact with their depravity in its multiplied developements. We are astonished from time to time at the disclosure of their duplicity, dishonesty, trick, and cunning. Those only who have, or have had, the management of Negroes, know what the hardening effect is upon their own hearts. That man who takes possession of his property and commences the management of his people with that feeling of interest and tenderness which he has cherished for them from his childhood, and with a willingness to favor them in every way, must be watchful; otherwise, from their general character and behaviour, painfully exhibited to him, he will withdraw his confidence entirely and settle down into a state of indifference, his patience being exhausted and his feelings having undergone an entire change towards them.

Throw then these points together: we belong to distinct varieties of the human race, with the superiority on our side; a superiority rendered *more apparent* by the *relation* which we sustain to them as *masters*, and *more real*, both to them and us, when we become *managers;* and shall we be in no danger of cherishing, it may be, of cherishing unconsciously, a disrespect, if not a contempt for the Negroes, which may influence us to sink them lower in the scale of intelligence, morality and religion, than in truth and justice they should be?

A third disadvantage is *our latent, and in many instances manifest disinclination to the full disclosure of the moral and religious condition of the Negroes.*

The disinclination is in proportion to *the use* proposed to be made of the facts of the case, and arises from several causes.

One is *pride.* There are citizens in the free States who give, perhaps without any conscious design, an entirely false coloring to the moral character and prospects of the free Negroes among them, in order to support some favorite theory, or to shield the impotency of their own efforts, or themselves, from the ancient reproach " what do ye more than others? Physician heal thyself. "

In the South we spiritedly repel the charge of the injustice of the present constitution of society, by referring our opponents to the sacred scriptures, which afford us their support, and to the argument drawn from expediency and necessity. On the charge of inhumanity we appeal to the ample provision of food and clothing; to the attention paid to the sick and the aged; to the lightness of the labor and the punishments; and to the good health, the spirits, and increase of the people in question. We compare their physical comfort and the amount of labor which they perform, with that of the laboring classes in England and on the continent of Europe and elsewhere, and we do not suffer at all by the comparison.

But when the charge of their intellectual and moral degradation is preferred against us, we are inclined to put the best face on affairs, knowing that this is the darkest feature and the most vulnerable point. We discover this feeling in the class of factory and land owners in England, whose statements on the moral condition of their operatives cannot be taken but with many grains of allowance. They would not have it known to what an ignorant and degraded race of operatives they are indebted for the comforts and conveniences of their lives as individuals, and for whatever of prosperity they enjoy as corporations or communities.

But we are wrong, decidedly wrong. The moral and religious condition of the Negroes, is that subject which above all others, as a Christian people, we should desire most thoroughly to investigate and understand; and the truth coming from whatever quarter, will do us no harm, provided we allow it to have its proper effect upon us.

Another cause is *the fear of investigation itself, and of the consequences to which it may lead.*

The South, in view of the excitement on the general condition of the Negroes, in the North and West, has become sensitive. We have been thrown from necessity into an attitude of self-defence, and our strength consists in our union. Hence the public mind exercises a sleepless vigilance, that it may detect, either from abroad or originating at home, any sentiments or opinions hostile to our social constitution. There is less discussion, and less freedom of discussion, than in by-gone days. What we once bore from ourselves, is with difficulty borne now. That man runs the risk of losing popular favor whose candid statements and appeals, designed to do good *at home*, are seized upon with avidity, and perverted and made matter of accusation against us *from abroad*. He has to pass between Scylla and Charybdis. Under such circumstances there must be a strong inclination to silence; he will ponder well the proverb, " a time to keep silence, and a time to speak." As great interests are involved, should he speak, he will " ask wisdom of God who giveth liberally and upbraideth not."

Many are disposed to let all things continue as they are, and as they have been. There appears to be a misgiving that if we look diligently into the moral and religious condition of the Negroes, we shall make such discoveries that in order to satisfy conscience toward God and man, we shall be obliged to enter fully and vigorously upon the improvement of our people. New

cares, new troubles, new duties, new expenses array
themselves before us, and we recoil from them all.
Changes are inconvenient, even from bad to good.
Masters find it difficult to elevate their servants in their
regards after they have for so long a time been depressed.
To change their general course of treatment would be
virtually acknowledging to them and to all the world that
they have been in error; that they have not placed them
as high in the scale of intellectual and moral being as
they should have done; in short, that they have not done
them justice. Humility and self-denial are demanded,
but it is not easy to exercise these graces towards inferiors
and dependents. Masters see, as they suppose, in all
this, a lowering down of opinions, character, and dignity.
They think that they shall lose respect and authority —
the change will certainly inflate their servants, foster a
spirit of equality and disobedience, and in the end be
productive of no good.

There are others again, to whom the question recurs,
how far may we proceed in the religious instruction of
the Negroes without endangering our interests, our safety,
and our support? Say they, we know not when we
begin to do what may be necessary in the premises,
where we shall end or *how*. It will be hard to close the
door after it is once opened. We may safely confide in
those who undertake the work now; but what security
have we that their successors shall be men of like character? It is better, therefore, to cease from the matter
before it be meddled with. Their moral and religious
condition may not be as bad as some would have us
believe. We have been doing well in times past; apply
then the adage to the case in hand, "let *well* alone."

A fourth and last disadvantage, is the difficulty of obtaining an insight into the Negro character.

Persons live and die in the midst of Negroes and know comparatively little of their real character. They have not the immediate management of them. They have to do with them in the ordinary discharge of their duty as servants; further than this they institute no inquiries — they give themselves no trouble. The Negroes are a distinct class in community, and keep themselves very much *to themselves*. They are one thing before the whites, and another before their own color. Deception towards the former is characteristic of them, whether bond or free, throughout the whole United States. It is habit — a long established custom, which descends from generation to generation. There is an upper and an under current. Some are contented with the appearance on the surface; others dive beneath. Hence the diversity of impressions and representations of the moral and religious condition of the Negroes. Hence the disposition of some to deny the darker pictures of their more searching and knowing friends.

Besides all this, the moral perceptions of men differ · the eye of one man is " single," and the eye of another man is " evil." What *this* esteems bad *that* considers to be very good.

Nor have all the same opportunity of assisting their judgement by *comparison*. A man may greatly aid himself in attaining a correct opinion of the moral and religious condition of the Negroes in the United States, and especially of those in the slave States, by becoming from observation acquainted with the moral and religious condition of other masses of laborers, in other States and countries. It is not good to measure ourselves by

ourselves. One opportunity of faithful comparison, will
shed more light and carry more conviction into the mind,
ofttimes, than volumes of facts and arguments. The
only danger to be apprehended from such comparisons,
is that, becoming acquainted with that which is *worse*,
we may rest satisfied with that which is *bad*.

Here then are obvious disadvantages to be encountered
in an inquiry into the moral and religious condition of
the Negroes. The *first*, our intimate knowledge of their
degraded character; the *second*, our belonging to a
different variety of the human family and sustaining
towards them the relation of superiors; the *third*, our
disinclination to a full disclosure of their moral and
religious condition, arising from several causes; and the
fourth, the difficulty of obtaining an insight into the
Negro character. They must be borne in mind in the
progress of the inquiry. In regard to the moral and
religious condition of the Negroes we, especially of the
South, can have no just reason for remaining in ignorance
and inactivity. The subject involves our accountability
to them and for them, which we shall surely meet in that
world where all earthly distinctions are at an end; and it
involves their own eternal well-being, than which nothing
can be more valuable to them. Every sober and reflecting
mind should be impressed with the importance and
solemnity of the inquiry.

CHAPTER II.

Circumstances of the Negroes which affect their Moral and Religious
Condition.

The character of a people may be gathered from their circumstances.   A consideration therefore of the *circumstances* in which we find our Negro population, is a necessary and preparatory step to the inquiry we have in hand.

1. *The circumstances of the Slave Population.*

As habits of virtue and vice are formed, and character shaped, at a very early age, I shall begin with —

The Negro in his Childhood. — The formation of good character depends upon family government and training; upon religious instruction, private and public; access to the Scriptures and other sources of intellectual and moral improvement; the character of associates; modesty of clothing, and general mode of living.

If we take the mass of the slave population, properly speaking, we shall find but little *family government*, and for the reason that parents are not qualified, neither are they so circumstanced as to be able to fulfil perfectly the duties devolving upon them as such.   In the more intelligent and pious families, the children are taught to say their prayers, to go to church on the Sabbath, to attend

evening prayers on the plantation, and a few simple
rules of good conduct and manners. The majority of
church members, come short of this. The moral training of their children forms but a small part of their
effort in the family. There is not one family in a thous-
and in which family prayer is observed morning and
evening. Prayers are held in some families morning
and evening on the Sabbath day; in others in the evening
of every day. But a general meeting of all the members of the church as well as of worldly persons, for
prayer in the evening on plantations, conducted by
some prominent person among them, takes the place of
family worship — the plantation is considered one large
family. To this meeting children are required to come
or not, as the case may be. The hour is usually so late
that most of the children have retired for the night. If
such is the state of religious families what must be the
state of those which are irreligious? In multitudes of
families, both by precept and example, the children are
trained up in iniquity; taught by their parents to steal,
to lie, to deceive; nor can the rod of correction induce
a confession or revelation of their clearly ascertained
transgressions. Virtue is not cherished nor protected
in them. Parents put their children to use as early as it is
possible, and their discipline mainly respects omissions
of duty in the household; moral delinquencies are
passed by; and that discipline owes its chief efficiency
to excited passion, and consequently exists in the extreme
of laxity or severity. They ofttimes when under no
restraint, beat their children unmercifully.

As to direct *religious instruction*, we have seen that
the amount communicated *in families* is small. The
Negroes on plantations sometimes appoint one of their

number, commonly the old woman who minds the children during the day, to teach them to say their prayers,
repeat a little catechism and a few hymns, every evening.
The instances are however not frequent, and it is the
only approximation I have ever known to systematic
instruction for their children, adopted by the Negroes
themselves.

But how much religious instruction do the young
Negroes receive from their *Masters*, who sustain very
much the relation of parents to them? What is the
number of planters who have established plantation
schools? In other words, who have commenced a system of regular instruction for their Negro children;
conducting themselves that instruction daily or weekly,
or engaging the services of members of their own families, or even going to the expense of employing missionaries for the purpose?

Push the inquiry still further. How many *ministers*
assemble, at stated seasons, the colored children of their
congregations for catechetical instruction, exhortation,
and prayer? How many *churches* have established
Sabbath schools at convenient stations in the country,
or in towns and villages, for colored children and youth,
and do maintain them from year to year? To all these
questions it must in candor be replied that the numbers
are small compared with the whole.

Shall we speak of *public* instruction such as is communicated by a *preached* Gospel? Negro children do
not enjoy the advantages of a preached Gospel; for the
custom is, where no effort is made to alter it, for the
children to remain at home on the Sabbath. Multitudes
never having been taught to " remember the Sabbath
day to keep it holy," consider it in the light, purely, of

a holyday;—a day of rest, of sports, and plays. The distance to the house of worship is frequently considerable, too considerable for the attendance of small children; parents do not like the trouble of children; and, in short, should their children accompany them, the services being conducted for the most part for the special benefit of masters, do them no good, being above not only their comprehension, but even that of their parents.

Shall we speak of *access to the Scriptures?* The *statutes* of our respective slave States forbid all knowledge of letters to the Negroes; and where the statutes do not *custom* does. It is impossible to form an estimate of the number of Negroes that *read.* My belief is that the proportion would be expressed by an almost inconceivable fraction. The greatest number of readers is found in and about towns and cities, and among the free Negro population, some two or three generations removed from servitude. There are perhaps in all the larger cities in the South, schools for the education of colored children, supported chiefly by the *free* Negroes, and kept generally in the shade. On the one hand, therefore, the Negro children cannot be "hearers of the law," for oral instruction is but sparingly afforded to the mass of them; and on the other, they cannot "search the Scriptures," for a knowledge of letters they have not, and legally, they cannot obtain.

With whom is the young Negro *associated?* With children no better instructed and disciplined than himself, and the whole subjected to the pernicious examples of the adults. They are favored with no association calculated to elevate and refine.

Negroes, especially the children, are exceedingly inattentive to the preservation of their *clothing.* The habits, in the particular of dress, of their forefathers from Africa still cleave to them, especially in the warmer seasons of the year, when they are left to themselves. This very improvidence on the part of the Negroes presents an increase of expenditure on the part of owners for clothing. The waste is great. And indeed, once for all, I will here say, that the wastes of the system are so great, as well as the fluctuations in prices of staple articles for market, that it is difficult, nay, impossible, to indulge in large expenditures on plantations and make them savingly profitable.

Their *general mode of living* is coarse and vulgar. Many Negro houses are small, low to the ground, blackened with smoke, often with dirt floors, and the furniture of the plainest kind. On some estates the houses are framed, weather-boarded, neatly white-washed, and made sufficiently large and comfortable in every respect. The improvement in the size, material, and finish of Negro houses is extending. Occasionally they may be found constructed of tabby or brick.

A room is partitioned off for a sleeping appartment and store-room, though houses are found destitute of this convenience. In such dwellings privacy is impossible; and we may in a manner say that families live, sleep, and grow up together; their habits and manners being coarse and rude. Some owners make additions to the houses according to the number and age of the children of families.

Having now considered the circumstances of the Negro during his childhood, we may proceed and consider the circumstances of —

The Negro at Adult age. — He lives in a house similar to the one in which he passed his childhood and youth. He has the necessary and annual provision made for his wants; associates with fellow-servants of like character to his own. The seeds of virtue or vice sown in his youth, now blossom and bear fruit. He marries and settles in life, his children grow up around him and tread in his footsteps, as he did in the footsteps of his father before him.

The remarks on the *religious instruction of children* apply with equal correctness to *adults*. Stated religious instruction of adults *on plantations*, communicated by masters, ministers, or missionaries employed for the purpose, taking the slave States together, is not of frequent occurrence. The chief privilege enjoyed by thousands on plantations is *evening prayers*, conducted by themselves. If the individuals upon whom the conduct of the evening meeting devolves are able to *read*, a chapter in the Bible is read; a hymn is read and given out and sung; followed with prayer. If they cannot read, then a brief exhortation in place of the Scriptures founded, it may be, on some remembered passage, then a hymn from memory and prayer. There are thousands also, who, although freely allowed the privilege, do not embrace it, either from want of inclination, or of suitable persons to conduct the meetings. It is matter of thankfulness that the owners are few in number, indeed, who forbid religious meetings on their plantations, held either by their servants themselves, or by competent and approved white instructors or ministers. "All men have not faith." I have never known servants forbidden to attend the worship of God *on the Sabbath day*, except as a restraint temporarily laid, for some flagrant misconduct.

On special occasions, such as fast days, communion

seasons, and protracted meetings, a day or more is
allowed servants by many masters. Throughout the
slave-holding States the rest of the Sabbath is secured
to the Negroes, and on this day they have extensive
opportunities of attending divine worship, in town and
country. But it is well known to those who have atten-
tively observed the habits of this people, that large
numbers of adults remain at home or spend the day in
visiting or in ways still more exceptionable. Various
causes conspire to produce the effect. For instance;
it is their day of rest; the distance which they must
walk to church is considerable; the accommodations for
seats, in certain cases, are limited; the services of the
sanctuary are too elevated for them; they are not
required or encouraged to go; they have no exalted
ideas of the importance of religion, and in common with
all men, are naturally disinclined to it, and are easily
satisfied with excuses for the neglect of it; and other
causes which might be mentioned. 'Many, in settlements
that are and that are not supplied with Gospel ministrations, live and die without an adequate knowledge of the
way of salvation.

Nor can the adult Negro acquaint himself with duty
and the way of salvation *through the reading of the
Scriptures*, any more than can the child. Of those
that do read, but few read well enough for the edification of the hearers. Not all the colored *preachers* read.

Two other circumstances which have considerable
bearing on the moral and religious character of the
Negroes deserve attention. The first is that the *marriage state is not protected by law*. Whatever of protection it enjoys is to be attributed to custom, to the
conscientious efforts of owners, and the discipline and

doctrines of the churches; and also the correct principle and virtue of the contracting parties. But the relation is liable to disruption in a variety of forms, for some of which there is no remedy. The second is that *the government* to which they are subjected is *too much physical in its nature.* To discard an appeal to the principle of fear — the fear of punishment of *the person* of the transgressor in some form or other, would be running contrary to all governments in existence, both human and divine. While the necessity is admitted, yet the appeal should be made as seldom as possible and in the mildest form consistent with the due support of authority and the reformation of the transgressor. Man has a *spiritual* as well as an *animal* nature, and corrective influences, should be brought to bear upon that *directly* and in the *first instance*, as soon as he is able to discern between good and evil.

Such then are the circumstances of the slave population, which have an unfavorable influence upon their moral and religious condition. Those circumstances only have been referred to which prominently assist us in our inquiry. In conclusion it may be added that servants have neither intellectual nor moral intercourse with their masters generally, sufficient to redeem them from the adverse influence of the circumstances alluded to; for the two classes are distinct in their association, and it cannot well be otherwise. Nor have servants any redeeming intercourse with any other persons. On the contrary in certain situations there is intercourse had with them, and many temptations laid before them against which they have little or no defence, and the effect is deplorable.

2. *The circumstances of the free Negro population.*
The free Negro population is about equally divided
between the free and the slave states ; the balance may
be somewhat in favor of the slave states.

Their *locations* are chiefly in cities, towns and villages; they are but thinly scattered throughout the country. Unless diverted by some uncontrolable circumstance
they invariably find their way into cities, partly because
they there find most society of their own color, and
partly because they make out to live at less expense of
labor : have the means and opportunities of vicious indulgence more at hand, with less danger of detection,
and in every respect are under less supervision and restraint.

Their *station* in society as well as their *condition*, is
one of *inferiority.* Their freedom consists mainly, in
deliverance fiom *compulsory* labor. The *real estate*
owned by them taking the whole population, is very
trifling : their *personal property* is something greater ;
but as a class they are *poor.*

Here and there one may be found cultivating his own
land for a support, but the mass, are hired servants : —
waiters in private and public houses, stewards and cooks
and common hands on board steam boats, and merchant
vessels : some few on board men of war : mechanics,
tradesmen : shop keepers, porters, draymen : hour and
day laborers : " hewers of wood and drawers of water."
Multitudes have no visible means of living : no support
but that of vice.

They usually occupy some particular quarter of the
town, abandoned to them, with the exception of certain
poor and degraded white families and shop keepers.
The houses which they occupy are built cheaply for the

poorer class of renters ; and when of sufficient size, will sometimes accommodate from two to six families. On a personal inspection of the entire Negro quarters of one of the chief towns in the Northern states, I found white families mixed in with the black, a most motly assemblage : whole families, sometimes taking in *boarders*, lodged in *one* room, without partitions or screens. Their furniture coarse and scanty, and so was their every day clothing in which I found them. There were no gardens cultivated, where ground was accessible. There were no visible comforts : all things wore the appearance of poverty, improvidence, idleness, drunkenness and debauchery. They seemed to live, literally, " from hand to mouth ; " and to work only in obedience to stern necessity. There were a few, and but a few, creditable exceptions.

The conveniences and comforts to be found in their dwellings, the bountifulness of their diet and clothing, the number of friends which they have, or can command in seasons of sickness and suffering, all depend upon their own industry and uprightness of character. That character being generally bad, their physical condition is bad also. This is the testimony of all who have made observations on the condition of the free Negroes in the *free states*. Their physical condition in the *slave states*, on the whole, *is decidedly in advance* of what it is in the *free states*. There are more free colored *families* in the slave than in the free states : in the latter the young cannot marry, the support of a family, especially through the rigors of winter being difficult ; and consequently numbers of youth, abandon themselves to profligacy.

Their advantages for education, and consequently *access to the written word of God*, are more limited in the

slave than in the free states, on account of the existence
of laws against the education of colored persons; but
notwithstanding, in the slave states the free Negroes, do
have schools for their children, or some private instruction, and it would be difficult to decide whether as many
of them do not learn to read as in the free states. The
number of *writers* is less.

In the free states schools are established in the cities,
supported chiefly as *free* schools, for the education of
Negro children; in villages, provision is also made for
them; and their employers teach them   A few pass
through *College;* the professions opened to them are
Medicine and Divinity. The majority are ignorant of
letters.

Houses of public worship are erected in the chief towns
in the free and slave States, where they may have *access
to a preached Gospel:* in the free States for the use of the
free Negroes — in the slave States for the use of *free Negroes and slaves.* The officiating ministers either white
or colored. Negroes seldom if ever, worship in the *white*
churches of the free States, in the cities; for example,
in Boston, Providence, New York, Philadelphia, etc.
They are not expected to do so; neither is it thought
desirable by the people. Consequently their accommodations are poor and scanty. In the Southern churches
multitudes do; and the free colored population frequently
prefer it to worshiping in the colored churches. In like
manner there are *Sabbath schools* for the Negro children
and youth, in the free States, and in a number of places
in the slave States. But the free Negroes of the United
States do not possess houses of worship, nor ministers of
the Gospel, nor Sunday schools, *in sufficient number for
their accommodation.* They are left in sad destitution of

the means of grace. Children grow up, and adults live, estranged from the house of God — the Sabbath is with them a day of idleness — of vain and wicked pastime.

The amount of *family government and instruction* is limited; they associate with their *own color* or with *degraded whites;* and as to *prospects of advancement in society*, they may accumulate *wealth*, there is no other distinction, except that of influence among themselves, arising from skill and intelligence and zealous devotion in the professions of medicine and divinity. They can never rise above their *caste.*

Briefly as we have adverted to the circumstances of the free Negro population, it must be apparent that those circumstances exert an unfavorable influence upon the developement of good moral and religious character.

CHAPTER III.

Moral and Religious Condition of the Negroes in the United States.

We have refered to the *disadvantages* under which we labor for prosecuting our inquiry, and also, to the *circumstances* in which we find our Negro population. These preparatory steps being taken, we may now come intelligently, and with less surprise at the results, to a consideration of their actual moral and religious condition.

As to moral and religious character, the Negroes are *naturally* what all other men are. No attempt, therefore, will be made either to show that they are *more depraved* than another people would be in like circumstances, or to show that they are the *most degraded* of all people on the earth. To attempt the establishment of one or both these positions would argue contempt of the truth. It is my wish to present the truth on the subject, derived from observation and other sources; believing that nothing more, and nothing less, is required by the importance of it.

1. *The Moral and Religious Condition of the Slave Negro Population.*

Ignorance of the doctrines and duties of Christianity is prevalent among the Negroes.

Their notions of the Supreme Being; of the character and offices of Christ and of the Holy Ghost; of a future state; and of what constitutes holiness of life, are indefinite and confused. Some brought up in a Christian land, and in the vicinity of the house of God, have *heard* of Jesus Christ; but who he is, and what he has done for a ruined world, they cannot tell. The Mohammedan Africans remaining of the old stock of importations, although accustomed to hear the Gospel preached, have been known to accommodate Christianity to Mohammedanism. "God," say they, "is *Allah*, and Jesus Christ is *Mohammed* — the religion is the *same*, but different countries have different *names*."

The number of professors of religion, in proportion to the whole, is not large, that can present a correct view of the plan of salvation; although in many instances where they fail to do so, it is but just to observe, that their knowledge is greater than one not familiarly acquainted with them would conceive it to be. It exceeds their power of expression; since from the want of education and practice, they are unable to state accurately and readily their own views and feelings.

True religion they are inclined to place in *profession*, in *forms and ordinances*, and in *excited states of feeling*. And *true conversion*, in *dreams, visions, trances, voices* — all bearing a perfect or striking resemblance to some form or type which has been handed down for generations, or which has been originated in the wild fancy of some religious teacher among them. These dreams and visions they will offer to church-sessions, as *evidences* of conversion, if encouraged so to do, or if their better instruction be neglected. Sometimes principles of conduct are adopted by church members at so much variance with the Gospel that the " grace of God is turned into lasciviousness." For example, members of the same church are sacredly bound by their religion not to reveal each others sins, for that would be backbiting and injuring the brotherhood. And again, that which would be an abominable sin, committed by a church member with a worldly person, becomes no sin at all if committed with another church member. The brethren must "bear one another's burdens and so fulfil the law of Christ."

All the various perversions of the Gospel are to be met with, and more than probable, pushed to extremes. *Antinomianism* is not uncommon, and at times, in its worst forms. " Christ," is made "the minister of sin " — the christian is safe, do what he may.

To know the extent of their ignorance even where they have been accustomed to the sound of the Gospel in white churches, a man should make investigation for himself — the result will frequently surprise and fill him with grief. They scarcely feel shame for their ignorance on the subject of religion, although they may have had abundant opportunity of becoming wiser. Ignorance, they seem to feel, is their lot; and that feeling is intimately associated with another, every way congenial to the natural man, namely, a feeling of irresponsibility — ignorance is a cloak and excuse for crime. Some white ministers and teachers, in their simplicity, beholding their attention to the preaching of the Gospel, adapted to their comprehension, and hearing the expressions of

their thankfulness for the pains taken for their instruction, come to the conclusion that they are an unsophis-
ticated race; that they form one of the easiest and
pleasantest fields of labor in the world; and that they are
a people "made ready, prepared for the Lord;"—nothing
more being necessary than to carry them the Gospel
and converts will be multiplied as drops of morning dew,
yea, a nation will be born in a day.

Experiment shortly dissipates these visions, and well
is it if the sober reality does not frighten the laborer
away in disgust and disappointment. He who carries
the Gospel to them encounters depravity, intrenched in
ignorance, both real and pretended. He beholds the
Scripture fulfilled, "having the understanding darkened,
being alienated from the life of God through the ignorance that is in them, because of the hardness of their
hearts."—*Eph.* 4, 17—19. He discovers deism, skepticism, universalism. As already stated, the various
perversions of the Gospel, and all the strong objections
against the truth of God; objections which he may
perhaps have considered peculiar only to the cultivated
minds, the ripe scholarship and profound intelligence, of
critics and philosophers! Extremes here meet on the
natural and common ground of a darkened understanding
and a hardened heart. He is convinced that there is "a
spirit which ruleth in the hearts of the children of disobedience." "They are *wise* to do evil; but to do good
they have no knowledge."

Intimately connected with their ignorance, is their
superstition.

They believe in second-sight, in apparitions, charms,
witchcraft, and in a kind of irresistible Satanic influence.
The superstitions brought from Africa have not been

wholly laid aside. Ignorance and superstition render them easy dupes to their teachers, doctors, prophets, conjurers; to artful and designing men. When fairly committed to such leaders, they may be brought to the commission of almost any crime. Facts in their history prove this. On certain occasions they have been made to believe that while they carried about their persons some charm with which they had been furnished, they were *invulnerable.* They have, on certain other occasions, been made to believe that they were under a protection that rendered them *invincible.* That they might go any where and do any thing they pleased, and it would be impossible for them to be discovered or known; in fine, to will was to do — safely, successfully. They have been known to be so perfectly and fearfully under the influence of some leader or conjurer or minister, that they have not dared to disobey him in the least particular; nor to disclose their own intended or perpetrated crimes, in view of inevitable death itself; notwithstanding all other influences brought to bear upon them. Their superstition is made *gain* of by the conjurers and others like them. They are not only imposed and practiced upon to their hurt, by these more prominent characters, but by each other more privately, by " tricking," as it is called, for the gratification of revenge, or of lust, or of covetousness. A plain and faithful presentation of the Gospel, usually weakens if not destroys these superstitions.

Their sense of obligation to improve religious privileges is seriously defective.

Necessarily so, both with the church and the world, because they have never enjoyed to any great extent, early religious training. It is a matter depending pretty much upon the contingencies of the day or the hour whether they attend the house of God on the Sabbath or the meeting for prayer on the plantation. One of the first efforts of the Minister or Missionary should be to create a sense of obligation in respect to this very thing : to enlighten their consciences, and bring them to feel that they are responsible for the due improvement of their privileges ; and that the members of the church should be foremost in meeting that responsibility. They will now and then excuse their remissness, by pleading that their leisure is needed for rest : or that they have no time : that it is hard for them to serve their earthly and heavenly master too. It is but an excuse, for the Negroes in the South, in general, fall short at the least one third of what free white laborers perform. Yet as power may be, and sometimes is abused, we should look well to it, that by our exactions and treatment, we may not prevent our people from entering in to the kingdom of heaven.

They have but *a poor standard of moral character,* and are *indifferent to the general corruption of manners that prevails around them.*

Which is a strong evidence of their moral degradation: for a public sentiment in respect to various vices and improper customs, pervades with considerable force all societies advanced in some good degree in piety and virtue.

The standard of moral character is much higher among the members of the church, than among those who are not, but it is not by any means, what it might and ought to be. They say and do and tolerate what is plain evidence that their standard is low. To aspire to or hope for as elevated a morality as obtains among the whites

they think, can neither be expected, nor required of them
With the people of the world there is scarcely any
standard of moral character, strictly speaking, at all
They seem to feel that they have very little to gain or
lose either way they turn.

They take little interest in the moral improvement of
their own color. They live not together as communities having common ties and interests which would
prompt them to promote the public piety and virtue, but
very much as independent individuals and families.
Such a thing as their uniting to suppress any particular
vice, or to promote any good object, has not been known
among them, if we except a few Temperance societies
formed of late years. They regard not the evil influence which they may exert over their neighbor, nor the
injury which they may do him in his character, in his
family, or property, if their lust or malice or avarice be
gratified.

They follow their own inclinations and interests, having respect to consequences mainly, as they may bring
them into collision with the laws and regulations of the
plantation or household. Should they escape the master, the difficulties with their own color will be easily
adjusted, if cared for at all.

But the Negroes are scrupulous on one point; they
make common cause, as servants, in *concealing* their
faults from their owners. Inquiry elicits no information
no one feels at liberty to disclose the transgressor; all
are profoundly ignorant; the matter assumes the sacred
ness of a "professional secret:" for they remember
that they may hereafter require the same concealmen:
of their own transgressions from their fellow servants
and if they tell upon them *now*, they may have the like

favor returned *them ;* besides, in the meanwhile, having their names cast out as evil from among their brethren, and being subjected to scorn, and perhaps personal violence or pecuniary injury.

The frequency of church discipline and the character of the crimes requiring it, cast light upon their moral and religious condition.

The discipline of colored members is involved, tedious, vexatious and disgusting. Many cases worthy of discipline never appear for it, because, at one time, they are secretly hushed up, and at another, testimony cannot be procured, as they avoid, if it be possible, becoming accusers or witnesses. Excommunications, however, and suspensions are of perpetual occurrence, for crimes shocking in character, and of themselves sufficient to show the general state of morals ; such for example as adultery, fornication, theft, lying, drunkenness, quarreling, and fighting. The *first three* are their most common vices. Out-breaking sins only are taken in hand. Their bitterness, wrath, clamor, evil-speaking, and profanity are seldom noticed, and for the reason that all passes away with the breath, and no man has his family invaded, his property consumed, or his bones broken.

I have heard the observation made by men whose standing and office in the churches afforded them abundant opportunity for observation, that the more they have had to do with colored members, the less confidence they have been compelled to place in their Christian profession. A great many whites are very incredulous on the point ; indeed, the Negroes themselves do not place a great deal of confidence in each other's Christian character, and they should be good judges, for they have a more intimate acquaintance with one another than

the whites possibly can have. Yet when we consider
that the Negroes are brought up in ignorance of religion
in multitudes of instances ; subjected ofttimes to the
incompetent teachings of men of their own color ; the
preaching and instruction in white churches above their
comprehension ; no access directly to the word of life ;
surrounded with depraved society ; subjected to manifold temptations; destitute to a considerable extent of
encouragement in ways of righteousness ; and a life of
active employment, I apprehend that our surprise will
be, not that there are *so many* spurious conversions and
so many defections, but that there are so *few;* and moreover, that in judging their Christian character, charity
demands that we should consider their condition and
circumstances and make very great allowances.   Hence
considering their condition and circumstances, and com-
paring them with the more improved and favored class
of white members, I could not say that the amount and
degree of piety were remarkably in favor of the one
over the other.   I have seen the Scriptures abundantly
fulfilled amongst the Negroes — " hath not God chosen
the poor of this world rich in faith and heirs of the
kingdom, which he hath promised to them that love
him." — *Ia.* 2, 5.

But a brief view of the *prevailing vices* of the Negroes will best reveal their moral and religious condition.

Violations of the marriage contract.

The divine institution of marriage depends for its
perpetuity, sacredness, and value, largely upon the protection given it by the law of the land. Negro marriages
are neither recognized nor protected by law. The
Negroes receive no instruction on the nature, sacredness,
and perpetuity of the institution; at any rate they are

far from being duly impressed with these things. They are not required to be married in any particular form, nor by any particular persons. Their ceremonies are performed by their own watchmen or teachers, by some white minister, or as it frequently happens, not at all ; the consent of owners and of the parties immediately interested, and a public acknowledgment of each other, being deemed sufficient.

There is no special disgrace nor punishment visited upon those who criminally violate their marriage vows, except what may be inflicted by owners, or, if the parties be members, by the church in the way of suspension and excommunication.

Families are and may be divided for improper conduct on the part of either husband or wife, or by necessity, as in cases of the death of owners, division of estates, debt, sale, or removals, for they are subject to all the changes and vicissitudes of *property*. Such divisions are, however, carefully guarded against and prevented, as far as possible, by owners, on the score of interest, as well as of religion and humanity.

Hence, as may well be imagined, the marriage relation loses much of the sacredness and perpetuity of its character. It is a contract of convenience, profit, or pleasure, that may be entered into and dissolved at the will of the parties, and that without heinous sin, or the injury of the property or interests of any one. That which they possess in common is speedily divided, and the support of the wife and children falls not upon the *husband*, but upon the *master*. Protracted sickness, want of industrious habits, of congeniality of disposition, or disparity of age, are sufficient grounds for a separation. While there are creditable instances of conjugal fidelity for a long series of years, and until death; yet infidelity in the marriage relation and dissolution of marriage ties are not uncommon.

On account of the changes, interruptions and interferences in families, there are quarrelings and fightings, and a considerable item in the management of plantations is the settlement of family troubles. Some owners become disgusted and wearied out, and finally leave their people to their own way; while others cease from the strife ere it be meddled with, and give it as an opinion that the less the interference on the part of the master the better. A few conscientious masters persevere in attempts at reformation, and with some good degree of success.

Polygamy is practised both secretly and openly; in some sections where the people have been well instructed it is scarcely known; in others, the crime has diminished and is diminishing; it is to be hoped *universally so.* It is a crime which among all people and under all circumstances, carries, in its perpetration, vast inconveniences and endless divisions and troubles : and they are felt by the Negroes as well as by others, and operate as a great preventive. Polygamy is also discountenanced and checked by the majority of owners, and by the churches of all denominations.

Uncleanness. — The sin may be considered universal. The declaration will be sufficient for those who have any acquaintance with this people in the slave-holding States or in the free States; indeed, with the ignorant laboring classes of people wherever they may be found. It is not my object to institute comparisons, if it were, I could point to many tongues and people, in civilized governments, upon the same level of depravity with the Negroes.

The sin is not viewed by them as by those of higher intelligence and virtue, so that they do not consider character as lost by it, nor personal degradation as necessarily connected with it. A view which, however it may spring from vitiated principle, preserves the guilty from entire prostration.

Intimately connected with this view is the crime of *Infanticide :* — a crime restrained in good measure by the provision made for the support of the child on the part of the owner, by the punishment in case of detection, and by the moral degradation of the people that takes away the disgrace of bastardy.

Theft. — They are proverbially *thieves.* They bear this character in Africa; they have borne it in all countries whither they have been carried; it has been the character of slaves in all ages, whatever their nation or color. They steal from each other; from their masters from any body. Cows, sheep, hogs, poultry, clothing; yea, nothing goes amiss to which they take a fancy; while corn, rice, cotton, or the staple productions, whatever they may be, are standing temptations, provided a market be at hand, and they can sell or barter them with impunity. Locks, bolts, and bars secure articles desirable to them, from the dwelling of the master to that of the servant, and the *keys*, must always be carried.

Falsehood. — Their veracity is nominal. Duplicity is one of the most prominent traits in their character, practiced between themselves, but more especially towards their masters and managers. Their frequent cases of *feigned sickness* are vexatious. When criminal acts are under investigation, the sober, strenuous falsehood, sometimes the direct and awful appeal to God, of the transgressor, averts the suspicion, and by his own tact or collusion with others, perhaps, fixes the guilt upon some innocent person. The number, the variety and ingenuity of falsehoods that can be told by them in a few brief moments, is most astonishing. Where opportunity is given they will practice imposition. Servants, however, who will neither steal nor lie, may be found, and in no inconsiderable numbers.

Quarreling and Fighting. — The Negroes are settled in some quarter of the plantation, in houses near each other, built in rows, forming a street. The custom is to give each family a house of its own. The houses sometimes have a partition in the middle and accommodate a family in each end. These are called *double-houses.* Living so near each other, and every day working together, causes of difference must necessarily arise. Families grow jealous and envious of their neighbors; some essay to be *leading* families; they overhear conversations and domestic disagreements; become privy to improper conduct; they depredate upon each other; a fruitful source of tumult is the pilfering and quarreling of children which involve their parents. The women quarrel more than the men, and fight oftener. Where no decisive measures are taken to suppress these practices, plantations sometimes become intolerable, might gives right; the strong oppress the weak. Every master or manager has the evil under his own control.

They come to open breaches too, with their neighbors on adjoining plantations, or lots, if they live in towns. The Sabbath is considered a very suitable day for the settlement of their difficulties. However, with truth it may be said, there are fewer personal injuries, and manslaughters, and murders among the Negroes in the South, than among the same amount of population in any part of the United States; or, perhaps in the world.

Insensibility of Heart. — An ignorant and degraded people are not wont to exhibit much of the milk of human kindness.

Unless the Negroes are carefully watched and made accountable for power lodged in their hands, it will be abused. Parents will beat their children, husbands their wives, master-mechanics their apprentices, and drivers the people. In sickness, parents will neglect their children, children their parents ; and so with the other social relations. They cannot be trusted as *nurses.* Hence they must be *made* to attend upon the sick, and then *watched* lest they neglect them ; which ultimately brings the whole care of the sick upon the master or manager. It is a saying of their own, "that white people care more for them than their own color ;" and again, " that black people have not the same feeling for each other that white people have." It is an indisputable fact that when Negroes become owners of slaves they are generally cruel masters. They will over-load, work-down, bruise and beat, and starve all working animals committed to their care, with careless indifference.

Profane Swearing — is indulged in by both men and women ; and in certain districts to a most fearful extent. The vile habit is not so much under the notice of masters as some others, because servants restrain themselves in their presence and hearing, so that a plantation may be notorious for its profanity and the owner be ignorant of the fact. With profane swearing may be connected their *vulgar and obscene conversation, songs, and jests,* which tend to the early ruin of delicacy, modesty, and virtue.

Drunkenness — is more prevalent in towns and cities because facilities for procuring ardent spirits are greater than in country places. Drunkenness is easily detected and rarely escapes punishment, and the Negroes stand in fear. But immense quantities of ardent spirits are sold in the Southern States to the Negroes, by *retailing shops*, established for the express purpose of *Negro-trading*, wherever such trade may be secured. These shops injure the pecuniary interests of the country; they corrupt the morals, injure the health and destroy the lives of many of the Negroes; and are the *greatest nuisances and sources of evil tolerated in the country*. Had the Negroes access to ardent spirit they would speedily become a nation of drunkards.

Sabbath-breaking.—From all that has been said on the moral and religious condition of the Negroes, it is not necessary to enlarge on their Sabbath breaking. If they go not to the house of God, as multitudes do not, they spend the day in visiting, in idleness and sleep, or in hunting, fishing, or, sometimes, in thieving or working for their own convenience and profit; and where Sunday markets are tolerated, in trading. The necessity for the few Sunday markets which may exist, is laid in the cupidity and selfishness of those in authority; and the deeper condemnation of the iniquity will be visited upon them. The labor which the overwhelming mass of the Negroes perform in the South, especially in the cotton growing districts, leaves them abundant time for their own domestic affairs, if they have any disposition to improve it. Hence the general fact that the Negroes who keep the Sabbath, are the most thrifty and well-to-live. If a master so works his people as to compel them in a measure to labor for themselves on the Sabbath, or if he requires for himself any labor from them, on that holy day, the burden of the sin is upon his shoulders;

nor can such conduct be spoken of in terms of too severe reprobation; and it merits the attention of the civil authorities, and the severest penalties provided in law. But if a master be humane, and makes every arrangement to promote the prosperity of his people, if they will do that which they know is wrong, the blame is theirs and not his. There is, indeed, *a limit* to the responsibility of masters, as well as of others in authority. I am aware that there are exceptions in favor of members of the church, among Negroes, and in favor of particular parts of our country, wherein efforts have been made to secure a better observance of the Sabbath, but taking the country generally, our Sabbaths are profaned.

Our observations have, thus far, had direct reference to *country*, or *plantation*, Negroes, and *exceptions to our general view, are always implied if not expressed.* Variations may be discovered in their character and circumstances in different States and in different parts of the same State.

The moral and religious condition of *town and city Negroes*, may be disposed of in a few lines.

They admit of division into four classes: *family servants*, or those who belong to the families which they serve; *hired servants*, or those who are hired out by their owners to wait in families, or to any other service; *servants who hire their own time*, and work at various employments and pay their owners so much per day or month; and *watermen*, embracing fishermen, sailors, and boat-men.

Town and city Negroes are *more intelligent and sprightly* than country Negroes, owing to a difference in circumstances, employments, and opportunities of improvement. Their *physical condition* is somewhat improved; and they enjoy *greater access to religious privileges.*

On the other hand, they are exposed to greater temptations and vices; *their opportunities of attending upon places of pleasure and dissipation are increased;* they have *stronger temptations to theft, and idleness, and drunkenness, and lewdness; and the tendency to Sabbath breaking* is equally great. Their moral and religious condition is precisely that of plantation Negroes, modified in some respects and aggravated in others, by peculiarity of circumstances. They are more intelligent but less subordinate; better provided for in certain particulars, but not more healthy; enjoy greater advantages for religious improvement, but are thrown more directly in the way of temptation; and, on the whole, in point of moral character, if there be any pre-eminence it is in favor of the country Negroes; but it is a difficult point to decide.

I shall, now, having brought to a close the moral and religious condition of the slave Negro population, present *a few extracts from various and recent authors,* corroborative of the view which I have taken of it.

Edwin C. Holland, Esq., in his, " *Refutation of Calumnies circulated against the Southern and Western States:*" Charleston, 1822, says, page 59; "If it be asked why those in the lower country are *allowanced,* while those of the interior are not; the answer is, that such are the facilities of transportation to market, and the disposition to thievery so innate to the blacks, that a planter's barn would in a very short time become bankrupt of its wealth, and the whole of his substance vanish like unsubstantial moonshine."

Dr. Dalcho, of the Episcopal church, in his "*Practical Considerations, etc.;*" Charleston, 1823, p. 6. "Ignorant and indolent by nature, improvident and depraved by habit, and destitute of the moral principle, as they generally appear to be, ages and generations must pass away before they could be made virtuous, honest, and useful members of society."

Gen. *Thomas Pinckney,* in his "*Reflections, etc.;*" Charleston, 1822; pp. 20, 21. "Every thing consigned to the management of the slave, who has neither the incitement of interest, nor the fear of certain punishment, is neglected or abused; horses and all inferior animals left to their charge are badly attended; their provender finds its way to the dram shop, and they are used frequently without discretion or mercy; their carriages and harness are slightly and badly cleaned; the tools of the mechanics are broken and lost through neglect; their very clothing becomes more expensive through their carelesness arising from the knowledge that they must be supplied with all these articles, as well as their subsistence, at their masters expense; and waste, that moth of domestic establishments, universally prevails."

The Honorable Charles Cotesworth Pinckney; "*Address before the Agricultural Society of South Carolina;*" Charleston, 1829, second edition, pp. 10, 12.

"There needs no stronger illustration of the doctrine of human depravity than the state of morals on plantations in general. Besides the mischievous tendency of bad example in parents and elders, the little Negro is often taught by these his natural instructers, that he may commit any vice he can conceal from his superiors, and thus falsehood and deception are among the earliest lessons they imbibe. Their advance in years is but a progression to the higher grades of iniquity. The violation of the seventh commandment is viewed in a more venial light than in fashionable European circles. Their depredations of rice have been estimated to amount to twenty-five per cent on the gross average of crops, and this calculation was made after fifty years experience, by one whose liberal provision for their wants left no excuse for their ingratitude."

Thomas S. Clay, Esq., of Bryan county, Ga. "*Detail of a Plan for the Moral Improvement of Negroes on Plantations;*" 1833; pp. 8, 9; speaks of "vice and impurity, as the inheritance, for ages, of this degraded race," and enumerates "quarreling and fighting, lying and indecency," among their vices.

The Honorable Whitemarsh B. Seabrook: "*Essay on the Management of Slaves :*" Charleston, 1834: *pp.* 7, 8, 12, &c. "As human beings however slaves are liable to all the infirmities of our nature. Ignorant and fanatical none are more easily excited. Incendiaries might readily embitter their enjoyments and render them a curse to themselves and the community." — "The prominent offences of the slave are to be traced in most instances to the use of intoxicating liquors. This is one of the main sources of every insurrectionary movement which has occurred in the United States, we are therefore bound by interest as well as the common feeling of humanity, to arrest the progress of what may emphatically be called the contagious disease of our colored population. What have become of the millions of freemen who once inhabited our widely spread country ? Ask the untiring votaries of Bacchus. Can there be a doubt, but that the authority of the master alone prevents his slaves from experiencing the fate of the aborigines of America?" — "At one time polygamy was a common crime: it is now of rare occurrence." — "Between slaves on the same plantation there is a deep sympathy of feeling which binds them so closely together that a crime committed by one of their number is seldom discovered through their instrumentality. This is an obstacle to the establishment of an efficient police, which the domestic legislator can with difficulty surmount."

The executive committee of the Kentucky Union for the moral and religious improvement of the colored race, in their "*Circular* to the ministers of the gospel in Kentucky" — 1834, say — "We desire not to represent their condition worse than it is. Doubtless the light that shines around them, more or less illuminates their minds and moralizes their characters. We hope and believe that some of them, though poor in this world's goods, will be found rich in spiritual possessions in the day when the King of Zion shall make up his jewels. We know that many of them are included in the visible church, and frequently exhibit great zeal; but it is to be feared that it is often 'a zeal without knowledge:' and of the majority it must be confessed, that 'the light shineth in darkness and the darkness comprehendeth it not.' After making all reasonable allowances, our colored population can be considered, at the most, but semi-heathen." — *Western Luminary.*

Bishop Meade of Virginia in his admirable, *"Pastoral Letter to the Diocese of Virginia,"* urges the duty of affording religious instruction to those in bondage, on the ground that they are degraded and destitute. *Alexandria, D. C.* 1834.

Bishop Ives of North Carolina, (same pamphlet, Appendix pp. 27 – 28,) takes the same ground in his *Address to his Convention.*

C. W. Gooch Esq., Henrico county, Va. *Prize Essay on Agriculture in Virginia.*

" The slave feels no inducement to execute his work with effect. He has a particular art of slighting it and seeming to be busy when in fact he is doing little or nothing. Nor can he be made to take proper care of stock, tools, or any thing else. He will rarely take care of his clothes or his own health, much less of his companion's when sick and requiring his aid and kindness. There is perhaps not in nature a more heedless, thoughtless human being than a Virginia field Negro. With no care upon his mind, with warm clothing and plenty of food under a good master, is far the happier man of the two. His maxim is, ' come day, go day, God send Sunday.' His abhorrence of the poor white man is very great. He may sometimes feel a *reflected* respect for him, in consequence of the confidence and esteem of his master and others. But this trait is remarkable in the white, as in the black man. All despise poverty and seem to worship wealth. To the losses which arise from the *dispositions* of our slaves, must be added those which are occasioned by their *habits. There seems to be an almost entire absence of moral principle among the mass of our colored population.* But details upon this subject would be here misplaced. To steal and not to be detected is a merit among them, as it was with certain people in ancient times, and is at this day, with some unenlightened portions of mankind. And the vice which they hold in the greatest abhorrence is that of telling upon one another. There are many exceptions it is true, but this description embraces more than the majority. The numerous *free* negroes and worthless dissipated whites who have no visible means of support, and who are rarely seen at work derive their chief subsistence from the slaves. These thefts amount to a good deal in the course of the year and operate like leeches on the fair income of agriculture. They vary, however, in every county and neighborhood in exact proportion as the market for the plunder varies. In the vicinities of towns and villages they are the most serious. Besides the actual loss of property occasioned by them, they involve the riding of our horses at night, the corruption of the habits and the injury of the health of the slaves; for whiskey is the price generally received for them."

These extracts selected at random, are sufficient. A multiplication of them would be but a tiresome repetition. After all, the best testimony, *is the observation and experience of all persons who are intimately acquainted with them.* That the Negroes are in a degraded state is a fact, so far as my knowledge extends, *universally conceded.* It makes no difference if it be shown, as it might be, that they are less degraded than other portions of the human family, the fact remains true in respect to them, *they are degraded,* and it is *this fact* with which we have to do.

2. *The moral and religious condition of the free Negro population. Conclusion of the subject.*

They are *emphatically, lovers of pleasure and of show.*

All kinds of amusements, except those which involve labor or reflection, possess great attractions for them, and their indulgence is limited only by their means of access to them.

With a passion for dress, they frequently spend all

they make, in fine clothes; their appearance on the Sabbath and on public days, is any thing else but an index of their fortunes and comfort at home. They hire clothing for set occasions if they have none sufficiently good.

Proverbially idle, the majority work not except from necessity, and as soon as they collect a little money they must enjoy themselves upon it. They have been known to refuse employment, because not exactly out of money. Their love of ease overcomes that of gain. This propensity to idleness exposes them to manifold temptations, plunges them into numerous vices and subjects them to great privation and suffering.

They are amazingly *improvident*. One melting ray from a summer's sun, dissipates every remembrance of a long and dreary winter of suffering. The golden season of labor is passed in lounging along the streets and basking in the sun, or in lazy, bungling, and fitful attempts at work. Those that have regular trades and employments do better. *Profane swearing, quarreling, fighting and Sabbath-breaking*, are such common vices that they require no special notice.

Drunkenness, with its attendant woes, hurries large numbers of them to sudden and untimely ends. Low, dark, secluded, and filthy dram shops, are favorite resorts; often the depositories of stolen goods. I have seen them living upon a few crackers a day and as much whiskey as they could procure; their life spent in idleness, nightly revels, drunkenness, and debauchery.

Theft is still with them, in a state of freedom, a *characteristic vice*. Their petty larcenies are without number, and they advance to burglaries and give constant employment to police officers. Let any one attend the city courts in our chief towns in the *free* States, or read the reports of cases in the newspapers, and he will be surprised at the number of colored persons. Stabbing and murder have of late years not become infrequent.

Lewdness is without bounds. Great numbers, both in the slave and free States, not only pursue the vice, but are trained up to it, as a means of living. Infanticide, and the crimes and wretchedness connected with the vice, are found among them: the crime of infanticide is far more common among the free Negroes in the *free*, than in the *slave* States. Indeed it is by no means common among the free Negroes in the slave States. Their *marriage relations* too, are subject to dissolutions from infidelity and various other causes. It is a remarkble fact that a large proportion of those of a marriagable age, *remain single*, especially in the free States, where the support of a family is difficult. This fact has a considerable bearing on their state of morals.

With a *few extracts from different publications*, this branch of our inquiry shall be dismissed.

"The experience of the States north and east of the Susquehanna, with regard to this class of persons, is not on the whole much more encouraging." (i. e. than that of the Southern States, where it is bad.) "The number of respectable individuals is considerably greater indeed, but the character of the mass nearly the same. Nor can it be urged that they are here debared access to the ordinary means of moral and intellectual regeneration. On the contrary, schools are established for them; they are aided in procuring the conveniences of religious instruction and divine worship; they are united in societies adapted to produce self-respect and mental activity; exemplary attention is paid in numerous instances to the regulation of their habits and principles. They have every facility which is enjoyed by the laboring classes among the whites, of acquiring a plain education and a comfortable subsistence and of making provision for their children. They have the same legal security in person and property and generally, the same political rights as the rest of the community." — *Walsh's Appeal.*

"Taken as a whole the free blacks must be considered the most worthless and indolent of the citizens of the United States. It is well known that throughout the whole extent of our Union, they are looked upon as the very *drones and pests* of society. Nor does this character arise from their disabilities and disfranchisement, by which the law attempts to guard against them. In the non-slaveholding states, where they have been more elevated by law, this kind of population is in a worse condition and much more troublesome to society than in the slave-holding and especially in the planting States. Ohio, some years ago, formed a sort of land of promise for this deluded class, to which many have repaired from the slave-holding States; and what has been the consequence? They have been most harshly expelled from that State and forced to take refuge in a foreign land. Look through all the Northern States and mark the class upon whom the eye of the police is most steadily and constantly kept; see with what vigilance and care they are hunted down from place to place; and you cannot fail to see that idleness and improvidence are at the root of all their misfortunes. Not only does the experience of our own country illustrate this great fact, but others furnish abundant testimony." — *President Dew.*

Governor Giles, upon a calculation based on the average number of convictions in the State of Virginia from the penetentiary reports, up to 1829, shows that "crimes among the free blacks are more than three times as numerous as among the whites, and four and a half times more numerous than among the slaves," and that the proportion of crime is still not as great among the free blacks in Virginia, as in Massachusetts. Hence is it inferred that they are not so degraded and vicious in Virginia, a slave State, as in Massachusetts, a free State." —*Ibid.*

"We are not to wonder that this class of citizens should be so depraved and immoral." "Idleness, and consequent want, are of themselves sufficient to generate a catalogue of vices of the most mischievous and destructive character. Look to the penal prosecution of every country and mark the situation of those who fall victims to the laws; and what a frightful proportion do we find among the indigent and idle classes of society! Idleness generates want, want gives rise to temptation, and strong temptation makes the villain. Mr. Archer of Virginia well observed in his speech before the Colonization Society, that the free blacks were destined by an insuperable barrier, to the want of occupation, thence to the want of food, thence to the distresses which ensue that want, thence to the settled depravation which grows out of those distresses and is nursed at their bosoms." — *Ib.*

A colony of free blacks was expelled from Ohio, in 1832, on account of their dissoluteness and dishonesty and misery; being considered in the light of vagabonds and nuisances. A college for free negroes was projected in New Haven about the same time, and the respectable citizens opposed and suppressed it, because the increase of that class of population was considered an evil. "Few of them, (the free Negro population,) are engaged in trade or commerce or have any hopes of elevating themselves to that situation. Nine-tenths of them are in subordinate and menial situations and likely thus to remain, at low wages. That they labor under the most oppressive disadvantages which their freedom can by no means counterbalance is too obvious to admit of doubt."

"I waive all inquiry whether this be right or wrong. I speak of things as they are; not as they might or ought to be. They are cut off from the most remote chance of amalgamation with the white population, by feelings or prejudices, call them what you will, that are ineradicable. The situation of the majority of them is more unfavorable than that of many of the slaves. 'With all the burdens, cares, and responsibilities of freedom, they have few or none of its substantial benefits. Their associations are and must be chiefly with slaves. Their right of suffrage gives them little if any political influence, and they are practically if not theoretically excluded from representation in our public councils.' No merit, no services, no talents, can ever elevate the great mass of them to a level with the whites; occasionally an exception may arise, a colored individual of great talents, merits, and wealth, may emerge from the crowd. Cases of this kind are to the last degree rare. The colored people are subjected to legal disabilities more or less galling and severe in almost every State in the Union. *
* * * * And there is no reason to expect that the lapse of centuries will make any change in this respect, (i. e. 'the jealousy with which they are regarded.') They will always, unhappily, be regarded as an inferior race." — *Carey's Letters*, *Let*. 12.

"Mr. Everett, in a speech before the Colonization Society, 1833, says, "the free blacks form in Massachusetts about one seventy-fifth part of the population; *one sixth of the convicts in our prisons are of this class."*

A memorial presented to the Legislature of Connecticut, in 1834, states "that not a week, hardly a day passes, that they (the free colored people,) are not implicated in the violation of some law. Assaults and batteries, insolence to the whites, compelling a breach of the peace, riots in the streets, petty thefts, and continual trespasses on property are such common occurrences resulting from the license they enjoy, that they have ceased to become subjects of remark. It is but recently that a band of Negroes paraded the streets of New Haven, armed with clubs and pistols and dirks, with the avowed purpose of preventing the law of the land from being enforced against one of the species. Upon being accosted by an officer of justice and commanded to retire peacably to their homes, their only reply consisted of abuse and threats of personal violence. The law was overshadowed and the officer consulted his own safety in a timely retreat." The memorial then proceeds to show that the evil complained of has so rapidly progressed that the whites have become the subjects of insult and abuse whenever they have refused to descend to familiarity with them: that themselves, their wives, and children, have been driven from the pavements, where they have not submitted to personal conflict; that from the licentiousness of their general habits, they have invariably depreciated the value of property by their location in its neighborhood: and that from their notorious uncleanliness and filth, they have become common nuisances to the community."—*Memorial.*

From the report of the warden of the Connecticut state prison, 1838, it appears "that the number of blacks in confinement compared with the whites is ten or twelve times greater than is the proportion of the black to the white population in the State." — *Journal of Commerce*, *May* 16, 1838.

" The records of crime in the free States show a frightful disproportion in the numbers of white and black offenders, and most especially in those States where there are no disabilities or restrictions by law imposed upon the blacks."

" In Massachusetts they are one seventy-fourth part of the population, yet they are in the proportion of one sixth of the convicts in the state prison. In Connecticut one thirty-fourth part of the whole, one third of the number in the penetentiary. New York one thirty-fifth and one fourth of the convicts. New Jersey one thirteenth, and one third. Pennsylvania one thirty-fifth, and one third. In Ohio the black population is one to one hundred and fifteen white; convicts seven to one hundred. Vermont, by census of 1830, contained 277,-000 souls; 918 were Negroes. In 1831 there were seventy-four convicts in the prison, and of these twenty-four were Negroes! When compared with what is reported of the prisons of the slave-holding States, it is shown that the proportion of Negroes in the penetentiaries of the free States is in the ratio of more than ten to one in favor of the slave-holding States. * * * The free Negroes in Ohio, in the aggregate, are in no better condition, therefore, than the slaves in Kentucky. They are excluded from social intercourse with the whites, and whatever of education you may give them will not tend to elevate their standing to any considerable extent." — *Report of the Committee on the Judiciary, relative to the repeal of laws reposing restrictions and disa-*

bilities on blacks and mulattoes, by Mr. Cushing, Feb.
21, 1835. Agreed to unanimously. Legislature of
Ohio.

The view which has now been taken of the Moral
and Religious Condition of the Negroes of the United
States, will, we believe, justify us in the following *gene-*
ral conclusions.

1. They are intellectually and morally a degraded
people; the most so of any in the United States; — and
while from their universal profession of the Christian
system, and their attendance upon its ordinances of
worship, and the absence of all fixed forms of idolatry,
they cannot, strictly speaking be termed *heathen;* yet
may they with propriety be termed *the heathen of our*
land.

2. The majority of them have access to some kind of
means of grace, either among themselves or in connection with the whites; but they are not as efficient means
as their necessities require; while multitudes of them
are almost wholy destitute. Nor has the colored population, bond and free, either ability or will to supply
themselves with the Gospel of the grace of God; but
are left in next to absolute dependence upon the permission, the countenance and assistance of the whites.

3. They are living in manifold and gross sins; their
iniquities are aggravated and great before the Lord, and
not the least of them is their neglect and contempt of
spiritual mercies and privileges within their reach.
Thousands are annually descending to the grave and
eternal misery, and they demand and ought to excite the
benevolent feelings and efforts, for their salvation, of the
churches of Christ throughout the Union.

PART III.

OBLIGATIONS of the Church of Christ to attempt the Improvement of the Moral and Religious Condition of the Negroes in the United States, by affording them the Gospel.

CHAPTER I.

The Obligations of the Church to afford the Gospel to the Negroes.

There are one or two positions upon which the argument under this head is based, and as preliminary thereto demand attention.

The Gospel is the gift of God to our lost and ruined race. Our Divine Lord " was made *flesh* " — *John* 1 : 1–14. He took upon himself our nature : — *Heb.* 2 : 11 – 18; for our benefit. That benefit is *eternal life.* " In him was life, and the life was the light of men. — *John* 1 : 4, 17, 3. " For God so loved the world that he gave his only begotten Son, that whosoever believeth in him should not perish, but have everlasting life." — 3 : 16. " Thanks be unto God for his unspeakable gift."— 2 *Cor.* 9 : 15.

It hath pleased the Almighty, in his sovreignty, to bestow the Gospel upon but a portion of the human race. He has, however, chosen to employ human agency in extending the knowledge, and the consequent blessings of this glorious gift, to all mankind, in fulfilment of his expressed designs, and his own most precious promises. He has made it the *duty* under the most solemn commands, of all who *possess* the Gospel *to impart it to those who are destitute of it.* The possession of the gift implies the obligation to impart it. No man may question this position who allows himself to be guided by the conviction, of reason, the dictates of conscience, or the declarations of the word of God.

In attempting to fulfil this duty, the general and the just rule of action is, that we impart the Gospel to those of our fellow-men who are *most dependent* upon us for it — who are *most needy and most accessible.*

These three peculiarities meet in the case of the Negroes; and consequently they stand *first* in their claims upon our benevolent attention. And our remarks in confirmation shall be directed,

1. *To the Negroes in the Slave States.*

They are *the most dependent of all people upon us for the word of life.*

A glance at the civil condition and connection of this people with us, will demonstrate the point. They are, in the eye of the law, *property;* over which there is an absolute control as such, excepting in so far as they are human beings, and by law are protected in life and limb. The law, however, makes no provision for their religious training, and all the privileges of religion are regulated by the customs of society and the will of owners; nor is it in the power of any one to interfere between the master and the servant, and dictate what privileges his servant ought and must enjoy, any more than he may interfere between parent and child.

Throw these facts together. By law or custom, they are excluded from the advantages of education; and by consequence, from the reading of the word of God: and this immense mass of immortal beings is thrown for religious instruction upon *oral* communications entirely. And upon whom? Upon their *owners*. And their owners, especially of late years, claim to be the *exclusive guardians* of their religious instruction, and the almoners of divine mercy towards them, thus assuming the responsibility of their *entire* christianization!

All approaches to them from abroad are rigidly guarded against, and no ministers are allowed to break to them the bread of life, except such as have commended themselves to the affection and confidence of owners. I do not condemn this course of self-preservation on the part of our citizens. I mention it only to show more fully the point in hand; the *entire dependence* of the Negroes upon *ourselves* for the Gospel.

While this step is taken, another has already been taken, and that of a long time; namely, *Negro preachers* are discouraged, if not suppressed, on the ground of incompetency and liability to abuse their office and influence to the injury of the morals of the people and the infringement of the laws and peace of the country. I would not go all the lengths of many on this point, for from my own observation, Negro preachers may be employed and confided in, and so regulated as to do their own color great good, and community no harm: nor do I see, if we take the word of God for our guide, how we can consistently exclude an entire people from access to the Gospel ministry, as it may please Almighty God from time to time, as he unquestionably does, to call some of them to it "*as Aaron was.*" The discouragement of this class of preachers, throws the body of the people still more in their dependence upon ourselves, who indeed cannot secure ministers in sufficient numbers to supply our own wants.

Nor have the Negroes any *church organizations different from or independent of our own.* Such independent organizations are, indeed, not on the whole advisable. But the fact binds them to us with still stronger dependence And, to add no more, we may, according to the power lodged in our hands, forbid religious meetings, and religious instruction on our own plantations; we may forbid our servants going to church at all, or only to such churches as we may select for them; we may literally shut up the kingdom of heaven against men, and suffer not them that are entering to go in!

It is not too much, therefore to say that the Negroes are in a state of almost absolute dependence upon their owners for the words of eternal life.

They are the *most needy* of any people in our country. This is very evident, from the exposition which we have given of their dependence; as well as of their moral and religious character. They have no education, no immediate access to the word of God, no competent teachers of their own color, no competent number of white teachers, and are in a state of great ignorance and moral degradation.

And lastly, they are the *most accessible.* They speak the same language with ourselves; dwell in the same land, at our own doors; and are members of our house-

holds. No law forbids the religious instruction of the
Negroes, *orally*, by proper instructers, either during the
week or on the Sabbath day ; and any minister of the
Gospel, or any owner, may undertake the good work,
and prosecute it as largely and as long as he pleases.

We are prepared now to take up *the obligation of the
church of Christ in the slave-holding States to impart
the Gospel of Salvation to the Negroes within those
States.*

1. That obligation is imposed upon us in the first
instance *by the providence of God.*

This follows undeniably from all our previous statements, in the history of their religious instruction, and
in the sketch of their moral and religious condition.
But it may be of some service to be particular under
this head. It was by the permission of Almighty God,
in his inscrutable providence over the affairs of men,
that the Negroes were taken from Africa and transported
to these shores. The inhabitants of the Colonies at
their first introduction had nothing to do with the infa-
mous traffic, and were, we may say, universally opposed
to it. The iniquity of the traffic and of their first introduction, rests upon the Mother Country.

Being brought here they were brought as *slaves ;* in
the providence of God we were constituted *masters ;*
superiors ; and constituted their *guardians.* And all
the laws in relation to them, civilly, socially, and religiously considered, were framed by ourselves. They
thus were placed under our control, and not exclusively
for our benefit but for theirs also.

We could not overlook the fact that they were men ;
holding the same relations to God as ourselves — whose
religious interests were certainly their *highest and best*

and that our *first* and *fundamental duty* was to provide to the extent of our ability, for the perpetual security of those interests. Our relations to them and their relations to us, continue the same to the present hour, and the providence of God still binds upon us the great duty of imparting to them the Gospel of eternal life.

2. The obligation is imposed upon us *by the word of God.*

As already evinced from general principles and commands; the sum of all is, that the Gospel is the gift of God to men, and those who possess it are bound to bestow it upon those who do not.

A few passages of a *general character* may be advanced, bearing strongly on the point in hand.

"Go ye into all the world and preach the Gospel to every creature." Our Lord in this command recognizes, men, not as of a particular nation or color, but collectively, as the intelligent and accountable creatures of God. "God hath made of one blood all the nations of men." It is therefore necessary that the Gospel be preached to the Negroes as well as to the other varieties of the race, and seeing that they have not put it from them, nor judged themselves unworthy of everlasting life, we cannot, we dare not, neglect them and turn to others.

"Though shalt love thy neighbor as thyself." And who are our neighbors if the Negroes are not? They are members of the same great family of men; and members of our own communities and parts of our very households; and spend their days in our service. If we see them stripped of necessary religious privileges, and lying in their depravity, helpless, and exposed to eternal death, shall we be neighbors unto them if we look upon

them and see their misery and pass by without affording
them what relief may be in our power?

"All things whatsoever ye would that men should do
to you, do you even so to them." Were we in the condition of the Negro and he in our own; able to read
and to appreciate the word of God, and to impart it to
us, would we not think it his duty to do it? Yes. And
if he neglected that duty we should consider him deficient both in humanity and religion.

But we advance a step further. *The word of God
recognizes the relation of master and servant, and
addresses express commands to us as masters.*

In the constitution of his visible church on earth
Almighty God included the *servants of families;* commanded the sign of his everlasting and gracious covenant to be made in their flesh, and thereby secured to
them, as well as *to children* the privileges and blessings
of the same. He would have them trained up in the
knowledge of his most holy name and for his service:
nor must they be neglected, nor excluded. Gen. 17:
12–13. "And he that is eight days old shall be circumcised among you, every man child in your generations, he that is *born in the house* or *bought with money*
of any stranger, which is not of thy seed;" and the
command is *repeated,* to show his tender regard for the
poor, and that his covenant embraces them. "He that
is born in thy house and he that is *bought with thy
money* must needs be circumcised; and my covenant
shall be in your flesh for an everlasting covenant." In
obedience to this command Abraham "in the self-same
day circumcised his son Ishmael and all that were *born
in his house,* and *all that were bought with his money.*"
v. 23. He apprehended the will of God as expressed

in the covenant, and received the divine approbation :. "for I know him that he will command his children and his household after him, and they shall keep the way of the Lord to do justice and judgment, that the Lord may bring upon Abraham that which he hath spoken of him." *Gen.* 18: 19.

The rest of the Sabbath was secured to servants in the Decalogue : "in it thou shalt not do any work, thou nor thy son, nor thy daughter, thy *man-servant* nor thy *maid-servant.*"—*Exod.* 20: 8–11. The *sacred festivals* were opened to them, and along with their masters they were to rejoice before the Lord : they were also to present *sacrifices and offerings* to the Lord, in the appointed place and eat of them "before the Lord," with their masters. "Thou mayest not eat, within thy gates, the tithe of thy corn, or of thy wine, or of thy oil, or the firstlings of thy herds, or of thy flocks, nor any of thy vows which thou vowest, nor thy free will offerings, or heave offering of thine hand : but thou must eat them before the Lord, in the place which the Lord thy God shall choose, thou and thy son and thy daughter, and thy *man-servant* and thy *maid-servant,*"—*Deut.* 12: 17, 18. "And thou shalt keep the *feast of weeks:* and thou shalt rejoice before the Lord thy God, thou, and thy son, and thy daughter, and thy *man-servant*, and thy *maid-servant.*" So also "the feast of *tabernacles.*"—*Deut.* 16: 1–16.

Thus in the *Old Testament*, the law of God, and the Sanctuary and all its privileges, were opened to servants and secured to them by the declared will of God : and it was the duty of masters to command their households after them, that they should keep the way of the Lord to do justice and judgment : otherwise the Lord would not bring upon them the promised blessings.

The *New Testament* is, if possible more explicit.

In several epistles, the relation of master and servant is recognized, and the mutual duties of each arising out of that relation mutually insisted upon. Masters and servants are addressed as *belonging to the same churches* and heirs of the *same grace of life :* 1 *Tim.* 6 : 1 — 5. Eph. Col.

What kind of servants are intended ? *Slaves :* the original teaches us so, while the very duties enjoined upon servants and the observations made upon their condition, (1 *Cor.* 7 : 20 — 12,) confirms the fact that they were *literally Slaves.* And the kind of slavery that existed among the Jews was that allowed in the Old Testament; which may be considered identical with that which prevails amongst us at the present time; and no one will deny that the slavery which existed among the Greeks and Romans and Gentile nations, was identical with our own. All authentic history, and the codification of the Roman laws made in the reign of Justinian, prove it. The slaves were more heterogenous in their national origin, than ours. Among them however existed *Negroes :* and in no small numbers. Indeed a traffic in Negro slaves had been carried on for centuries before Isabella gave permission for their transportation to these western shores ; and they were sold and scattered over all the east.

When therefore the New Testament addresses commands to *Masters,* we are the *identical persons* intended. We are Masters in the New Testament sense. We are addressed as directly and as identically, as when we are *Fathers,* and it is said " *Fathers* provoke not your children to wrath."

And what are these commands ? "And ye *Masters,*

do the same things unto them, forbearing threatening : knowing that your Master also is in Heaven : neither is there respect of persons with him." *Eph.* 6 : 9.

As servants are exhorted to fulfil their duties to their masters, " as the servants of Christ, doing the will of God from the heart : " having respect to their accountability to God ; so also masters are exhorted to do the same things, to fulfil their duties to their servants, from the same principle of obedience to God and respect to future accountability.

" Masters give unto your servants that which is just and equal : knowing that ye also have a Master in Heaven." *Col.* 4 : 1. Masters are here required to treat their servants justly and equitably, in respect, of course, to all their interests, both for time and eternity ; for they shall account to God for the same.

Thus doth God put his finger upon us as *Masters.* He holds up before our faces our servants and our duties to them. He commands us to fulfil those duties under the pain of his displeasure. He tells us that in the performance of duty he does not respect *us* more than he respects *them.*

Can any one doubt that among the duties of Masters, is that of imparting, and causing to be imparted to them the Gospel of Salvation ? Supposing Masters gave unto their servants that which was just and equal for this present life — and *gave no more :* would that come up to the spirit and power of the command ? Would it be just and equal for masters to suffer them to remain in ignorance of the way of salvation, to die and be eternally lost ? Surely not. Says Job. " If I did despise the cause of my man-servant or of my maid-servant, when they contended with me : what shall I do when God riseth up? And when he visiteth what shall I answer him? Did not he that made me in the womb, make him? And did not one fashion us in the womb?" If we neglect to evangelize our servants, they may justly have a controversy with us; and if we continue to despise their cause, in the day when God riseth up for judgement, we shall be speechless.

Thus by the *providence* and *word* of God are we under obligations to impart the Gospel to our servants.

It may be added, that we cannot disregard this obligation thus *divinely imposed*, without forfeiting our humanity, our gratitude, our consistency, and our claim to the spirit of christianity itself.

Our Humanity.

Humanity is that kindness and good will towards our fellow creatures which prompts us to sympathize with them in their necessities and sufferings, and to exert ourselves for their relief.

The Lord Jesus has furnished us with the most beautiful and striking illustrations of this virtue. "What man shall there be among you, that shall have one sheep, and if it fall into a pit: will he not lay hold on it and lift it out?" "Doth not each one of you, loose his ox or his ass from the stall and lead him away to watering? And ought not this woman being a daughter of Abraham, whom Satan hath bound, lo these eighteen years, be loosed from this bond?" *Matt.* 12: 10—13 *Luke* 13: 14—16, 14; 2—6. Apply the reasoning: "How much then is a man better than a sheep or an ox?" When our servants are sick and diseased, we do not suffer them to want; we physic and nurse them. But are not their *souls* more precious than their *bodies*? Much more then should we lift our servants from the pit of ignorance, moral pollution and death into which they have fallen. Much more should we strive to loose them (bound for so many years!) from the bonds of sin and satan and lead away their famishing souls to the water of life.

Our Gratitude. They nurse us in infancy, contribute to our pleasures and pastimes in youth; and furnish us with the means of education. They constitute our wealth, and yield us all the comforts and conveniences of life; they may in a degree adopt towards us, the language of Jacob to Laban, "thus I was: in the day the drought consumed me, and the frost by night and my sleep departed from mine eyes:" they watch around our languishing beds in sickness; share in our misfortunes, weep over us when we die; prepare us for the burial and carry us to the house appointed for all the living.

The obligations, the sacrifice and service are not to be all on one side, in the relation of master and servant. If we have been made partakers of their *carnal* things, our duty is also to minister unto them in *spiritual* things, *Rom.* 15: 27. 1 *Cor.* 9: 11. And shall we consider it "a great thing" to fulfil this duty? The kindest and the most grateful return which we can make them, is to put them in possession of the richest gift of God to men, the Gospel of our Lord and Saviour Jesus Christ.

If we neglect to do this, we shall forfeit also our *consistency.*

Consistency is the correspondence of our conduct or practice with our professed principles. *Ezra* 8: 22. And it is an exceedingly rare virtue.

As philanthropists and christians, we are contributing of our substance; and offering up our prayers, that

Christ's kingdom may come, and that his Gospel may be preached to every people under heaven. We have indeed assisted in sending missionaries to the heathen, thousands of miles from us; and to multitudes of destitute white settlements in our own country; in founding Theological Seminaries and filling them with students, that the demand for laborers in the great harvest might be supplied. We have assisted in having the gospel preached in our public prisons; in the harbors of our sea-port cities, and along the lines of our canals and the shores of our lakes and rivers, to those who do business on the great waters. We have assisted in gathering the children of parents of every condition into Sabbath Schools; and in efforts to stay the swellings of the fiery waves of intemperance. We have been printing Bibles and tracts and religious works, with which to supply every family and every individual in our land, and also to meet the urgent demands for the same from other lands. This is all as it should be. But what have we done publicly, systematically and perseveringly for the Negroes, in order that they also might enjoy the gospel of Christ? Why are they as a class overlooked by us in our benevolent regards and efforts? What blindness hath happened to us in part, that we cannot see their spiritual necessities and feel the claims which they undeniably have upon us? Our Lord in view of our works, will say to us, "these ought ye to have done and not to leave the other undone."

We cannot cry out against the Papists for withholding the Scriptures from the common people and keeping them in ignorance of the way of life, for our inconsistency is as great as theirs, if we withhold the Bible from our servants, and keep them in ignorance of its saving truths, which we certainly do while we *will not* provide ways and means of having it read and explained to them.

The celebrated John Randolph, on a visit to a female friend, found her surrounded with her seamstresses, making up a quantity of clothing. " What work have you in hand ? " " O sir, I am preparing this clothing to send to the poor *Greeks*." On taking leave at the steps of the mansion, he saw some of her servants in need of the very clothing which their tender-hearted mistress was sending abroad. He exclaimed, " Madam, madam, *the Greeks are at your door !* "

If we neglect to impart the Gospel to the Negroes, our inconsistency will be most glaring and shameful.

And furthermore, we shall *forfeit our claim to the spirit of Christianity itself.*

The remarks under the head of *consistency* evidenced this position, but nevertheless it will allow of a distinct consideration.

This spirit is *love.* " Thou shalt love the Lord thy God with all thy heart, with all thy mind, and with all thy strength ; and thy neighbor as thyself." Love is of God. " He that loveth is born of God, for God is love." " In this was manifested the love of God towards us, because that God sent his only begotten Son into the world, that we might live through him," — 1 *John* 4 : 7 – 11. His love has respect to the immortal souls of men ; their everlasting salvation. For this our Lord Jesus Christ came into the world and labored, suffered and died on the cross. The *same spirit* is wrought in the hearts of all who are *truly his disciples.* Their chief joy *is the glory of God in the salvation of men ;* the increase of the church upon the earth. The cherished and ever-living desire of their soul is that men may be converted to God. To effect this conversion they willingly labor and submit to sacrifices, even, if need be, unto death. This is the spirit which burns and glows in all the word of God; unquenchable—invincible in its progress, because originated and sustained by the grace and power of the Almighty.

"I am a debtor both to the Greeks and to the Barbarians, both to the wise and to the unwise. So, as much as in me is, I am ready to preach the Gospel to you that are at Rome also. For I am not ashamed of the Gospel of Christ; for it is the power of God unto salvation, to every one that believeth; to the Jew first and also to the Greek." "I say the truth in Christ, I lie not, my conscience also bearing me witness in the Holy Ghost; that I have great heaviness and continual sorrow of heart. For I could wish that myself were accursed from Christ for my brethren, my kinsmen according to the flesh."—*Rom.* 1: 14–16, *and* 9: 1–3. "For the love of Christ constraineth us because we thus judge that if one died for all, then were all dead: and he died for all that they which live, should not henceforth live unto themselves, but unto him which died for them, and rose again." — *2 Cor.* 5: 14–15. "I will very gladly spend and be spent for you (for your souls,") — 12: 15. "Yea, and if I be offered (i. e. my *strength and life* offered up,) upon the sacrifice and service of your faith, I joy and rejoice with you all." — *Phil.* 2: 17.

Where then *this spirit is wanting, there is wanting the very spirit of Christianity itself.*

"The salt has lost his savor; wherewith shall it be salted? It is thenceforth good for nothing, but to be

cast out, and to be trodden under foot of men!"—
Mat. 5: 13–16.

The idea that we possess the spirit of Christianity in
its perfection, while we constantly and directly neglect
the evangelization of the Negroes, when it lies within our
power, is preposterous in the extreme. We are neither
"the light of the world:" nor "the salt of the earth."

Reverse the order of Providence. Let us recur to
the illustration already adduced. Were we in the condition of the Negro, and he in our condition, able to
read and to appreciate the Gospel: experimentally acquainted with it: a partaker of its privileges and of its
eternal hopes; would we consider it his duty, (a duty
which he was well able to perform,) to make us partakers with himself in the Gospel: that Gospel to which
we have a right as the gift of God to all men; and which
we could claim at his hands as the divinely appointed
almoner of God's mercy to us: that Gospel which is
every thing to perishing sinners and which alone could
yield us happiness in our humble lot? Certainly we
should. Suppose he *would* or he *did* not? *Could* we
believe that he sincerely felt all the amazing and soul-
stirring truths which the Gospel contains? *Could* we
believe that he possessed the *spirit of the Gospel?* No,
no! we could not!

"There is that scattereth and yet increaseth; and
there is that withholdeth more than is meet, and it tendeth to poverty. The liberal soul shall be made fat, and
he that watereth shall be watered also himself. He that
withholdeth corn, the people shall curse him; but blessing shall be upon the head of him that selleth it."—
Prov. 11: 24–26. "Now if any man have not the
spirit of Christ, he is none of his."—*Rom.* 8: 9.

"Whoso hath this world's goods and seeth his brother have need and shutteth up his bowels of compassion from him, how dwelleth the love of God in him?"—1 *John* 3 : 16–20. With more tremendous emphasis let it be asked "Whoso hath the *word of eternal life* and seeth his brother have need, and shutteh up his bowels of compassion from him, how dwelleth the love of God in him? Let this question be answered to that God who without respect of persons judgeth according to every man's work!

Such are the considerations which we must address to ourselves, who reside in the Southern States, in order that we may be awakened to the great duty of imparting the Gospel to the Negroes.

2. We now turn *to the Negroes in the free States.*

And our remarks on the duty of affording *them* the Gospel, need not be protracted after what has been said.

It is the duty of the white churches in the free States to afford the Gospel to the Negroes, for the following plain reasons among others.

1. Because of their *general poverty.*

They are, as a class, *a poor people;* among, if not, "*the* poor of the land." And consequently are not able to give suitable encouragement to the institutions of religion; not able to build churches, support ministers, or buy books and maintain Sabbath schools. The means must come from purses other than their own. Such has been *the fact* in the majority of instances where the Gospel has received an adequate support among them. More than the majority have little or nothing to give; they barely make out to obtain the necessaries of life.

2. Because of *their moral degradation.*

This has been in a measure demonstrated. The statements already made need not be repeated. They are a proper field for missionary effort; and have been to a great extent, very strangely overlooked. Such a mass of ignorance and vice can in no way be desirable in any community, whether we view them in a civil or religious light. Their corrupting influence in cities, where they chiefly congregate, has never been inquired into, nor duly appreciated.

3. Because of their *entire dependence upon the whites for their every improvement.*

They have almost *no spirit* of moral improvement among themselves; it is not to be expected from them considering their character and circumstances. They have *no men of influence, no leaders of their own color,* who are able to sway the people; to project and execute plans for their general religious improvement. Nor have they *societies* of their own for the purpose. The truth is, they do not look to themselves; they do not depend upon themselves. They look up to and depend upon the whites. The feeling of subjection and dependence which they had in a state of slavery, is hereditary and is kept alive by the frequent accession of Negroes, escaped from servitude or set free. Then the vast superiority of the whites in point of numbers, intelligence, morality, and station, cherish it. Hence the efforts of the whites for their benefit are received with special favor and relied upon. At least it was so in times past. They have of late years been taught to distinguish between *friendly* and *hostile* whites; and they have been inflated with high notions of their perfect equality with the whites in wisdom, standing, rights, and importance. The effect has been, and it should not be deemed extraordinary, that they have become rather heady and high-minded; some of their friends have not been able to do them the good that they wished; and others disguted, have ceased to feel and to act for them. Whether they will be ultimately benefitted by this increase of knowledge and sense of importance, remains to be seen.

4. Because of *consistency.*

The efforts for the moral and religious improvemen of the Negroes in the free States, do not correspond with *the profession* of interest in them, as a class of people.

With some, the bestowment of *freedom* is the sum of all duty. And *freedom* is the grand catholicon for all the evils which harrass and oppress the colored man. It has not proved exactly so, in the free States. There are districts in Rhode Island, in New Jersey, New York, and Delaware, once peopled with Negroes. They were emancipated on the soil, and now there is scarcely one to be seen. They have been scattered and driven off, and have melted away before the whites. Their few descendants are "making out to live" in cities, and in country situations, here and there. At the present day the Negroes are not reached as a class by education and religion. They are not a desirable population—so confessed on all hands; and their intelligence, morality and thrift in the free States, give but poor encouragement to the doctrine of emancipation in those parts of the Union where they are held to service.

The overwhelming majority in the free States are whites. They possess all the intelligence, wealth, and power; and move on without disturbance from the few

Negroes among them.   The weight of the Negroes upon
the wheels of society is scarcely felt.   But what would
be the state of things if the whites were in the *minority*
and they the *majority?*   I shall not undertake to furnish
an answer to the question which every man of ordinary
consideration can do for himself the moment after it is
put to him.   The great duty of the churches and friends
of the Negroes in the free States, is to attempt, more
systematically and efficiently, their moral and religious
improvement.

CHAPTER II.

EXCUSES.

I shall proceed immediately to the *excuses* in relation to a discharge of the obligations now proved to rest upon the church of Christ in the United States, to attempt the improvement of the moral and religious condition of the Negroes, usually advanced *in the slaveholding States.* In giving them a candid consideration those made in the free States may in a measure be anticipated.

The Negroes *have the Gospel already.*

They have access to the churches on the Sabbath, and hear the same preaching that their masters do; they are favored frequently with services from the ministers, expressly for their instruction; they are received into, and are under the watch and discipline of the white churches; there are some Sabbath schools for them; they have plantation prayers, and numerous preachers and exhorters of their own color, and some of them are able to read; nor do they know any other religion but the Christian religion.

It is true they have access to the house of God on the Sabbath; but it is also true that even where the privilege is within their reach, a minority only, (and frequently a very small one) embrace it. There are multitudes of districts in the South and Southwest, in which the churches cannot contain one-tenth of the Negro population ; besides others in which there are no churches at all. It must be remembered also that in many of those churches there is preaching only once a fortnight, or once a month, and then perhaps only one sermon. To say that they fare as well as their masters does not settle the point ; for great numbers of masters have very few or no religious privileges at all.

The direct preaching of ministers to the Negroes is well, and is a great benefit. But the number who do this is far smaller than it should be. The ordinary preaching to the whites makes little impression upon the blacks, being above their comprehension and not made applicable to them. Hence their stupid looks, their indifferent staring, their profound sleeps, and their thin attendance. What is there to light up the countenance with intelligence ; to rivet attention ; to banish drowsiness, so common to laboring men and men unaccustomed to think when sitting still ; what is there to attract them to the house of God ? Nothing but sound and show. Solid instruction, pungent appeals to the conscience, will bring men to the house of God and retain them in attendance there, and nothing else will. But divine truth is not thus adapted to the Negroes, by ministers, in their sermons to the whites ; and those Negroes who enjoy such a dispensation of the Gospel as this, upon careful examination, are found to be sadly deficient in a knowledge of religion, and we are surprised to find Christianity in absolute conjunction with a people and yet conferring upon them so few benefits.

The general preaching to the whites will not answer the purpose. The Negroes require preaching specially adapted to them. It is true they are received into, and are under the watch and care of, white churches; but that fact does not prove that they are properly enlightened, and are continued under courses of instruction, so that they go on unto perfection. In hundreds of instances the very reverse is the fact; their ignorance, superstition, and deception are complained of. Their piety is taken upon trust; and the numerous and perplexing cases of discipline for gross immoralities sufficiently prove that the complaints uttered against them are well founded. A man must not stand on the *outside* of a church and judge of the church character and standing of these people, he must go *within*.

The Sabbath schools for their exclusive benefit, taking the entire population, need scarcely be named. Their plantation meetings serve to keep alive religion among them, but contribute little to the increase of their intelligence; while there are hundreds of plantations where there are no such meetings at all, there being few or no church members to conduct them.

We have colored ministers and exhorters, but their numbers are wholly inadequate to the supply of the Negroes; and while their ministrations are infrequent and conducted in great weakness, there are some of them whose moral character is justly suspected and who may be considered blind leaders of the blind.

It is true there are no forms of idolatry prevalent among them, nor have the *corruptions of Christianity* made progress among them, the field being too low and poor to enlist the sympathies of the leaders and advocates of such corruption, except the Papists, who in

some of our chief towns have proselyted some of them ;
yet Christianity, as understood and professed by them, is,
as I have already attempted to show, exceedingly imperfect, and needing great improvement.

*The Negroes are incapable of receiving religious
instruction, except to a very limited extent.*

From the manner in which their religious instruction
is neglected, it would appear that their incapacity is
taken for granted.   Appealing to our own experience
in their instruction, we should judge the objection to be
a mistake.   They are capable, even under oral instruction, and that not enjoyed in any high degree of perfection, of making very considerable advances in religious
knowledge.

But if they are capable of receiving instruction sufficient to make plain to them the way of salvation, then
their capacities should be filled to overflowing, to that
extent.   In all reason and conscience deny it not to
them, for it is their everlasting life.   The mind of man
is created so as to admit of eternal expansion and progression in knowledge and holiness.   The good work
which is done for them in time will be carried forward
unto perfection in eternity.

But to pursue the excuse a step further.   It is customary with many to entertain low opinions of the
intellectual capacity of the Negroes.   Whether this be
right or wrong we leave every man to judge for himself
after a due investigation of the subject ; and to judge,
likewise, whether their mental weakness is to be attributed to the circumstances of their condition, or to any
difference as made by the Author of their existence
between them and other men.   *If* God has made such
a difference, it cannot be proved to be any impeachment

either of his wisdom, goodness, or justice. Such a difference exists between *individuals* without any such impeachment, and may exist in like manner between the *races* of mankind. But to suppose the Negroes too stupid to comprehend the essential doctrines of Christianity is certainly to disregard the testimony of God's word, the witness of his Spirit, the evidence of facts.

What saith the Scripture? " He hath made of one blood all nations of men that dwell on all the face of the earth;" and again, "God is no respecter of persons; but in every nation he that feareth him and worketh righteousness is accepted with him."—*Acts* 10 : 34, 35. What then can be plainer than that all men have one common origin, and that all are capable of exercising proper affections towards God; and this necessarily implies a *capability of understanding* the divine law. If it be allowed that the Negroes are men, then these things are true in regard to them, and thus by the word of God does it appear that they are capable of understanding the Gospel. And does not the Spirit of God bear witness to their capacity? Are there not great numbers who have been enlightened, regenerated, and sanctified by him? Their ignorance of divine subjects is owing to their want of proper instruction, and not at all to any defect of mental constitution.

The Gospel meets with little success among them.

Grant the fact to be so ; from the view which has been taken of the limited instruction of the Negroes and their extremely ignorant and vicious condition, and the feeble encouragement which many receive in their efforts to lead a religious life, our wonder more naturally might be, not that the Gospel meets with *little success* among them but that it meets with *any success at all.*

The excuse indicates a want of patience and proper feeling and consideration. If the Negroes in a state of ignorance and vice are not made intelligent and pious in a few days, we are ready to cry out that labor is vain; the field must be abandoned as an unprofitable one. We act unreasonably and uncharitably. We expect more of them than of ourselves or any other people. *They who would evangelize servants must " let Patience have her perfect work."*

It certainly comes with a very ill grace from us to speak of the little success of the Gospel amongst the Negroes. That little success is our condemnation; for what great efforts have we made that we should expect great success. Where we bestow little labor, we must expect but little reward.

But I apprehend that in the judgment of charity, considering the circumstances of the Negroes, the Gospel, when adequately preached to them, meets with as good success as among any other people to whom it may come. Why should it not? Can it be shown that they are given over to judicial blindness of mind and hardness of heart? Can it be shown that a work of grace in them is more difficult to the Omnipotent Spirit, than in another people?

If the Gospel has met with *any success at all*, it should operate as an encouragement to us, to make more vigorous efforts. Putting that success at the lowest point *the salvation of but one soul*, it is certainly great. For were it now revealed to us that the most extensive system of instruction which we could devise, requiring a vast amount of labor and protracted through ages, would result in the tender mercy of our God in the salvation of the soul of *one poor African*, we should feel warranted in cheerfully entering upon our work, with all its costs and sacrifices; for our reward would exceed all our toil and care above the computation of any finite mind.

But to set aside the excuse at once, if the Gospel met with *no success at all*, that would be no reason why we should withhold it from the Negroes. For if we certainly determine (as we have already done,) that it is our *duty* to give them the Gospel, we as certainly should do it. The *success* of our efforts *belongs to God;* nor are we to limit his sovreignty in granting or withholding a blessing, to any *particular time.* We are to labor *in faith*, and we are to labor *on.* "In due time we shall reap if we faint not." Thus acting, their blood will not be required at our hands; we have delivered our souls. This is the view which every Christian should take of the subject. And it becomes us to observe that God has manifestly been speaking to us in favor of our servants. He has called many of them into his kingdom and made them rich in faith, as we do know. We have not as yet listened to his voice. It is time that we should. He tells us that he is willing to bless the Gospel to their salvation. Shall we neglect them? Shall we despise God's voice?

We have not the means of supplying them with the Gospel.

The whites themselves are destitute; we cannot obtain ministers in sufficient numbers to supply our own destitutions; and when ministers may be obtained, we are not at all times able to *support* them. Servants cannot expect to fare better than their masters. Great numbers must necessarily continue destitute of the Gospel.

There is much truth, and painful truth, in the excuse. Our destitutions are very great! "The harvest truly is plenteous, but the laborers are few;" and few, indeed, in comparison with our wants, seem to be coming forward. But the excuse cannot be admitted as valid, where *suitable efforts* have not been made to procure a minister, and *suitable compensation* offered for his services, when such compensation can be afforded by those who call for his services. There is criminal neglect in both particulars in many neighborhoods and even organized churches. There is too an error in the excuse, that of *separating* the spiritual wants of the owners from those of their servants. They form one community, one household, and he that ministers to one, should to the other. The loaf should be divided, yea, if it be but *half* a loaf.

There are multitudes of Negroes in certain locations left wholly destitute of religious instruction : and where are their owners? In some city, or at some healthy retreat, enjoying the privileges of the Gospel with their families and a small number of their servants, while the great body of them, who supply all their wealth and comfort, are at a distance, and not one dollar appropriated, nor one effort made to procure their religious instrucion! Yea, some estates are in this condition, whose income would warrant the employment of a chaplain or missionary the year round! Is this rendering to servants that "*which is just and equal?*" Our means are more abundant and may be more enlarged and multiplied than we are aware of. An enumeration of them 1 omit for the present.

There are peculiar and great difficulties to be overcome.
Such for example as the ignorance, indifference, and in some instances, the opposition of masters; and the

want of funds — of missionaries — of ministers willing
to labor for the Negroes — of systems of instruction;
the stupidity, and viciousness, and hypocrisy of the
people themselves; confinement to *oral* instruction; the
unhealthiness of the climate, and so forth We ask, will
these and other difficulties that might be mentioned be
removed by being let alone? Are there means now in
operation for their removal? Will they ever be fewer in
number than they are at the present time?

There are difficulties in every enterprise of benevolence; and if we wait in our efforts to do good until
men cease to multiply excuses and objections, and until
all difficulties are removed, we shall never commence.
Times have suddenly and strangely altered in the world
if Christians can do good and perform their duty, without
encountering much that will try the purity and firmness
of their purposes. Shall we cower and retire before
difficulties? By no means. We are to encounter them
patiently, kindly, perseveringly; casting our care upon
God. He calls us to the duty. The work is his. In
his strength we labor. Do difficulties present themselves?
Remember God is great. Difficulties appear large in
the distance, but the nearer and more resolute our advance the smaller they become, until when in the strength
of the Lord we encounter them they vanish out of sight.
But *of whose creation* are these difficulties? *In themselves*, we meet with no difficulties but such as arise
from the natural enmity of the heart to the truth. The
difficuties lie mainly at our own door, and it is unjust
that they should be made the innocent sufferers.

Before this head of excuses is closed there are a few
sometimes urged by *owners* and *ministers*, which may
better be disposed of in this place than in any other.

I am a master, but no Christian, and am therefore excused from the duty.

Not at all. If the fact of being no Christian excuses you from obedience to the divine command of rendering to your servants that which is just and equal, then may you be excused from obedience to every other divine command addressed to you in your various circumstances and relations in life. The commands of God in themselves considered, are no more obligatory upon the man that *is a Christian,* than upon the man that *is not a Christian.* If you have not the necessary character and qualifications of a religious friend and teacher of your servants because you have failed to secure them, through grace, by "repentance towards God and faith in the Lord Jesus Christ," the greater is your sin and condemnation. You not only have the punishment of your own impenitency to bear, but all the consequences of it upon those around you, especially as it disqualifies you for a proper discharge of your duties to them. A most distressing situation truly. The excuse will not bear the light. Pursue it a little further. You feel it to be your duty to afford religious instruction to your *children,* and to support the institutions of the Gospel for the *sake of society at large.* As far as you are able you will get *others* to do for your family and friends and neighbors, what you cannot do for them *yourself.* This is commendable and just. Now act in the same way towards your *servants.* Make efforts to have that religious instruction communicated to them by others which you cannot communicate yourself, and give them every encouragement to attend upon it and to profit by it, in your power.

Although I hope I am a Christian, yet I am not qualified to instruct my servants.

You are not, in giving them saving instruction from the word of God, either expected or required to give them *a theological education*: or a *complete understanding of the whole Bible.* The grand points of doctrine and of duty; the things essential to be believed and to be done, are what you understand and have experience of, if you are a Christian; and if you will be at a little pains you may be able to make others understand them also; and you can give them the reasons why they should embrace them, for the reasons had weight with you and operate in their influence upon you continually. The very least expected of a Christian, is that he read the scriptures and pray in his family day by day. If you can do no more, you can assemble your servants and read a portion of scripture and pray with them, if not every day, then as frequently during the week as your circumstances will admit of.

This religion which allows a man to live *in the habitual neglect of the religious instruction of his servants,* when he is qualified or may qualify himself to attend to it, however much he may seem to be engaged in his own family or church, admits of the most serious question as to its reality.

But *I live away from my people;* I see them twice or thrice during the week; sometimes not for a month, or months.

The system of *non-residence,* whether from necessity on account of health; or from choice, to be free from care, or to be in the midst of society for the advantages of education and religion, is one of the greatest obstacles with which we have to contend in both the physical and religious improvement of the Negroes. And the system prevails to a great extent. It is easier to see the

evils, than to remedy them. To meet the excuse it need
only be said, when you are with your people take some
interest in their religious state; speak to them on the
subject; notice the members of the church; meet with
them at evening prayers. When you are away at your ease,
full of health and pleasure and privileges, do not forget
those who by their daily labor enable you to enjoy all these
blessings, and be at trouble and expense to procure for
them the services of some settled minister in their vicinity or some missionary. Let them have that which will
not empoverish you, but enrich them for ever!

*The management and the religious instruction of
servants cannot be united in one person.*

How do you reconcile such an assertion, in excuse for
neglect of duty, with *the holy Scriptures?* The management and the religious instruction of servants are *united*
in the *master* by them. — *Gen.* 18 : 19. The relations
of master and servant are recognized, and the duties of
them enjoined; and the duties *must be performed,* otherwise the scriptures are not fulfilled. How do you reconcile your assertion, with the *experience of some masters?'*
There are masters who have succeded in uniting the two
and with advantage every way.

You reply, *my instruction seems to do my people little
good; they are more disposed to receive instruction from
strangers than from myself.*

This may all be true; and true for very good reasons.
Your own practice may contradict your precepts. When
you call upon them to fulfil *their* duties they will expect
you to set the example by a fulfilment of *your own.*
They can discern consistency of conduct as well as
other men, and particularly in cases which involve their
own interest and happiness. If you do not labor and be

at some sacrifice of time and means to improve their *physical condition* by providing more liberally and to the extent of your means for their comfort in good houses, good clothing and good food; if you do not regulate *your discipline* so as to maintain authority without injustice, and secure to every family and every individual just rights and privileges; in short, if you fail to impress your people with the belief that you are really their friend, and desire their best good for this world as well as for the next, and that you honestly intend to promote it, as far as lies in your power, they cannot, they will not value your instructions. They will view your efforts as hollow-hearted, *purely selfish*, intended for *effect*. You desire them to be Christians that you may have less trouble in their management, your work more honestly done, and your pecuniary interest more prospered. " Thou, therefore, which teachest another, teachest thou not thyself?" " First cast out the beam out of thine own eye."

Or, your *manner* of instruction may be improper. You may look at them and speak to them, and pray for them in your meetings, with harshness and haughtiness. God resisteth the proud in religion, and so doth man. You may make them feel at an infinite remove from you and that there is no common ground in Christianity, upon which master and servant may happily meet. Or, falling into the other extreme, you may come to them with undue familiarity and affectation of regard — in simpering, canting tones and expressions — elevating them to an equality with yourself, not as a Christian, but as a master. As a consequence the dignity of your relation towards them perishes, and with it your respect and influence. Christianity is neither to be professed nor taught, so as to break down the orders in society established in the providence of God, and distinctly recognized by it.

You may lack regularity and perseverance in your instructions.

Instruction to do much good, should be regular in its occurrence, and *persevered in.* Learn to be patient, and to moderate your expectations.

Again, *when I instruct my people they presume upon it; and if I have occasion to correct one of them immediately he absents himself from meeting, and thus ends religious instruction with him.*

Admitting the objection to be true, as it often unquestionably is, yet it presents no *bar*, but a *difficulty*, in the way of the discharge of duty; a difficulty which must be encountered and overcome in the best manner possible. You have to contend with the bad temper of children after correction sometimes, and so will you with that of servants.

See to it, first of all, that your plantation or family discipline *be just*, then *carry it into effect*, in all necessary cases, with all authority, without fear or partiality, and ere long you will be borne out by the consciences of your people. They know, as well as you do. that a servant who knows his master's duty and will not do it must be made to do it; and that this is the doctrine both of religion and reason. A steady, just, and efficient discipline conduces to the happiness of both master and servant. Some of your people in the beginning of your efforts, through ignorance and viciousness, may presume upon your instructions; but persevere in them. and in ordinary and necessary discipline, annexing rewards to good conduct, and the result will be satisfactory.

There are owners whose experience accords with what we have now advanced.

A minister of the Gospel says, I cannot preach to the Negroes; I am not able to make myself understood; I have no turn for it.

A sad confession, and an excuse never to be admitted. Your *Divine Master,* "preached the Gospel to the poor." — *Matt.* 11 : 5. He was not above noticing poor servants, and visiting them in their sickness, and even performing miracles for their healing. — *Matt.* 8 : 5 – 13. His spirit was poured out upon them as well as upon others, and they were called into the glorious liberty of the Gospel and made "the Lord's freemen." — 1 *Cor.* 7 : 22. His *Apostles* were "forward to remember the poor;" spiritually and temporally. They preached the Gospel to servants, and many were born into the kingdom of God through their instrumentality. They baptized and received them into the churches along with their masters, and addressed commands to them in their letters to the churches. — *Eph.* 6 : 5, *Col.* 3 : 22. Yea, the great Apostle to the Gentiles, receives as a son the *runaway,* Onesimus, "begotten in his bonds," and kindly writes his master Philemon, a letter of intercession, and sends him back with it. — *Epistle to Philemon.*

The Apostles make it the duty of *their successors* in the ministry to give religious instruction to servants, and to inculcate upon them the duties of their station. — 1 *Tim.* 6 : 1 – 5, "let as many servants as are under the yoke count their masters worthy of all honor," — "These things teach and exhort." And again in *Titus* 2 : 9 – 10. Surely with these examples and precepts before him, that "workman" "*needeth to be ashamed,*" who surrounded with servants in perishing need of the Gospel, cannot

" rightly divide to them the word of truth." He should " *study* to show himself approved unto God," in this department of his labor. Woe to him, if he fails to do so through sloth, or indifference to the worth of the soul, or through pride, feeling that one of his cultivation and improvement would injure his style of composition and manner of delivery, and would lower his respectability in his own eyes and in the eyes of the world, by condescending to labor among Negro servants, and by adapting his preaching to their capacities!

To pass by the *sin*, it is an absolute *disgrace* to a man "called of God as was Aaron," not to be able to make the Gospel intelligible to all that hear him. To all those who make this excuse, we apply the ancient adage, " where there is *a will* there is *a way*."

Once more : the minister says, *my church allows me no time to preach to the Negroes. I am willing to do so, if I could.*

In the first place, have you *requested* time to do so, after presenting to your church the obligation of affording particular religious instruction to the Negroes connected with it? Yea, when met by lukewarmness, or it may be, by objections, have you upon your conscience, as a minister of the Gospel, *insisted* upon it? There is scarcely a church in the South which would not, upon a proper consideration of the duty, yield to the wishes of its minister in this respect.

And again : when you accepted the call to the pastoral office, why did you not give the church to understand, distinctly, that you would devote a just proportion of your labors to the servants attached to the families of the congregation ; that you would consider yourself the pastor of the servants as well as of the masters, parents and children ?

Such an interest in the religious instruction of servants would be hailed with joy by many churches, and while it would endear their ministers to them, it would give them increased confidence in their piety and a stronger hope of being benefited by their labors.

Should it so happen that you are *forbidden* to preach to the Negroes by the people over whom you are settled, *from no fault of your own*, but from sheer opposition to the work of religious instruction, your course undoubtedly will be to reason the case, calmly, conscientiously, and decidedly, and wait patiently for a time, and when hope of change expires, withdraw to another field. The commission is, "go ye into all the world and preach the Gospel to every creature :" and no minister ought to be influenced, either by the fear or favor of men, to go contrary to that high command. It is set down among the aggravated offences of the Jews, and as filling up the measure of their sins, when wrath would come upon them to the uttermost, *that they forbid the Apostles " to speak to the Gentiles that they might be saved."* — 1 *Thes.* 2 : 14 – 16. But while these remarks are made, it becomes me to say as a matter of fact and of justice to the Southern churches, that I have never known nor heard of any such instance. Efforts for the religious instruction of the Negroes have been in some churches *suspended* for a season, on account of the excited state of public feeling, to be *resumed* when that excitement should pass away.

We have occupied sufficient space on these *excuses*. *Excuses* we have none. Do not let us make them ; but faithfully inquire if the reason of our neglect of duty, does not arise from ignorance on the one hand, or indisposition on the other ?

CHAPTER III.

OBJECTIONS.

THE *Objections* to the religious instruction of the Negroes in the slave States, turn upon two grounds; — *the first*, that religious instruct.on tends to the dissolution of the relations of society as now constituted ; and *the second*, that it will really do the people no good, but lead to insubordination.

When it is remembered that these objections have united for their support, the interests, the passions, the prejudices, and the fears of the objectors, and I may add, a certain degree of ignorance and of opposition to religion itself, it will be seen that they are very strong, and require to be met with perfect frankness and with sober reason.

For myself, in urging the great duty of the religious instruction of the Negroes in the slave States, I have no concealments to make. My grand, exclusive object has ever been to put them in possession of that which confers *peace with God in time and blessedness with him in eternity.* I do not, therefore, pursue religious instruction as a *means* to an *earthly end;* so that while I am *professedly* seeking to improve their *spiritual* condition, I am *actually* laboring to effect changes in their *temporal* condition. I have not so learned Christ. As an honorable man, as a minister of the Gospel, I utterly repudiate such a course of conduct. The preaching of the Gospel for the salvation of the souls of men is one thing; the changes in their civil relations in this present life, effected by the influence of its spirit and its principles, is another. The *former* is the office of the ministry — the *latter*, the office of Divine Providence. I am not ashamed of the Gospel in respect to the former; I am not afraid to trust God in respect to the latter.

The first objection is this. *If we suffer our Negroes to be instructed the tendency will be to change the civil relations of society as now constituted.*

To which let it be replied that we separate entirely their *religious* and their *civil* condition, and contend that the one may be attended to without interfering with the other. Our *principle* is that laid down by the holy and just One: "render unto Cæsar the things which are Cæsar's and unto God the things that are God's." And Christ and his Apostles are our *example*. Did they deem it proper and consistent with the good order of society to preach the Gospel to servants? They did. In discharge of this duty, did they interfere with their civil condition? They did not. They expressed no opinion whatever on the subject, if we except that which appears in one of the Epistles to the Corinthian Church. (*1st Epistle, c.* 7: *v.* 19–23.) There the Apostle Paul considers a state of freedom preferable to one of servitude, and advises slaves if they can lawfully obtain their freedom, to do it; but not otherwise. He does not treat the question as one of very great moment in comparison to the benefits of the Gospel. "Art thou called being a servant, care not for it, but if thou mayest be made free, use it rather ; for he that is called in the Lord being a servant is the Lord's freeman," etc. May we not follow in the footsteps of our Saviour and his Apostles, and that with perfect safety too? Yea, and without proceeding as far as did the Apostle Paul? We maintain that in judicious religious instruction there will be no necessary interference with their civil condition. The religious teacher must step out of his way for the purpose.

The objection, it will be perceived, is levelled against the *influence of the Gospel itself ;* and if the Gospel will subvert the institutions of our society then we should fear to be instructed in it *ourselves,* and banish it altogether. And who would entertain such a monstrous proposition?

But the Gospel is to be preached " to every creature ;" the knowledge of the Lord is to fill the earth; Almighty God has so promised, and he will make it good. We cannot, therefore, resist the progress of the Gospel. We can exclude its light no more than we can that of the sun. It is destined to, and will ultimately, reach every Negro in our land. And what influences its spirit and principles are in the providence of God to produce upon their condition shall be produced ; but the precise nature and extent of those influences it is impossible to determine. We may reason from one principle to another, and draw out conclusion after conclusion, into one grand result, and the concatenation of the whole, in our view, be perfect; and yet the sovreignty of God like a disturbing force may enter in and preserve the present constitution of our society substantially the same. The subject is one of those "secret things" which belong to God alone.   His providential dealings towards the nations of the earth are a great deep.   They constitute the wonders of History.   It is enough for every reasonable and every Christian man to know that the Gospel, like the sun, sheds down its influences upon mankind decidedly yet calmly, and that it causes all its fruits to spring forth and to mature in their season without noise, or violence, or injustice, if men will but allow to it its perfect way; and that those influences will fill up the measure of the angelic song: "Glory to God in the highest and on earth peace, good will towards men." —*Luke* 2: 14.

If we are in a strait, in view of the objection, let us make the pious choice of David, "let us fall into the hand of the Lord, for his mercies are great;" let us do what he so clearly defines to be *present* duty, then shall we cast ourselves and our servants into his hands, and confidently rely upon him to reveal to us what may be our *future* duty, and to guide us and our servants quietly and intelligently in the way that we should go.   The path of *present* duty, on this as well as on all other subjects, is the path of safety.

The second objection is — *If we suffer our Negroes to be religiously instructed, the way will be opened for men from abroad to enter in and inculcate doctrines subversive of our interests and safety.*

In this objection *the Gospel* is not feared, but *the agents* by whom it is preached.   Our views in reply, shall be briefly and we hope satisfactorily given.

There are men, who, if the door of access to the Negroes in the South were thrown open indiscriminately to all, would enter in to send among us not "peace," but literally "a sword."   Men who fall under the Apostle's description in 1 *Tim.* 6: 1–5, and from whom, in obedience to his command we would "withdraw ourselves." Against the introduction of "*such*" there cannot be too much vigilance observed.

The field of labor among the Negroes in the South, is one, in many respects, of no ordinary difficulty; and it is the dictate as well of benevolence as of prudence to inquire into the character and qualifications of those who enter it. They should be *Southern men;* men entitled to that apellation; either those who have been born and reared in the South, or those who have identified themselves with the South, and are familiarly acquainted with the structure of society; in a word, men having their interests in the South. Such men would possess the *confidence of the community;* for they would not act in their official connection with the Negroes, in such a manner as to breed disturbances, which would inevitably jeopard their own lives and tend to the utter prostration of their families and interests. They would also, from their experience and observation and knowledge, *be competent and profitable instructers of the Negroes.*

But the very spirit which prompts the objection refutes it. For how is it possible when such a wary vigilance is manifested, for ministers or religious teachers, entire *strangers* in community, to come in, have access to the Negroes privately and publicly, and sow the seeds of discontent and revolt? It is impossible. They cannot come unless we permit them.

Indeed, the most effectual method to *preclude* the introduction of improper teachers, is for us to *take the religious instruction of our Negroes into our own hands, and to superintend it ourselves.* We shall then know *who* their teachers are, and *what* and *when* and *where* they are taught.

A third objection is — *The religious instruction of the Negroes will lead to neglect of duty and insubordination.*

I ask how can it? You reply: why the very attention you bestow upon them: the very instructions you give them elevates them in their own consideration, prompts them to assume an equality with their masters and teaches them, practically at least, to neglect their work and to resist discipline. You teach them that "God is no respecter of persons;" that "he hath made of one blood all the nations of men;" "thou shalt love thy neighbor as thyself;" "all things whatsoever ye would that men should do to you, do ye even so to them;" what use, let me ask, would they make of these sentences from the Gospel?

Let it be replied that the effect urged in the objection might result from *imperfect* and *injudicious* religious instruction; indeed religious instruction may be communicated *with the express design* on the part of the instructer to produce the effect referred to, instances of which have occurred. But who will say that neglect of duty and insubordination are the *legitimate* effects of the Gospel purely and sincerely imparted to servants? Has it not in all ages been viewed as the greatest civilizer of the human race? As the most powerful of all causes in allaying the wild and stormy and rebellious tempers of the mind, and reducing men to habits of cheerful industry, domestic virtue, submission to authority and law, and peaceful intercourse in society? He is but poorly read in the history of his race who knows not and who believes not this fact. I grant, and I do rejoice

in it, that religion is a great enlightener of the human
mind, that it does tend to give an elevation to character,
and dignity and importance to men; and to afford a
knowledge of, as well as a protection to, their interests
and rights in their connection one with another. But
religion, at the same time, teaches all men submission
to the will of God expressed both in his Word and in
his Providence ; and by its life giving spirit, influences
them to fulfil the duties of their respective callings faithfully and quietly. It is by our Lord compared to salt;
it *preserves* as well as *purifies*.

The Gospel recognizes the condition in which the
Negroes are, and inculcates the duties appropriate to it.
Ministers are commanded by the Apostle Paul to " exhort
servants to be obedient to their own masters and to please
them well in all things; not answering again, not pur-
loining; but showing all good fidelity, that they may
adorn the doctrine of God our Saviour in all things;
for the grace of God, that bringeth salvation, hath appeared to all men ; teaching us that denying ungodliness
and worldly lusts, we should live soberly righteously
and godly in this present world." — *Titus* 2 : 9 - 12.
Again : " Let as many servants as are under the yoke
count their masters worthy of all honor, that the name
of God and his doctrine be not blasphemed. And they
that have believing masters let them not despise them,
because they are brethren; but rather do them service,
because they are faithful and beloved, partakers of the
benefit. These things teach and exhort." And the
Apostle is very positive with ministers that they impress
these duties upon servants, for in the next verse he adds,
— " If any man *teach otherwise*, and consent not to
wholesome words, even the words of our Lord Jesus

Christ, and to the doctrine which is according to godliness, he is proud, knowing nothing, but doting about questions and strifes of words, whereof cometh envy, strife railings, evil surmisings, perverse disputings of men of corrupt minds, and destitute of the truth, supposing that gain is godliness ; *from such withdraw thyself.*"
—1 *Tim.* 6 ; 1-5.

Writing to the church at Ephesus, he saith, " servants be obedient to them that are your masters according to the flesh with fear and trembling, in singleness of your heart, as unto Christ. Not with eye service as menpleasers ; but as the servants of Christ, doing the will of God from the heart, with good will doing service, as to the Lord and not to men ; knowing that whatsoever good thing any man doeth, the same shall he receive of the Lord whether he be bond or free."— *Eph.* 6: 5-8.
A similar passage occurs in his Epistle to the church at Collosse. "Servants obey in all things your masters according to the flesh, not with eye-service, as menpleasers, but in singleness of heart, fearing God; and whatsoever ye do, do it heartily, us to the Lord and not unto men ; knowing that of the Lord ye shall receive the reward of the inheritance, for ye serve the Lord Christ. But he that doeth wrong shall receive for the wrong which he hath done, and there is no respect of persons."— *Col.* 3 : 22-25.

The Apostle Peter is equally decided. "Servants be subject to your masters with all fear; not only to the good and gentle, but also to the froward. For this is thankworthy, if a man for conscience towards God endure grief, suffering wrongfully, For what glory is it if when ye be buffeted for your faults ye shall take it patiently ? But if when ye do well and suffer for it, ye take it patiently, this is acceptable with God. For even hereunto were ye called ; because Christ also suffered for us, leaving us an example, that ye should follow his steps." — 1 *Pet.* 2: 18 – 25.

Such are the commands of the Gospel to servants, as comprehensive of their duties as any master could desire; and all excuses for unfaithfulness and insubordination carefully guarded against. Yea, we hear the Apostle Paul exclaim, "let every man abide in the same calling wherein he was called. Art thou called being a servant? Care not for it; but if thou mayest be free choose it rather. For he that is called in the Lord being a servant, is the Lord's freeman; likewise also, he that is called being free is Christ's servant. Ye are bought with a price, be not ye the servants of men. Brethren let every man wherein he is called, therein abide with God." — 1 *Cor.* 7: 20 – 24. And what do we see the same Apostle do? He restores the " unprofitable " Onesimus to Philemon his master, though he had escaped from him to a great distance. Thus putting into practice his own views and precepts. He calls the converted slave "a brother beloved," now to be specially regarded by Philemon, not only as a servant "in the flesh," but as a Christian servant " in the Lord." The Apostle Paul holds the most perfect fellowship with his master, as a truly christian man; in whose household there was a company of believers — "a church " — for whom he prayed " always;" in whose " faith and love toward the Lord Jesus and toward all saints " he had " great joy and consolation." He calls him " brother " — " our dearly beloved and fellow-laborer." He felt no scruples in receiving and laboring with him in the Gospel. His letter to Philemon for its Christian courtesy, delicacy, and tenderness, is above all praise.

We now ask, will the duties of servants to their masters be neglected, and their authority despised, by instructions of this sort, and by a careful adherence to the example of the Apostle Paul on the part of the ministers of the Gospel? No never. Is not the discharge of duty made more sure and faithful, and respect for authority strengthened by considerations drawn from the omniscience of God and the retributions of eternity? The fact is not to be questioned. Joseph exclaimed, " how can I do this great wickedness and sin against God?" And what was the reply of the Christian Negro when the ground of his obedience and fidelity to his master was inquired into? "Sir, *I fear God*, whose eyes are in every place beholding the evil and the good; therefore do I obey and am faithful as well behind my master's back as before his face."

What parent considers the religious instruction of his children, as having a tendency to make them more wicked and rebellious? Should neglect of duty and insubordination ensue upon the religious instruction of servants, the fault will be discovered in imperfect instruction, or in the mismanagement of the master.

A fourth objection. *The Negroes will embrace seasons of religious worship, for originating and executing plans of insubordination and villany.*

This might be the case if they were allowed to congregate on plantations at night, and at places of worship on the Sabbath without a proper regulation of their assemblies, or any supervision of a responsible white teacher, or of planters themselves. And for the reason that masses of men, especially of ignorant and vicious men, coming together under little or no restraint, naturally, yea, inevitably, fall into excesses and riots. But

a proper regulation of the times and places of meeting,
and the faithful supervision of religious teachers, assisted
by deacons and elders, or planters, would preclude all
serious disorders. An experience of some eight years,
confirms me in the opinion. For in five or six hundred
meetings upon plantations during the week, and at
stations for preaching on the Sabbath, with congregations
varying from twenty to five hundred and more, I have
never been disturbed during a single meeting with any
noise or riot, and not more than three times have I had
occasion, after services, to interfere in checking disor-
derly conduct; and in the instances referred to, they
were private quarrels, the parties meeting and in a
moment of passion, assaulting each other. As it so
happened, in each instance, I was alone amidst hundreds
of them, and a single command quelled the disturbance
instantly. Wherever religious meetings have been embraced for purposes specified in the objection, on inquiry
it will be found that the people were left to themselves
and so fell into temptation.

But why are men so tenacious of *religious meetings*
and of *religious teachers,* as though the Negroes had
no other kind of meetings and no other kind of teachers?
Are they not privileged to assemble for feasting and
merriment?   Do they not have their balls and parties of
pleasure, in town and country?   Are they not collected
for miles around to *huskings* and other kinds of job-
labor, where they drink and sing and revel like baccha-
nals?   What troops of them walk our streets in idle
search for labor? or sit in market places all day long?
Are there not portions of all our chief towns inhabited
chiefly by them, with the most perfect communication
from house to house at all hours, and to whom men of

various characters and designs may find an introduction? Do they not rendezvous at low tippling shops, on terms of companionship with their vicious keepers; some of which are complete Negro exchanges, where all that transpires in the social, the religious, the civil, and the political world, is regularly made known and sagely discussed? "Judge not according to the appearance but judge righteous judgement." — *John* 7: 24.

A fifth objection is *religious instruction will do no good; it will only make the Negroes worse men and worse hypocrites?*

It will be unnecessary to dwell upon this objection, since it has been answered by much that has already been advanced; and because those who urge it, do not (as charity bids us conclude,) really believe in its truth ; unless indeed, they be avowed and malicious infidels; and we have reason to be thankful there are very few such amongst us.

Who are we? In what age and in what country of the world do we live that we should question the excellency of the Gospel, the propriety of preaching it "to the poor;" What is the Gospel? Is it not, "the grace of God that bringeth salvation ; teaching us that denying ungodliness and worldly lusts, we should live soberly, righteously and godly in this present world; looking for that blessed hope and the glorious appearing of the great God and our Saviour Jesus Christ, who gave himself for us, that he might redeem us from all iniquity and purify unto himself a peculiar people, zealous of good works?" — *Titus* 2: 11-14. This is the Gospel. These are the things which we are to teach and exhort. And is it under *such* teaching and exhortation that men will increase in crime and hypocrisy? Why should the

Gospel produce an effect on Negroes, contrary to that which it is designed to produce, and which it actually produces on all other men, and on some whose condition is worse than theirs? Who may limit the power of the Holy Ghost the Third Person of the adorable Trinity? Is any thing too hard for Him, in the regeneration and sanctification of men? The immortal mind may be darkened and polluted with ignorance and sin, yea, sunk to the lowest depths; — but the immortal mind is there, and that precious jewel, by the omnipotent and gracious energies of the Holy Ghost, through the word of God, may be regenerated, cleansed of its defilements, filled with light and purity and fitted for the highest and most honorable uses both in this world and in that which is to come.

The objection is not supported by a solitary fact. Wherever Negroes have *really* enjoyed, for any reasonable time, *the privileges of the Gospel*, in point of general intelligence, morality and order, they are in advance of those who have not enjoyed them. Is it not conceded that a truly pious servant gives less trouble and is more profitable than one who is not? Is there one master in a thousand who does not desire such servants? Is it not true, that the most pious servants exert the happiest influence in promoting honesty and good order on plantations and in communities?

That there is a large number of *nominal* christians among the Negroes, I do not deny. But why is it so? Are they made hypocrites by faithful instruction? No. The abounding of spurious religion, results from a deficiency of faithful instruction; and a too hasty admission into the church after a profession of conversion, and pretty much an entire neglect of their further instruction after being admitted. A reformation on our part in regard to these particulars, would produce a happy effect upon the purity and permanency of their religious character. Nominal Christianity abounds most in churches where the instruction and discipline are most imperfect and weak, and from which the influence of competent white instructers is most withdrawn.

But one or two irregularities in their meetings, one or two defections from profession, are sufficient to prejudice the minds of many against the religious instruction of the Negroes. Because they remain impenitent and pervert the Gospel and deceive their fellow men, therefore are they unworthy of it? Who then would be worthy, if God should deal with men according to this rule? Where is there a church on earth in which all the members are pure? What did the Apostle say of some of the members of the churches at Corinth and at Philippi; and of the churches in Galatia? Did not our Lord himself say that when the householder sowed *wheat* his enemy sowed *tares;* that the net cast into the sea gathered of every kind, both bad and good?

Admit the objection to be true, in its fullest extent, and what then? Does it annul our duty? Far from it. Let them harden themselves and grow worse under the means of grace; whether they will hear or forbear, we are to do our duty; we are to obey God; we are to throw the responsibility of their salvation upon their own shoulders, and clear our garments of their blood.

The objections now considered, we do not deem of sufficient weight to alter the conclusion to which we have already come, that it is our duty to impart sound religious instruction to our colored population in the slave States.

CHAPTER IV.

BENEFITS.

LET us proceed to the more agreeable employment of showing *the Benefits*, which would flow from the religious instruction of the Negroes.

There would be a better understanding of the relation of master and servant : and of their reciprocal duties.

Not much has been *published* in our country on the relation and duties of master and servant. And it seems strange that it should be so, and since that relation has existed so long and become so extensive; since so much involving private and public happiness, depends upon the faithful discharge of the duties of it. Not much *inquiry and discussion*, in the way of *conversation* has been indulged in, on the general subject; and not much *preaching* upon it from the pulpit.

There are many of our owners who have never given themselves the trouble, with the Scriptures in their hands for a guide, solemnly and prayerfully to inquire into the number and nature of those duties which they owe to their servants and are in reason and in conscience bound to perform. Nor do we think that there are many servants who have been instructed and understand their

duties towards their masters and from what motives they
should discharge them.   What is the consequence?
Why, ignorance and indifference exist both on the one
part and on the other.   Too much is left to custom, to
chance, to interest and convenience, to impulses.   The
principle which regulates the relation and its duties, I
have heard defined thus: on the part of *the master*,
" *get all, and give back as little as you can ;* " and on
the part of *the servant*, " *give as little, and get back all
you can.*"   And what is the principle thus defined?
Pure selfishness!   Considering what human nature is
and observing the conduct of masters and servants, we
have ground to fear that there is too much truth in the
existence and influence of this principle.   But we constantly see the severity of it mitigated, even by itself,
lest it should over-shoot its own ends, and especially by
feelings of attachment and benevolence that spring up
between superiors and inferiors.

There is something, however, above all this, that is
needed, and that something is *the introduction of religion.*   Religion will tell the master that he is a master
"according to the flesh," only ; that his servants are
fellow-creatures, and he has a master in heaven to whom
he shall finally account for his treatment of them.
Religion will tell the servant " to be obedient to masters
according to the flesh, with fear and trembling, in singleness of heart as unto Christ; knowing that whatsoever
good thing any man doeth, the same shall he receive of
the Lord whether he be bond or free."   The master will
be led to inquiries of this sort.   In what kind of houses
do I permit them to live ; what clothes do I give them
to wear ; what food to eat; what privileges to enjoy ?
In what temper and manner, and in what proportion to

their crimes do I allow them to be punished? What care do I take of their family relations? What am I doing for their souls' salvation? In fine, what does God require me to do to, and for them and their children, in view of their happiness here and hereafter? Light will insensibly break into his mind. Conscience will be quickened, and before he is aware perhaps, his servants will be greatly elevated in his regards, and he will feel himself bound and willing to do more and more for them. The government of his plantation will not be so purely selfish as formerly. His interest will not be the sole object of pursuit, nor offences against that visited with sorer punishment than offences against God himself. He will have an eye to the comfort, the interest of his people, and endeavor to identify their interest with his, and also to make them see and feel it to be so. It will be a delight to him to see them enjoy the blessings of the *providence* and the *grace* of God.

Such an attempt at a discharge of duty on religious grounds, will produce favorable influences, upon the feelings and conduct of servants. Religion will cause them to understand their duties better, and to perform them more perfectly and cheerfully.

The pecuniary interests of masters will be advanced as a necessary consequence.

I do not mean that the introduction of the Gospel upon a plantation in and of itself puts new life and vigor into the laborers and the soil which they cultivate, and necessarily makes them more profitable to owners, than plantations where the Gospel is not introduced at all. By no means. Such a statement would be unfounded in fact. For there are owners who take no pains whatever to have their Negroes instructed; but who feed and clothe and lodge them well, and are humane and take the best care of them, and by careful, skilful and pushing management, go far beyond their religious neighbors in their incomes. But I mean, that religious instruction is no detriment, but rather a benefit: that, other things being equal, the plantation which enjoys religious instruction will do better for the interests of its owner, than it did before it enjoyed such instruction. Virtue is more profitable than vice; while this is allowed to be no discovery, no man will question its tru:h.

Increased attention to the temporal comfort of servants would improve their *health;* and the expense of lost labor by sickness, and of physicians' bills would be saved. Their wants being more liberally supplied and sharing more largely in the fruit of their labors, many temptations to *theft,* to which they are exposed, would be removed; and they would become more *industrious* and *saving. Crime* would be diminished. For teachers in order to reformation, would charge upon the Negroes the sins to which they are most addicted and expose their enormity and consequent punishment in the world to come. They are sometimes found guilty of notorious sins and scarcely know that they are sins at all. Religious instruction would lead them to respect each other more, to pay greater regard to mutual character and rights; the strong would not so much oppress the weak; family relations would be less liable to rupture; in short, all the social virtues would be more honored and cultivated. Their *work* would be *more faithfully done;* their *obedience* more universal and more cheerfully rendered. The genuine effects of religion upon them would be, "with good will doing service, as to the Lord and not unto men."

And who can tell the pleasurable feelings of a humane and Christian master, in view of a moral reformation of his servants? He will thank God that he is, if not wholly, yet measurably relieved from perpetual watching, from fault-finding and threatening and heart-sickening severity; and that he can *begin* at least to govern somewhat by the law of love. The good character of his people render them more valuable as property; and even should he not make as much as formerly, the loss is more than balanced by what he sees his people enjoy and by the comfort and satisfaction which he possesses himself.

The religious instruction of the Negroes *will contribute to safety*.

"The thing that hath been it is that which *may* be;" and although, as a slave-holding country, we are so situated, that, so far as man can see, the hope of success on the part of our laboring class, in any attempt at revolution is forlorn, yet no enemy (if there be an enemy) should be despised, however weak, and no danger unprovided for, however apparently remote. Success may not indeed crown any attempt, but much suffering may be the consequence both on the one part and on the other. It is then but a prudent foresight, a dictate of benevolence and of wisdom, to originate and set in operation means that may act as a check upon, if not a perfect preventive of evil.

I am a firm believer in the efficacy of *sound religious instruction*, as a means to the end desired. And reasons may be given for that belief. They are to be discovered in the *very nature and tendency of the Gospel*. Its *nature is peace*, in the broadest and fullest extent of the word. Its *tendency*, even when its transforming influ-

ence upon character is *not* realized, is to soften down
and curb the passions of man; to make him more
respectful of another's interests, and more solicitous of his
favor; more obedient under authority, and patient under
injuries; and to enhance infinitely in his estimation the
value of human life. His conscience is enlightened and
his soul is awed. He knows God reigns to execute
judgment, and it will require greater effort to excite him
to unhallowed deeds. But when character *is* transformed
by the Gospel, its nature and tendency are perfected.
The servant recognizes a superintending Providence, who
disposes of men and things according to his pleasure;
that his Gospel comes not with reckless efforts to wrench
apart society and break governments into pieces, but to
define clearly the relations and duties of men, and to lay
down and render authoritative, those general principles
of moral conduct which will result in the happiness of
the whole, and in the peaceable removal of every kind
of evil and injustice. — To God, therefore, he commits
the ordering of his lot, and in his station renders to all
their dues, obedience to whom obedience, and honor to
whom honor. He dares not wrest from the hand of God
his own care and protection. While he sees a preference
in the various conditions of men he remembers the
words of the Apostle : — "Art thou called being a servant? Care not for it; but if thou mayest be free, use
it rather. For he that is called in the Lord, being a
servant, is the Lord's freeman : likewise, also, he that is
called being free, is Christ's servant. Ye are bought
with a price, be not ye the servants of men. Brethren,
let every man wherein he is called, therein abide with
God."

Besides the general and special influences of the Gospel now adverted to, safety will be connected with *the very dispensation* of it, in two particulars, which 1 would not omit to mention. The *first* is: — The very effort of masters to instruct their people, creates a strong bond of union and draws out their kindly feelings to their masters: kindness produces kindness: love begets its own likeness. The presence also of white instructers, settled ministers or missionaries, in their private as well as public religious assemblies and free intercourse with the people and with their influential men and leaders, exert a restraining influence upon any spirit of insubordination that may exist, and at the same time give opportunities for its detection. The Negroes are as capable of strong personal attachments to their religious instructers as are any other people; and of their own will are inclined to make confidential communications.

The *second* particular is, that the Gospel being dispensed in its purity, the Negroes will be disabused of their ignorance and superstition, and thus be placed beyond the reach of designing men. The direct way of exposing them to acts of insubordination is to leave them in ignorance and superstition, to the care of their own religion. Then may the blind lead the blind, and both shall fall into the ditch: then may they be made the easy and willing instruments of avarice, of lust, of power or of revenge. *Ignorance — religious ignorance —* so far from being any safety, is *the very marrow of our sin against this people, and the very rock of our danger.* Religion and religious teachers they must and will have, and if they are not furnished with the true they will embrace the false. And what, I would add, is the language of *facts* on the point under our notice.

In the conspiracy in the city of New York in 1712, Mr. Neau's school for the religious instruction of the Negroes was blamed as the main occasion of the barbarous plot. And yet, "upon full trial the guilty Negroes were found to be such *as never came to Mr. Neau's school*, and what is very observable, the persons whose Negroes were found most guilty, *were such as were the declared opposers of making them Christians* ! "

The rebellions in 1730 and the *three* in 1739, in South Carolina, were *fomented by the Spaniards in St. Augustine*, and religion had nothing to do with them. The ground of that in 1741 in New York city again, I do not precisely understand; but it is pretty well ascertained that it was not *religion*. It is questioned whether the whites were not wholly deluded. There is evidence to believe that there was no plot at all on the part of the Negroes, although they suffered terribly.

Of that of 1816, in Camden South Carolina, discovered and suppressed, Mr. F. G. Deliesseline writes : "Two brothers engaged in this rebellion could read and write, and were hitherto of unexceptionable characters. They were *religious*, and had always been regarded in the light of faithful servants. A few appeared to have been actuated by the instinct of the most brutal licentiousness, and by the lust of plunder ; but most of them by wild and frantic ideas of the rights of man, *and the misconceived injunctions and examples of Holy Writ !* " — E. C. Holland's Refutation, etc. p. 76.

Of that of 1822, in Charleston South Carolina, Mr. Benjamin Elliott writes : "This description of our population had been allowed to assemble for *religious* instruction. The designing leaders in the scheme of villainy availed themselves of these occasions to instil sentiments of ferocity *by falsifying the Bible!*" Then he proceeds to show how it was done and adds, "such was their *religion* — such the examples to be imitated." Further on Mr. Elliott remarks, — "Another impediment to the progress of conspiracy, will ever be the *fidelity of some* of our Negroes. The servant who is false to his master would be false to his God. One act of perfidy is but the first step in the road of corruption and of baseness; and those who on this occasion have proved ungrateful to their owners, have also been *hypocrites in religion!*" — *Same pamphlet, pp.* 79, 80. Referring to the same affair of 1822, Mr. C. C. Pinckney remarks — "On investigation it appeared that all concerned in that transaction, except one, had seceded from the regular Methodist Church in 1817 and formed a separate establishment, in connection with the African Methodist Society in Philadelphia; whose bishop, a colored man, named Allen, had assumed that office, being himself a seceder from the Methodist Church of Pennsylvania. At this period Mr. S. Bryan, the local minister of the regular Methodist Church in Charleston, was so apprehensive of sinister designs, that he addressed a letter to the city council, on file in the council chamber, dated 8th November, 1817, stating at length the reasons of his suspicion." — *Address, Note B. p.* 20.

The South Hampton affair, in Virginia, in 1832, was originated by a man under color of religion, a pretender to inspiration. As far back as 1825 the Rev. Dr. J. H. Rice, in a discourse on the *injury done to religion by ignorant teachers*, warned the people of Virginia against the neglect of the proper religious instruction of the Negroes, and the danger of leaving them to the control of their own ignorant, fanatical and designing preachers.

His prophecy had its fulfilment in South Hampton. If we refer to the West Indies we shall behold religion exerting a restraining influence upon the people; and particularly on one occasion all the Negroes attached to the Moravian Missionary Churches, to a man supported the authority of their masters against the insurgents.

Enough has been said to satisfy reasonable and Christian men that sound religious instruction will contribute to safety. There are men who have no knowledge of religion in their own personal experience, and who have not been careful to notice its genuine effects upon servants, and they will place little or no confidence in any thing that might be said in favor of it. They can place more reliance upon *visible preventives* of their own invention than upon *principles of moral conduct* wrought in the soul and maintained in supremacy by Divine Power, whose nature they do not understand, and whose influence, however good, is invisible, and for that very reason not to be trusted by them. Nor have they either the candor or willingness, to make a distinction between *false* and *true* religion. In their opinion the Gospel is no benefit to the world. Such men we are constrained to leave to the influence of time and observation, and invoke for them the influence of the Spirit of God. I shall never forget the remark of a venerable colored preacher, made with reference to the South Hampton tragedy. With his eyes filled with tears, and his whole manner indicating the deepest emotion, said he, " Sir, it is the Gospel that we, ignorant and wicked people need. If you will give us the Gospel it will do more for the obedience of servants and the peace of community than all your guards, and guns, and bayonets." This same Christian minister, on receiving a packet of inflammatory pamphlets through the Post-office, and discovering their character and intention, immediately called upon the Mayor of the City and delivered them into his hands. Who can estimate the value in community of one such man acting under the influence of the Gospel of peace ?

The religious instruction of the Negroes will *promote our own morality and religion.*

That the Negroes are intellectually and morally, in a degraded state, I trust will not be denied; and of course no man acquainted with human nature, will deny that constant connection and intercourse with a degraded people, will exert a deleterious influence upon persons of more elevated character, if there be not some peculiar causes in existence, or some special effort made, to counteract it. I do not hesitate to say that the influence of the Negroes on the *general* intelligence and morality of the whites is not good. There are those who deny it. I differ with them, and am happy in believing that the majority of my fellow citizens are with me. We are so accustomed to sin in the Negroes (which in them appears a matter of course,) that our sensibilities are blunted.

When we cease to "abhor that which is evil," we shall not long "cleave to that which is good." "First endure —then embrace;" is as true in sober prose as in flippant poetry. Planters will generally confess that the management of Negroes is not only attended with trouble and vexation from time to time, but with provocations to sin. Masters and mistresses of families have their trials. And the kind of influence which Negroes exert over our children and youth, when permitted to associate with them, is well known to all careful and observing parents.

Now we shall defend ourselves from the injuries to our moral and religious character, received through our colored population, by their religious instruction, at least in very large measure. And on the principle or promise of the word of God, "he that waters shall be watered also himself." God bestows his blessing *immediately* upon those who do their duty. There is also a *rebound* for good, in benevolent action. The effort to do good, strengthens the principle from which it proceeds. The way to strengthen and increase holiness in the soul is to abound in works of holiness. It is by giving our talents to the exchangers that we gain other talents.

By taking in hand the religious instruction of the Negroes, an ample field will be opened for the most vigorous exercise of the piety and zeal and talents of the church; a great proportion of which is now rusting for want of use. And when it pleases God to give success to our labors, and we see them assuming a higher standard of morals; the current of their opinions turning against ignorance and vice, their appearance and deportment becoming more respectable, we shall be favorably affected ourselves. As the one class rises so will the other; the two are so intimately associated they are apt to rise or fall together; to benefit servants, evangelize the masters; to benefit masters, evangelize the servants.

Much unpleasant discipline will be saved to the churches.

The offences of colored communicants against Christian character and church order are numerous, and frequently heinous; the discipline of delinquents is wearisome, difficult, and unpleasant. Excommunications are of frequent occurence : and are usually followed, a short time after, by applications for re-admission. There will never be a better state of things, until the Negroes are better instructed in religion, both before and after their reception into the church.

The souls of our servants will be saved.

This is the crowning benefit; the grand and final aim of religious instruction. Where is the church in our land that would refuse to have its number of elect ones increased by the addition of these souls ready to perish? Where is the minister who would refuse to have them for the crown of his rejoicing "in that day?" Where is the master who would keep the cup of salvation from the lips of his own servants?

From the success which has attended the preaching of the Gospel in its purity to the Negroes, we infer that the "set time" to favor them has come; and that the Lord will succeed our faithful endeavors with the converting and sanctifying influences of his Holy Spirit. And when we remember their multitudes — the hundreds and thousands of immortal souls that are passing into an eternity for which they are unprepared; and when we remember their condition and circumstances in this world, and how much they stand in need of the supports and consolations of religion, who that has a heart to feel can hesitate to forward the work of their religious instruction? "All souls are mine," saith the Lord, and his glory is promoted as well in the salvation of the soul of an African as in that of any other man of any other country.

Without proceeding further, such are the benefits which we should realize in the slave-holding States by the faithful and general religious instruction of the Negroes.

I can conceive of no ground whatever upon which to found *an objection* to their religious instruction in the free States; doubtless *excuses* may sometimes be made, but as they must arise generally from corrupt sources and be of limited prevalence, I shall pass them by. The *benefits* arising from their religious instruction have been in some locations so manifest, and must be so obvious to all, more especially indeed to those who have made the character and condition of the Negroes in the free States a matter of serious reflection, that I shall in like manner omit any notice of them.

I have now completed this Part of our subject. The *obligations* of the church of Christ in the United States to impart the Gospel to the Negroes I trust have been demonstrated; the *excuses* and *objections* to a discharge of those obligations stated and obviated; and the *benefits* briefly yet sufficiently exhibited.

PART IV.

MEANS and Plans for promoting and securing the Religious Instruction of the Negroes in the United States.

CHAPTER I.

THE Church of Christ must be made familiar with the duty and moved to its performance.

There is much ignorance, much indifference — indeed, much apathy in the churches on the subject of the religious instruction of the Negroes This people have never been brought up, as it were in *a body*, and presented to the churches, as a people demanding their prayers and efforts for their salvation. We need an all-pervading light and feeling in the churches on the subject. The work must begin *in the house of God.* Our first effort therefore must be to bring the spiritual condition and prospects of the Negroes in the United States and our duties toward them, before the minds of Christians. They will then discover *what is to be done,* and inquire *how shall it be done?*

I would in this place state distinctly that I see no necessity for the formation of associations or societies on an extensive scale embracing States, or even the whole United States, with central boards, appointing agents for the collection of funds and forming auxiliaries, employing and appointing ministers and missionaries, disbursing monies, in a word assuming the entire control of the great work. On the contrary I think I see some very strong objections to such a course, especially in the Southern States. It is unnecessary to offer these objections to the reader. The *impracticability* of forming such associations and conducting them with success, settles the question.

There are no objections to *local* associations, or societies: formed by the people interested, on the ground itself which they propose to occupy. Such associations, (the one in Liberty Country Georgia is an example,) have done and may do great good, and are always under control of their own members and officers.

I conceive that the churches *in their respective organized forms* are competent to undertake, and to prosecute the work to complete success. They are associations for doing good within themselves. Each denomination has its regular and constitutional organization, and can avail itself of that organization to execute its plans of benevolence. If a denomination chooses to appoint committees or boards and agents under prescribed regulations " over this business," there can be no objection ; it is this particular branch of the church acting in its organized capacity still.

The various denominations in the Southern States, so far as they have taken action on the religious instruction of the Negroes, have done so *within themselves*, thereby intimating their competency to the work, and expressing the opinion that no other organizations are necessary.

The first movement, dictated by wisdom, should be to bring the duty before *the bishops, elders, and deacons*, of all the various denominations of Christians, and through their instrumentality before church members and communities.

I would respectfully suggest the following as means to this desirable end which have in certain instances been used with success.

Let bishops, elders, and deacons, who have both knowledge and interest on the subject, *introduce it into their respective church judicatories for consideration and action.* Consideration will produce conviction and conviction action.

To illustrate the matter. At a meeting of *a presbytery* a member introduces the religious instruction of the Negroes, in a sermon or resolution, or in a report on the state of religion within a particular church or within the bounds of the body. The presbytery entertains the subject; it elicits remark; it grows in importance; the members feel that something must be done. Thus introduced it is suggested that they seek for more information, and it is moved that the subject be committed, or some branch of it, to different members to prepare reports, essays, or sermons, or dissertations, that presbytery may know more definitely the nature and extent of it.

The subject is then divided and members are appointed to prepare on such branches of it as we now mention : "*A statistical report* of the number of Negroes within the bounds of presbytery ; the number statedly attending public worship on the Sabbath day ; and the number of members in the several churches under the care of presbytery." "*Their moral and religious condition ; and access to the means of grace.*" "*What is done for their religious instruction,*— by ministers — by churches — by owners?" "What *kind* of instruction is needed ; and the *best mode* of imparting it?" "*Do servants form an integral part of a bishop's charge ;*

and what ought he to do for them?" " *The obligations* of churches and of owners to impart the Gospel to the Negroes." " *The necessity of Sabbath schools* and the *best plan* for conducting them."

Other branches of the subject will suggest themselves. I need not enlarge. These essays and reports, coming in from meeting to meeting will keep the subject before the presbytery, until a conscience is formed, enlightened and active, and then a regular system of efforts will be made from year to year, and the Negroes become the *permanent ob e ts* of Christian regard.

The presbytery will require its members to devote a part of the Sabbath or some portion of the week to their instruction; to bring the duty before the church sessions and congregations and endeavor to establish Sabbath schools for colored children and youth; and to report the number of members, extent and nature of efforts, and the success of them at every regular meeting of the body.

Thus the interest awakened in presbytery goes *down* to the *church sessions* and *congregations* within its bounds, and the whole community is acted upon. And again, through its reports *to synod*, the subject is introduced there, and being remarked, it is urged upon the attention of synod, and the members are impressed, (who form many presbyteries, covering a wide extent of country,) and through the action of synod thousands are affected. *Upward* the influence goes to the *General Assembly*, and from thence it is caused to flow *down again* over the length and breadth of the denomination, besides attracting the attention of *sister denominations* and enlisting them also in the work.

Substantially the same action may pervade the *Baptist*, *Methodist*, and *Episcopal* denominations, and with equal results.

Another means of awakening churches will be to *publish essays, reports, sermons, and tracts on the subject*, and give them a circulation as universal as possible. They will be like the seed which " the sower went forth to sow ;" much of it will fall upon good ground all over the country and effects both great and small will be the fruit.

And still another means, should it be practicable as well as advisable *the particular denomination* taking the work in hand, *may establish a committee or society to superintend it*, having some responsible individual engaged to visit the churches and to assist in establishing Sabbath schools, and to collect funds for the support of missionaries of approved character in places where they may be needed, and circulate information on the best plans for conducting the religious instruction of the Negroes.

By some such means as these the churches must be made familiar with the duty and moved to its performance.

CHAPTER II.

THE ways and means of imparting religious instruction to the Negroes.

OUR object should be to communicate the Gospel which bringeth salvation, to *the entire* Negro population of the United States, embracing the old and the young, the bond and free. The Gospel should be communicated *statedly*, at regularly appointed seasons ; and these seasons occuring as *frequently* as possible, at least once a week ; and in an *intelligible manner*, " for if the trumpet give an uncertain sound who shall prepare himself for the battle ? "

The Gospel should be communicated *in its fulness*, and every necesssary means used to that end ; such as *Sabbath schools* for children and youth, in which adults also may be included. *Preaching* to entire congregations on the Sabbath ; and *on plantations* during the week ; and where it is possible, holding a *weekly lecture*. *Visiting the sick ; attending funerals ; performing marriage ceremonies ;* maintaining *strict discipline in churches ;* appointing *watchmen* as assistants to conduct plantation prayers, and watch over the people and report cases of delinquency; and providing in the churches *committees of instruction* from among the white members to attend to all persons applying for admission, that they be not received without due examination and instruction; and finally, by *plantation instruction*.

But *who* shall communicate the Gospel in this manner to the Negroes? The question admits of an easy answer. We look, *first, to the bishops of churches.*

In the *free States*, if the Negroes have no distinct church organization of their own, and are dependent upon the whites, the ministers under whose influence they fall should make every suitable effort to improve their moral and religious condition.   There is no tie of early association and of sympathy, nor of interest, existing between the whites and the Negroes of the free States; the prejudice against color is very strong; the standing in society — the character and pecuniary resources of the Negroes, have no attractions; and many ministers find it difficult to get their feelings interested, or to make advances towards them.   And what makes the matter worse, is, that frequently the Negroes are independent in their degradation and spiritual necessities, and look upon the efforts of the whites in the light of a presumptuous interference with them and their own concerns.   In some of the chief towns there is a wide field for benevolent effort among this people, and much more ought to be done for them than is done.

In the *slave States*, the churches and congregations are universally composed of Negroes and whites — of bond and free; and ministers who are settled over the churches, *are* or *ought to be*, settled over *both classes*. *Servants* are as much a part of their charge as are *children*.   The churches are composed of *households:* parents and children, masters and servants; and ministers are in duty bound *to watch over the whole;* they are responsible for the whole. And yet how many churches employ their ministers, and never require them to give any attention at all to the Negroes connected with them and for whose religious instruction they are responsible to God! They come and go from the house of God month after month and even year after year, perfectly satisfied and quiet in conscience, feasting upon the provisions of that house, and their dependent servants starving for the bread of life! Yea, more, there are ministers of the Gospel who conceive themselves settled over the *whites only,* and are contented to have it so, and make their weekly preparations, from one year to another *for them only;* and the Negroes, although needing far more their labors, and for whose religious instruction they are responsible to God, are passed over! Where such a course of conduct is persisted in, after the light has been communicated for its reproof, it can but be considered monstrous injustice, and an evidence of a most defective, if not spurious Christianity.

Ministers settled over churches in the slave States should devote special attention to the colored portion of their charge.

They should devote *a portion of each Sabbath to regular preaching of the Gospel* to the Negroes: and at such time of the day as may be most convenient. They will secure larger congregations on this day than on any other, as it is the day of rest and religious worship.

They should, where it is possible, give a *lecture* to the Negroes, during the week on some evening; and in the country, where this exercise cannot be had, let them substitute, *one or two plantation meetings.* Such meetings may be connected with their *pastoral visitations* to the white families, and thus do good to the entire households. There are ministers who perform their duties in this manner, and thereby secure the warmest affections of their people. They should have in their churches *regular Sabbath schools for children and youth and adults,* which schools may be conducted by elders or deacons, or private members, and occasionally visited and catechised and addressed by themselves.

The great hope of permanently benefiting the Negroes is laid in Sabbath schools, in which children and youth may be trained up in the knowledge of the Lord. Such schools ought to be connected with every church in the Southern Country; and with ordinary effort may be kept up and conducted with success from year to year. I am acquainted with schools which have been in existence from seven to nine years, in which youth have grown up and married. Some continue after marriage in the schools, and retaining their interest, bring their little children with them. Those that leave, have their places filled by children that have become old enough to go to school. And thus the schools retain their usual number from year to year. The effect of them has been to increase in a high degree the religious intelligence of the people generally; to benefit their manners; to improve their morals; elevate their character; and make them greater respecters of the Sabbath, more regular in their attendance upon the public worship of God; more mindful of the various duties of life; and when converted, more lasting and consistent members of the church.

If a people are to be instructed *orally,* let the instruction be communicated to them in *early life.* It will then do them most good ; they will learn to use their memories and their reasoning powers and be prepared to profit by the more elevated services of the sanctuary. The amount of religious knowledge which may be communicated *orally*, can be conceived of by those only, who have made the experiment.

We may sometimes witness zeal and effort expended in keeping up in a church a Sabbath school of some fifteen or twenty *white* children, while immediately around and in connection with that church there are perhaps one hundred and fifty, if not two hundred *colored* children, growing up in ignorance and vice! How large an amount of religious instruction might be communicated to our colored population in the South, if in every regular place of worship Sabbath schools for colored children and youth could be originated and perpetuated? And how much good, and at how small an expense of time and labor, might numbers of private Christians in our churches accomplish (who now do comparatively, if not absolutely nothing at all,) if they would engage vigorously in schools of this character? A field great and wide is opened in the South for the establishment of Sabbath schools sufficient to employ all our zeal and effort in the good cause. And why may not ministers of the Gospel bring forward and present the claims of this field?

In addition to the regular Sabbath schools now recommended, ministers of churches ought to have *stated seasons for the gathering together of all the colored members*, that they may form a more intimate acquaintance with them ; and hold a conference of prayer and exhortation, at which time suitable instruction in Christian doctrine and duties may be communicated to them.

This is surely of great importance. For whatever pains may be taken to instruct candidates for church membership, the almost universal practice is to leave them to themselves after they become members, and no further efforts are made to advance them in knowledge. This is a great, a serious error. They require as much instruction *after* admission to the church as *before*.

At the seasons now spoken of *let the colored children of the church and congregation be assembled by the pastors, for catechetical instruction;* let them be thus assembled as often in the year as is convenient. It is the duty of pastors to "feed the lambs;" nor should Sabbath schools ever be made a substitute with pastors for these catechetical exercises with the children and youth of their charge. *They* are to instruct, them and become acquainted with them, as lambs of *their flock;* they are to teach the children to *look up to them* as their spiritual guides and rulers. The judgment and experience of the churches have approved and recommended and established these exercises for children and youth in all ages. If ministers are bound to assemble the *white* children, they are equally bound to assemble the *colored* children. This is the duty in churches of all denominations, especially in those denominations which hold to *infant membership* — the original and only constitution which God has given to his church on earth, in regard to its members — *believers, together with their infant children.*

There are some churches in which the infant children of colored members are regularly acknowledged by the rite of baptism, and their baptisms are recorded and preserved. The Episcopaleans are most faithful in this duty. But it cannot be disguised that there are very many churches in which the duty in respect to the Negro children, (however strictly it may be attended to in respect to the white children,) is wholly neglected; and for what reason it is impossible to say. Such churches lay themselves open to the charge of inconsistency, as well as want of proper regard for their colored members, and by their neglect lose the opportunity of securing a greater amount of interest in, as well as of instruction for, their children. It is the du y of these churches to have the infant children of all their colored members brought forward and baptized and enrol:d, and the children taken under the care and faithful instruction of the pastors; and where the duties of pastors and churches are properly fulfilled, the effects will be of the happiest kind. The churches will present an example to the world of consistency, unity, purity, and success.

Pastors should attend *the funerals* which occur in their colored congregations and particularly in their *colored membership.* They are children of affliction and sorrow as well as others, and need as much the consolations of religion, and the sympathies of Christian ministers and friends. It is cold, heartless, senseless heathenism that neglects death, and yields no balm to the wounded soul. But it is Christianity that invests that event with importance and comes to wipe away the tears of sorrow and bind up the broken heart. Our Lord never neglected the poor in their affliction; and no servant should be above his Lord.

They should also *solemnize their marriages;* and at their *own homes* and at such times as may best suit their convenience, for like the rest of mankind, they like to see their friends in their own houses, and give them on such joyous occasions, the best entertainment they can afford. Some ministers are in the habit of requiring for their own convenience, the people to appear and be married at the church. The consequence is, they are called upon very seldom; the people contrive to have their marriages solemnized at home. Church marriages are not more popular with the *lower* than with the *higher* classes in society.

The formal solemnization of their marriages is of great importance if their improvement in morals and religion is the object sought after. The effect is to elevate and throw around the marriage state peculiar sacredness. It is rendered "honorable in all." Polygamy and licentiousness are rebuked and overthrown. Masters protect families more, and make greater efforts to preserve them from separation.

That very great reforms can be made among the Negroes, in the sacredness and perpetuity of their marriage relations, admits of no question. The experiment has been tried and proven.

Another duty required of ministers is that *they attend with their sessions punctually and diligently to the discipline of colored members.*

Their discipline amounts to nothing at all in some churches, being left almost if not altogether to their colored watchmen; while in other churches it is most shamefully neglected. Cases are reported, (docketed or not as it may happen,) summarily disposed of, or deferred from time to time, until they are forgotten and never acted upon, or called up when it is too late to do any good. Ministers with their sessions should feel in duty bound to take sufficient time and exercise sufficient patience, and *never let cases accumulate on hand*, but promptly dispose of them when they are in possession of all the necessary facts and testimony. The Negroes stand as much in dread of church censures as any other class of members, and discipline punctually and efficiently executed produces the most desirable results.

Ministers with their elders and deacons should see to it that *committees of instruction* be appointed of the best members, not excluding themselves, to attend to *inquirers, and suspended and excommunicated members.* The committee should be distributed at different points in the congregations so as to suit the convenience of the Negroes, that they may not have too great a distance to walk for instruction. The churches also may make a rule to receive no person for examination for church membership, or for re-admission, who does not come *recommended* by some one of the committee.

I would add once more, that ministers *should endeavor to awaken their church members especially masters and mistresses, to the great duty of affording suitable instruction to the Negroes.*

They will necessarily be obliged to *preach* on the subject; and to converse on it in private. They ought not to be satisfied with preaching and conversing, but *suggest plans* and put the people upon an active discharge of duty and recommend and if necessary assist them, in establishing plantation instruction, in the way of weekly schools, and evening prayers. The work of religious instruction lies neglected in many a region of our country for no other reason than that those to whom the people look for guidance, are silent and inactive.

Is it said that this is imposing a great amount of labor on ministers, in addition to their care of the other class in their churches? Be it so. Is it imposing a single thing more than what ought to be done for the

Negroes? And are not ministers called in the Scripture, "*laborers?*" What else have they to do, who undertake pastoral charges, but to attend faithfully to them? If they find they have undertaken too large a charge let them seek a smaller one and give place to some one more able to fill their station. If this be impossible, let them endeavor to procure *assistants*. If the people will grant none, then make a proper division of time and efforts between both classes. *Do something* —almost any thing is better than the dead calm of indifference and idleness.

We are to look in the *second place*, to ministers of the Gospel, *employed as missionaries* to the Negroes.

There are extensive regions of country in the South and South-west, especially those bordering upon river courses and embracing river bottoms, and the most fertile lands, which are inhabited by a dense population of Negroes and by a small population only of whites, (which, indeed, is almost wholly withdrawn in the sickly season of the year.) Such regions, if ever to be supplied with the Gospel, must be supplied through the instrumentality of *missionaries*.

The missionaries should be *Southern men*, or men no matter from what country, yet *identified* in views, feelings and interests with the South, and who possess the *confidence of society*. Such missionaries better understand the civil condition and relations of the Negroes and their general circumstances, and are better qualified to preach the Gospel to them.

Men who feel that they cannot preach the Gospel to their fellow men, unless they are in some particular civil condition, and to bring them into that condition is with them more necessary than to bring them *to Christ;*

and upon which all their preaching and teaching must have a bearing to be in their estimation of any benefit; are the most unfit men in the world to come among us. Because they are, in the first place, dangerous to the peace and order of the country; and in the next place, are ignorant of the first principles of Christianity which is a religion adapted to mankind in all their various conditions, and is primarily intended to secure the salvation of the soul. Men of this stamp are always restless, fault-finding, impatient, unsuccessful ministers. I have known such obtain settlements in the South, but remain in them not long. They have left fields of great extent for missionary and ministerial labor, and have become wandering stars through one free State after another and finally settled in obscurity. Some of them having sold their servants and lands, and gathered all together, have shaken the dust off their feet, and become warm opponents of slavery; but have found no more peace than before. Such ministers have mistaken their own case. Their difficulties are not *external*, they are *internal*. The Southern people are, therefore, perfectly right in requiring missionaries of proper character, and not more with a view to their own peace, than to the profitable instruction of the Negroes themselves. Such individuals as would come under the garb of ministers and inculcate insubordination, and while they say to owners, "art thou in health my brother?" aim direct yet covert blows at their peace and prosperity, if not their very existence, are incendiaries of the worst order and for whom the laws provide very summary justice?

To supply the wants of the Negroes in the Southern States, large numbers of missionaries are required, but *where* shall they be obtained, and *how* shall they be

supported? Both melancholy questions, for they admit
of no satisfactory answer. "The harvest truly is plenteous, but the laborers are few; pray ye therefore the
Lord of the harvest that he will send forth laborers into
his harvest." Such is our Lord's command. We have
not missionaries in sufficient numbers to supply the destitute white population; we have churches able in part,
if not altogether able, to support their own ministers,
which find it difficult to obtain them. Yet, as in the
business world, if a demand is created for an article it
will shortly be produced to the extent of the demand, so
is it in the religious world. If a demand for missionaries be created, a supply will be obtained. The experience of the church in other fields of missionary labor
has demonstrated the fact.

We may, therefore, proceed to show *how* missionaries
to the Negroes may be *employed and supported* and this
may be the direct mode of finding out where they are to
be procured.

By *domestic missionary societies;* which exist in,
perhaps, all the denominations. The funds which are
contributed in the churches and by individuals, may be
judiciously applied to the support of missionaries to the
Negroes, as well as to the whites, and for the support of
ministers in feeble churches, to which numbers of
Negroes are attached. The particular denomination
employing missionaries through its own society will be
responsible for the same. Missionaries are now under
the employ of such societies in the South.

By *presbyteries, associations, conferences, and con-
vocations, without the agency of any society.*

The contributions are taken up in the churches and
collections made by order of the church judicatory acting

in the premises, and it appoints and is responsible for the missionaries. Some presbyteries and associations adopt this plan, and it succeeds very well. There are but few, indeed, of our church judicatories which could not, with suitable effort, support at least *one* if not *more* missionaries to the Negroes in such parts of their bounds as may need them.

By *one, or more churches uniting their contributions.*

Some churches, which for the wealth they contain, and the large annual income of their members, are of themselves abundantly able to support a minister for the white part of the congregation, and a minister for the colored part. And where the labor of attending to both classes is too great for one minister, they ought to have another. There are churches in no inconsiderable numbers, having a net income of from fifteen to fifty, and from fifty to eighty thousand dollars reckoning in members of the churches and congregations, and yet which give from five hundred to a thousand dollars for the support of *one* minister only; and that minister having within reach, from *fifteen hundred to three thousand Negroes!* — Surely the spiritual wants of the Negroes, should be attended to.

Two or more churches, of one or more denominations contiguous to each other, might unite and support a missionary to the Negroes connected with them; and the expense would be comparatively light upon each.

By *one or more planters, employing and supporting a Missionary for their own people.*

There are some planters, and some estates, whose immense incomes warrant the employment of a religious instructor from year to year. For example, there are net incomes, realized by individual proprietors, and by

estates, varying from *ten* to *thirty* thousand dollars, out
of which there is not contributed for the religious instruction of the Negroes, and I mean their *own* Negroes,
over *twenty-five* or *fifty* dollars, or perhaps *one hundred*;
and from some of these large incomes, *not one cent!*
And the Negroes, whose labor is thus profitable, are in
want of the word of life!

On such large plantations, as a mere matter of *gain*,
a religious instructor should be employed.

By planters in the same neighborhood *uniting*, the
support of a missionary is rendered light. Fix the salary of the missionary at *five hundred dollars*; and ten
planters at fifty dollars each, will pay it. The *board* of
the missionary if he be a single man might be *given* to
him by the different families; or locating with his family in some central point, by presents of provisions, his
living might be made cheap. The missionary thus employed could visit every plantation once in two weeks,
catechise the children and preach to the adults, besides
meeting all the plantations on the Sabbath, either at one
or more stations, and in like manner carry forward his
work of preaching and catechising.

I am persuaded that this is one of the most economi-
cal and successful plans of planters' supplying their people with adequate religious instruction. They employ
the men; they know their character and qualifications;
they regulate their operations; they control every thing.

We are to look in the *third place, to owners themselves,
to communicate the Gospel to the Negroes.*

Pious owners are intended; we cannot expect the
duty to be performed by those who are not pious. Should
both heads of the household be pious, so much the better; if *one* only, whether it be the master or mistress,
much may be done.

[1] The owner should impress upon his people *the great duty of attending public worship on the Sabbath,* and should use every proper effort to induce them to do so.

Frequent conversations with delinquents will have a good effect; and where it is necessary, suitable clothes should be given for the purpose.

[2] He should also, where a *Sabbath school* is conducted in his neighborhood, *make all the children and youth attend punctually.* To secure this end, let them be given in charge of some responsible person on the plantation on Sabbath morning to take them to church. In the absence of the owner or manager, let the driver be instructed to send the children. As they are careless with their clothing, and as parents neglect frequently to wash and to mend for them, it would be well for owners to supply the children with *a suit* to be worn *only on the Sabbath,* which might be kept either by parents or given in charge of some careful person.

[3] *The plantation should be brought under religious influences, and the physical condition of the people be improved.*

The owner, in order to success in the religious instruction of his people, must in all his intercourse and treatment of them exhibit the spirit of religion; otherwise his people will have no confidence in him and no respect for his efforts.

Let him begin with the improvement of their *physical condition.* Let him furnish them with *convenient and comfortable houses;* properly partitioned off, and well ventilated, and neatly whitewashed, and sufficiently large to accommodate the families resident in them; and furnished with necessary articles for house hold use.

Each house should also have a *small lot* for a garden, poultry yard, apiary, and other purposes, attached to it. Independent of this lot, the families should have *as much ground to plant for themselves* during the year as they can profitably attend; and also *the privilege of raising poultry and hogs;* indeed every privilege and opportunity allowed them to make themselves comfortable and to accumulate money. The greater the interest which they have at stake on the plantation, the greater security for their good behavior, and the greater prospect of their moral improvement.

I know plantations upon which industrious men improving their opportunities, sell during the year poultry, stock, and produce of their own raising, to the amount of thirty, fifty, and a hundred dollars.

The *clothing* of the people, both adults and children, should be attended to, and a proper care of their clothing required of all. *Habits of neatness* about their houses and lots, and *personal cleanliness*, should be insisted on.

The *provisions* of the plantation should be *sound* and *good* and *abundant*, and as *various* as the means of the planter will allow.

The *labor just;* securing the interest and prosperity of the plantation, and yet leaving the laborers fresh and vigorous in life and spirits. They should also have *sufficient time* and time *in its proper season* allowed them to work their own crops. The motto should be "live and let live."

Punishments should be inflicted upon those *proven guilty, (neither in anger, nor out of proportion to the offence,)* with as little resort to *corporal chastisement* as possible. Confinement and deprivation o privileges may be substituted, as well as other modes. Offences against

each other, against the laws of God and good neighbor-
ship with other plantations, should be punished as well
as against the authority and interest of the owner.

While punishments should be justly meted out, so
ought also *rewards*. And the rewards should be such
as consists with the means of the owner. A familiar
acquaintance with the character and circumstances of
each servant will enable the owner to judge what kind
of rewards would be most agreeable and advantageous.
There are many, who in their government, very much
neglect the fact that while they are "a terror to evil
doers," they should also be "a praise to them that do
well." The *sick* should be strictly attended to. But
impositions from cases of feigned sickness, as strictly
guarded against. Religion is no hiding place for laziness
and deceit.

The owner should, furthermore, *inquire into and
regulate and restrain the conduct of the people towards
each other:* teach them propriety of behavior, civility,
kindness, justice, virtue; and punish overt acts of
iniquity committed between themselves.

Cursing and swearing; breaking the Sabbath; quarreling and fighting; lying and stealing; the oppression
of the weak by the strong; neglect of children on the
part of parents, or of parents on the part of children,
or the neglect of one head of the family towards the
other; neglect of the aged and sick; cruel acts towards
dumb beasts; adultery and fornication; yea, all sins and
improprieties existing among them should be observed
and corrected. The feeling of some that they may do
and live among themselves just as they please, if they
will only *do their work*, belongs neither to humanity nor
Christianity.

There should also, be *a house erected* or *some suitable room*, always at command in the evening and on the Sabbath day, for *a place of worship* for the people on the plantation. What they familiarly call "*the prayer house.*" Let there be a *desk* or *stand* for the books and lights, and *good seats with backs*, and *sufficient room*. Let it be a *comfortable place*, in winter as well as in summer; and the style of its fixing up, such as will indicate a *respect* for religion and religious people.

In this *prayer house*, the evening prayers of the plantation; the plantation Sunday school; and the regular services of missionaries or ministers, may be conducted. It certainly, to say the least, looks most unfavorable for the character of owners, to go upon their plantations, —some of them extensive, in fine order, well filled up with houses of all kinds and for all purposes, and not even a *small room* appropriated to religious uses! The Negroes are crowded into one of their own houses, too small for their accommodation, on which account many do not attend prayers; and should the minister or missionary come, he is taken into some out house, prepared for the occasion, badly seated and cheerless at best; or the Negroes are taken into the *house of the owner*, where they are not sufficiently at home to be at ease. God has no tabernacle to dwell in on such plantations; and the Redeemer has not where to lay his head! It is the duty of every Christian master to see that his people are accommodated with a place of worship. A neat little chapel, with its tower or steeple and bell, while it is an ornament to a plantation, gives an air of stability and sobriety to it, awakens religious associations in the minds of the people, and produces the best of influences.

[4] *The owner must undertake the religious instruction of the people, himself.*

As our hope of permanently benefiting any people by religious instruction, lies in bringing children and youth statedly and constantly under it, the owner must *collect his Negro children*, and with some suitable book, carry forward their instruction from year to year. Let them be *collected into a school*, and taught for a short time daily, or twice or three times during the week, or on Sabbath evening; either by himself, his wife, or some member of the family. The children being required to come with clean faces and hands, their hair combed, and clothes in good order, and to behave quietly, and be attentive and obedient, soon relish the exercise and improve under it in disposition, manners, appearance, intelligence and morality. The master thus early becomes acquainted with the tempers and characters of the children and takes them thus early under discipline, and much trouble is saved in after life. Viewed merely as auxiliaries to plantation order and discipline they are of the first importance. The effect of these schools upon parents also, is highly beneficial. They feel grateful for the pains taken by their owners with them, and exhibit gratification and pride in their improvement. They endeavor also to fulfil their own duties to them better.

Having thus taken the children under instruction, he must not omit the *adults*.

With these he can meet every evening, or as frequently as possible in *the prayer house*. At the ringing of the bell, let teacher and people *be punctual*, and the *exercises pointed and short*. For example a *portion of scripture* read, with a few leading *questions* asked which will serve to keep up their attention, and a *remark or two* founded

on the passage; then a *hymn;* and the whole c'osed
with *prayer;* but not with *long* prayer. The time not
exceeding twenty or twenty-five minutes. The adults
(by varying the exercises,) may and indeed, ought to be
taught, the Lord's prayer, the ten commandments, the
creed and hymns, and instructed in singing. It will be
proper also to take them through some catechism.

Connected with this instruction the owner should as
occasion offers or at regular times, *converse privately*
with the people on the great subject of their souls' salvation. *The members of the church* should receive his
special attention. They may also be put under *the
watch* of some one of their own color of approved discretion and piety, who may report their general conduct
from time to time. Whenever there are any under
serious impressions, or hopefully converted, and are desirous of uniting with the church of God, particular pains
should be taken to have *them* properly instructed. These
are golden opportunities not to be omitted.

It will be the duty of the owner also, should he be a
believer in the infant membership with the visible church
of God, of the children of believers, to have the children
of such of his servants as are connected with his own
church *regularly presented in the assembly of God's
people and baptized.* Such baptisms should be recorded
by the church and he ought also to make a record of
them, as well as of the baptism of the other children of
his household. He should stand with the parents in
that interesting and solemn moment and the children
thus baptized should be under his special care and
instruction, and no means in his power should be left
unused to perfect as far as possible that religious education which he is under obligations to afford them.

It is much easier to neglect this duty than to perform it : and many shrink from the responsibilities imposed upon them by their own faith; and while they seriously neglect the spiritual interests of their people, they lay themselves and their church also, under the charge of great inconsistency. The Lord said of Abraham — " for I know him, that he will command his children and his household after him, and they shall keep the way of the Lord, to do justice and judgment; that the Lord may bring upon Abraham that which he hath spoken of him." —*Gen.* 18: 19. It is the faithfulness of the head of the household, which causes God to bring upon him, the fulness of his covenant blessings : " I will be a God to thee and to thy seed after thee."

But the owner, perhaps, interposes some *objections* to the duties now required of him. Some of these were considered in the *Third Part* of this work, and the reader is referred back to them.

The owner objects to the *amount of labor and care* involved in religious instruction conducted as now recommended. It would make the master the *greatest servant* on his own plantation.

The instances are extremely rare of a man's *over working* himself in this department of benevolent action, and I do not apprehend any danger from unfolding to owners the entire round of their obligations and duties to their servants, on that score. Can the owner place his finger upon a single thing recommended which would be better dispensed with than performed : or which does not appear to be his duty at all?

Looking at the gross, the amount appears, large, and is indeed large. But all the labors and cares and duties do not occur on one day, nor any two of them at one particular moment of time. They lie along the track of time, and the owner takes them up in the order of their occurrence. And if he be a man of system and energy he will have a place for every thing and every thing in its time, and although he may not accomplish all he desires or undertakes, yet he will accomplish a great deal, to the satisfaction of his own mind and conscience and to the peace and comfort of his people.

When a master is impressed with his obligations to his servants, and acts in view of eternity, he will find himself strengthened and made willing not only to undertake but to do a great deal for them. It should, however, not be disguised that that planter who undertakes the religious instruction and moral improvement of his people, must look upon it in the light of *a labor*. He necessarily undergoes, at least for a time, *greater trials and expense,* than the planter who does not. He is obliged to correct all the bad habits of government, all the debasing thoughts in relation to the Negroes which may unconsciously prevail *in himself.* He is obliged to correct what is manifestly wrong in his own deportment on his plantation, and to live up to that Christianity which he would teach. Thus one grand means of elevating his own moral and religious character will be an attempt to improve that of his servants! But this self-discipline is laborious and painful. And further, in promoting the moral improvement of his people, as already remarked, he must *improve their physical condition* — an almost interminable work. In the progress of his efforts the master will have painful evidence of the idleness, carelessness, ignorance, deceit, and degradation of his servants. He will experience disappointments and mortifications in respect to servants whom he deemed the most virtuous, honest, and obedient. He may even encounter opposition to moral reform from some of them. They may sport with his instructions, pervert his motives, corrupt the children and youth, and be guilty of improprieties on purpose to irritate and induce him to forego his attempt to bring the plantation under religious influence, to which their natural feelings are opposed. These are difficulties and trials, but ought not to deter a master from doing his duty.

There are planters who think that they confer a *favor* on their people by giving them instruction. It is a favor in one sense, but not in another — strictly speaking he who discharges his *duty* to another confers no *favor*. They think also that they confer a *favor* on the minister or missionary, by granting him permission to preach on their plantations. Religious instruction is that wich they may *give* or *withhold* according to their good pleasure. There must be an entire revolution in the views and feelings of such owners before they will conscientiously undertake and prosecute the religious instruction of their people.

We are to look in the *fourth place to elders and lay men*, to afford religious instruction to the Negroes.

Elders and laymen, of good spirit and qualifications, in churches *destitute* of pastors or stated supplies, might originate and continue Sabbath schools and Sabbath instruction for the *Negroes* as well as for the whites.

They might also, by some arrangement visit a plantation once a week and hold evening prayers with the people. They might read and expound a portion of Scripture, and converse with the members of the church and with those under serious impressions. By uniting with pastors in labor of this sort, they would become most valuable auxiliaries. There have been associations whose members have for some considerable time exerted themselves with self-sacrifice in doing good in this manner.

The instruction of the Negroes by missionaries, by owners, and by elders and laymen of the church, is liable to many delays and interruptions, and in the present state of the work and the subject in our country, our *main dependence* must be upon the *settled pastors and stated supplies of our churches :* and I venture to speak further on this point, at the risk of repetition.

The churches should convert their pastors, somewhat into *missionaries,* and they would then provide, with little or no additional expense, *permanent* instruction for the Negroes. *The religious instruction of the Negroes properly and officially devolves, and in large measure, depends upon settled pastors ;* and if all pastors and stated supplies in the several denominations would perform their duty to the Negroes attached to their congregations, there would be comparatively speaking, over immense tracts of country, but little need of missionaries ; religious instruction would pervade the South, the reproach of the neglect of our colored population, would be wiped away, and blessings temporal and eternal be conveyed to thousands now ready to perish. It is an encouraging fact that pastors are directing their attention to this field more than ever, and that our young ministers when they settle, seem disposed to devote, and that conscientiously, a reasonable portion of their time to the colored part of their charges.

CHAPTER III.

The Manner in which the Gospel should be communicated to the Negroes, so as to meet the character, condition, and circumstances of the people.— Conclusion.

The concluding chapter I shall throw into distinct heads, embracing several particulars relating to the religious instructon of the Negroes, which could not with propriety be introduced before.

1. *Manner of Preaching.*

As *preaching* depends upon the *preacher*, it will not be amiss to inquire *what kind of preachers are needed for the Negroes?*

Certainly not *ignorant* preachers. It is the opinion of some, that *any body* will do to preach to the Negroes, which is an erroneous opinion — the child of ignorance itself. No inconsiderable a part of that misery into which the fall brought mankind, is a *darkened understanding.* It is not more true that "the world lieth in wickedness," than that they have "the understanding darkened being alienated from the life of God through the ignorance that is in them." There is *the blindness of the mind and the hardness of the heart;* and they act and re-act the one upon the other. Our Lord has taught

us also, that men "*love* darkness rather than light;"
— this very state of blindness and haidness. They do
not like to "retain God in their knowledge." Hence
the more ignorant they are of God the more wicked
they are. And the more ignorant and wicked, the
greater the difficulty of enlightening and elevating them.
It will be seen that the difficulty is increased a thousand
fold, when the only access which the people have to the
light, is through the *living* teacher.

The primary work of a minister is to dissipate this
natural blindness of men's minds in respect to God, by
pouring in upon them in the most suitable manner, "the
light of the knowledge of the glory of God in the face
of Jesus Christ," and in this way quickening the conscience and moving the heart. To put men to this work
who are not only *unlearned* but *ignorant*, is to put the
blind to lead the blind; and as a result, "both shall fall
into the ditch." Shallow vessels are soon emptied.
When the watchmen are blind — are all ignorant; they
quickly become dumb dogs, that cannot bark. They
become weary with their own noise, and ashamed of the
little impression they make upon men; — their intellects
are stagnant. They are mere dreamers in knowledge,
and a spirit of indifference and inefficiency creeps over
them, and they are "lying down, loving to slumber." —
Isa. 56 : 10, 11. *Our Divine Lord* is the *great teacher*
that has come from God, and ever has been and ever
will be the "*light of the world.* His *ministers* after
him he calls and requires to be "*the light of the world.*"
"To be *instructed* unto the kingdom of heaven;" and
he sends them unto their fellow men, "to open their
eyes and to turn them from darkness to light and from
the power of Satan unto God." — *John* 1 : 4. 3 : 2 – 19.
8 : 12. *Matt.* 5 : 14. 13 : 52. *Acts* 26 : 17, 18.

We need for the *continued* and *successful* instruction of the Negroes, as well educated and as intelligent ministers and as good preachers as the churches can supply. It is the experience of all those who can lay claim to these qualifications, who have entered upon the work of the religious instruction of the Negroes, that instead of requiring less talents and learning, they have needed more than they possessed, and that they found the benefit of all the knowledge they had acquired.   Some preachers, really ignorant and unfurnished for their office, quickly expending their stock of knowledge, and exhausting all their manœuvres and invention to keep the people interested, have first been deserted by the people, and then have deserted themselves.   Others, well qualified in every respect, setting their standard of sermonizing and of intellectual effort *low*, have thought " *any sort of a sermon* " would do for the *Negroes*, and the Negroes have been *wise* enough to estimate their powers upon their own showing, and *proud* enough not to be put off with *any sort of a sermon*, and have therefore stayed at home or gone where they have thought they could do better. The preachers in the mean while have wondered at the falling off in their congregation — at the carelessness, hardness and indifference of the Negroes, and have perhaps given over effort, saying "it is of no use; they will not come," their consciences perfectly satisfied and at rest, "they have done what they *could!*"

Ministers in preaching to the Negroes, sometimes say, "they cannot interest them; they have no turn for it; they cannot make themselves understood." They have felt like exclaiming with Dr. Chalmers on a certain occasion, when laboring to put the inhabitants of Kilmany in possesion of some of his ideas, "I would make it plainer to you if I could!"

No one will deny that an acquaintance with the character, condition, and circumstances of a people, and some practice in addressing them, are highly advantageous to him who preaches to them. But it is the duty of ministers to attain to a thorough understanding of the doctrines and duties of Christianity, and to cultivate such a facility of expression and of language, as to be able to unfold both doctrines and duties intelligibly to the weakest hearer. When a minister is not able to do the *latter*, he may be suspected of not having attained the *former.* The knowledge of some men is general and indistinct. They are able to say much on subjects, call them by their right names, and use the ordinary phraseology; but are not masters of the *subjects themselves*, so that they can take them to pieces, show the different parts and put all together again. One boy draws his figure, demonstrates his problem, and thinks he understands it perfectly. Now take his book away and rub out his lines and letters, and set him to the demonstration and call upon him for the principles upon which the problem is constructed, and he is at fault after taking but one or two steps. Another boy takes the problem *into his mind,* lays hold of the thing itself; gets entire possession of it, and is able to demonstrate it, in any manner desired, resolve it into its first principles, and construct it again. This is but an illustration of what we meet with in theological studies. The nomenclature of the science is acquired; the order of subjects; and general notions of doctrines, and not much more. The preacher may perhaps interest what he terms enlightened audiences, but when required to *analyze* truth and present it in a plain way to plain people he cannot do it. The more he explains and defines, the more visible becomes the darkness of his own mind. He takes a passage of scripture and studies it; thinks he understands it; rises in the desk to deliver an exposition of it; but he does not succeed, and he cannot tell why.

The *general deportment* of the minister to the Negroes deserves attention. He should have reference to the character, condition, habits and feelings of the Negroes. His address and intercourse should be polite, frank, condescending and uniformly kind, and at the same time independent. Self-respect and the honor of the Gospel will dictate these virtues, and the people will quickly discover and rightly appreciate them. In order to secure the confidence and respect of the people, he must treat *them* with respect and manifest in word and in deed his interest in them. Whining and simpering, familiarity and a courting of popularity will destroy his influence. He must speak and be accessible to all, and forget not to extend charity as occasion offers, to the old and infirm. He should notice the children and youth a great deal, cultivate their acquaintance and the acquaintance also of the more prominent, pious, and influential members of the church and congregation. Scrupulously avoid personal disputes and quarrels with them, and be no party in such troubles between them. Act prudently, hear both sides, decide justly, and show the reasons for the decision. He should avoid making himself the repository of tales and difficulties between individuals and on plantations, and hear no tales at all respecting owners and matters which belong to their civil condition. — *Luke* 12 : 13 – 14.

He should be among them as their spiritual adviser, guide, and friend, and let the people look up to him as *their minister*. He should put himself to inconvenience to meet their calls for his services, in times of sickness, at weddings and at funerals; show them that he is their friend, and is neither ashamed of them nor their service. His *language* should be as pure *Saxon* as he can make it: and not accommodated in any degree whatever to their *broken English*, if he would escape contempt.

The minister to the Negroes should pay attention to *the manner, style, and character of his preaching.*

His *manner* should be grave, solemn, dignified, free from affectation, hauteur, or familiarity, yet ardent and animated. The people like gestures but not grimaces. His manner should be respectful. He should not endeavor to impress them with the fact, (should he unfortunately believe it himself,) that there is an infinite distance between him and them, and between his intelligence and theirs; and that he has humbled himself amazingly to take their instruction into his hands. He must not treat them as if they were a parcel of children, or a people perfectly stupid. Poor people have feelings as well as rich people; and if people are ignorant, and, if you please, fools, yet they do not like to be told of it. No good comes of it. It is enough for the minister to know what they are; let him go on and make them better. Nor must he be perpetually scolding and fault-finding, if they happen to come a little late to church, if a door slams, if a dog comes in, if a child cries, if a man sleeps, if they do not pay undivided attention, and so on. No people are perfection. Great allowances are to be made for the Negroes; and many things wrong among them may be owing to the minister himself. He on the contrary ought to proceed upon the principle of *kind encouragement.*— they greatly need it; and he should remark and praise all that he sees commendable. Praising a virtue is a condemnation of the opposite vice; and in many instances is the most effectual mode of condemning it. Encouragement stimulates a people to effort, and when they see that their minister notices and commends their efforts they will exert themselves the more. It would do some ministers a great deal of good to read frequently 1st and 2d *Thessalonians.* They might learn how highly they ought to think of God's people, and how much they ought to praise them for their works of faith and labors of love; and how proper it is to deal in kind encouragement.

Style and character of preaching. Sermons should be plain in language, simple in construction, and pointed in application, and of any length *from a half hour to an hour and a quarter,* according to the subject and the interest of the people. Like all other hearers, they have no objection to *long* sermons if they be *good* sermons and treated well. The reasoning in the sermons may be logical and close, if *abstract propositions and learned arguments* are excluded, and the reasoning short and made evident *by illustrations,* which is no very hard matter, if a man understands himself what he wishes to teach to others. As to the *subjects* of sermons, they may embrace the *whole round of the doctrines and duties of Christianity;* dwelling chiefly upon those most applicable to the people. There is not a single doctrine, however elevated, or as some express it, deep and mysterious, which may not be profitably exhibited. In my opinion the preacher with proper pains can speedily carry them, ignorant as they are conceived to be, to the limits of our actual knowledge of the doctrines of Christianity; and what is more, make them know and feel it. The human mind, if I may so express myself, is *conscious*

when it arrives at the boundaries of religious truth, and
is there disposed to stop; though pride and impiety, and
subtle leaders may tempt it to cross them. A little black
boy returning from Sabbath school was asked by his
little master, what he had been learning. He answered,
I have been learning about *God*. And what did you
learn about God? Why, that he *made me*. And what
else did he make? He made *all things*. Then said his
little master — but who made *God?* He replied, *no
body*. How then did God come at all? Why, he did
not come at all: somebody must be *first* and *begin* every
thing; and that *must be God*. But *how* can God be *first*
and *begin* every thing? The little black boy answered,
finally, "I *do n't know;* but it *must* be so; and *'t is so*."

To make my meaning plain that the most elevated
doctrines may be exhibited, and profitably exhibited, to
ignorant and illiterate people (which certainly is the
duty of every faithful steward of God,) and that in the
way of *illustration*, suppose I wished to bring forward the
doctrine of election: that God is *the author* of our salvation and bestows it *upon whom he pleases?* I would take
up *the history of the Apostle Paul*, and show *who* and
what he was *before* his conversion; and that out of his
own mouth. Next, show *when* and *where* and *how* he
was converted: that the thought or wish of becoming a
Christian *never had entered his mind:* that he was smit-
ten to the ground by the brightness of the glory of the
Lord Jesus, in the full career of his iniquity: and that
God overpowered him *by his Spirit, and shined into his
heart*, to give him the light of the knowledge of the
glory of God in the face of Jesus Christ. And last of
all, I would show that there was the *most wonderful and
perfect change wrought in the man*, which continued to

his dying day; and that, as Paul himself tells us, *it was wrought in him by God;* and for *no reason whatever,* but that it was *the good pleasure of his will.* Who can resist the force of the truth thus presented? Who can resist the inference and application? The *same way* which God took to bring *this chief of sinners* into his kingdom is *the same way* he takes to bring *all sinners* into his kingdom. The reason which moves him in one case moves him in all. The reason *is in himself.* "Even so Father for so it seemeth good in thy sight!" "Not unto us, O Lord, but unto thy name be all the glory."

Suppose again I wished to bring forward "*free agency and accountability;* there is the *history of Judas:* or "that *election to eternal life, includes the means thereto,*" there is *the shipwreck of Paul;* or, "*the divinity and humanity of Christ* — two natures in one person;" there is the *storm at sea* and many other of his wonderful works; or, "*justification by faith alone,*" there is the *penitent thief,* who had not righteousness enough to save him from death at the hands of *men,* much less, at the hands of *God.* And thus I might enumerate every doctrine and duty of the Holy Scriptures, with their appropriate and striking illustrations. The doctrines are thus fastened to the illustration; or rather the illustrations are fastened to the doctrines; and all are *nails driven in a sure place.* They are argued and decided, and laid away in the mind as *appeal cases.*

When the preacher takes a doctrine in hand, let him call it *by its right name;* and never be afraid to *use God's own word* to give it expression. Does he wish to express the awful condition of men before God? Paul offers him his text: "*By nature* children of *wrath.*" Does he wish to make known the entire depravity of the human race? Our Lord commands him to say, "that which is *born of the flesh is flesh.*" Does he wish to prostrate the guilty sinner before God and lead him to feel his inability to renew his own heart, and awaken him to look for power not his own? Let him take the declaration of our Lord, "*no man can* come unto me except *the Father* which hath sent me *draw him.*" Let him go all the height, and length and breadth and depth of the word of God openly, strongly, whether they will hear or forbear, yet humbly and meekly, not invading the province of the divine spirit, and vainly endeavoring to smooth off the angles of truth and to lay it quietly into men's minds and let it transform them, they know not how nor why. *The Divine Spirit will take care of his own truth*, plainly and believingly delivered : it is designed for saints and sinners, it suits their state ; they know it, they feel it ; and he will according to his good pleasure, make it a fire and a hammer to break the flinty rock in pieces.

From the foregoing observations it will be gathered, that the preacher to the Negroes, ought to deal much in *parables, historical events; biographies;* and in *expository preaching.* And his expository preaching may and ought to assume some *system.*

Should he select *parables,* he may take up our Lord's parables *in order;* should he select *biographies,* he may go through the life of our Lord, one event succeeding another, to the last sad catastrophe. Or, the lives of the Apostles as far as know.., — notices of persons whose history is introduced in the New Testament. Does he desire to enter upon *expository preaching?* He may take up the Gospels and expound them in order; the Acts of the Apostles ; and various chapters in the Epistles. Then there is the whole *Old Testament,* with the creation, fall, flood; the lives of the Patriarchs; the entire history of the church of God, filled with extraordinary characters and events. A studious man and one alive to his work, can never be without matter, as well new as old, for the instruction of the people. *The bible, the bible,* is the great store house of truth — an ocean without a bottom or a shore.

The practice of expository preaching recommended, is one eminently calculated *to advance the people in knowledge,* and of different kinds of preaching is *the most improving to the minister.* He will acquire an intimate and extensive acquaintance with the Scriptures; discover the dependence of every part and the union of the whole. He will have light falling directly and indirectly upon doctrines, and they will become clear to his mind, and he cannot tell his various steps to the pleasant conclusion. He will gather up a vast variety of subjects, and illustrations cf doctrines and duties; and finally know that "*all Scripture* is given by inspiration of God, and is profitable for doctrine, for reproof, for correction, for instruction in righteousness: *that the man of God may be thoroughly furnished unto all good works.*" — 2 *Tim.* 3: 16 – 17.

But it may be said by some that it is *laborious* and *difficult* preaching; and that but a few have a talent for it. He who would succeed well must *labor;* and it is worth all the labor expended for it. He must expect to encounter *difficulties,* but they are not *insurmountable;* and the reason why it is discovered that but *few* have a talent for it, is because there are but *few* who *perseveringly practice* expository preaching.

There are many works which will aid a minister as acquiring the tact and the mode — such, for example, in

Henry's Commentary, Andrew Fuller's Lectures on
Genesis, Porteus' Lectures on Matthew, Scott's Commentary, Stuart on Hebrews, Hodge on Romans, Hall's
Contemplations on the Old and New Testament. The
list might be extended, but students do not require it,
and to those who are not students it would be of no
avail. I mention these few because they are standard
works and of easy access, and are sufficient as a
specimen.

Every imitator is a slave and a bungler. A minister
should be familiar with the works of eminent men of
God who have preceded him, and take into his mind
their great and good thoughts, that it may be expanded
and sanctified thereby. He ought to study with care
the sermons of those who have been most successful in
winning souls to Christ, searching into the manner of
their *construction,* and especially into the principles
involved in their *application.*

But after all he must discipline himself and do his
own thinking and make his *own sermons,* and learn to
teach and to preach *for himself.* He must proceed
always upon *the principle of improvement.* What he
may not do well to day *perseverance* may enable him to
do better to-morrow. Then let him know no *discouragement.* "The thing *can* be done; *by divine aid I will
do it."*

The character of the Negroes both private and public
in a state of freedom and in a state of slavery; their
habits of thought, superstitions and manners, should be
carefully studied by the preacher, so that he may adapt
his preaching to them. He will perhaps frequently find
it necessary to follow the advice of Paul to Titus as to
the manner in which he should reprove the *Cretians,* and
for the same reasons. *Titus* 1: 12, 13. But let him

avoid the most distant approximations to *coarseness*, and follow the rule laid down in *Eph.* 5 : 11, 12.

The *strictest order* should be preserved at all the religious meetings of the Negroes, especially those held on the Sabbath day, and *punctuality* observed in commencing them at the appointed hour. No *audible* expressions of feeling in the way of groanings, cries, or noises of any kind, should be allowed. To encourage such things among ignorant people, such as they are, would be to jeopard the interests of true religion, and open the door to downright fanaticism. They are *bad* at best, among any people — they go from *worse* to *worst* as we descend in t 'e scale of intelligence.

Close attention should be paid to *their deportment*, lest they choose the seasons of public worship for seasons of business and pleasure ; and what is more, for settling up their disputes in *regular combats*. Disturbers of the public peace should be noted down ; the cases investigated and summary punishment inflicted by the proper authorities on the guilty. It is the minister's duty in all such cases to make a report and see justice done. The pious and more orderly and intelligent Negroes will always discountenance and oppose such unruly conduct. On dismissing his Sabbath congregations he should always *remain*, until he sees them pretty well on their way homeward.

2. *Manner of conducting Sabbath Schools.*

Notice of the *formation* of the Sabbath school for colored children and youth should be carefully and generally given, together with the *time* and *place* of meeting, and the *manner* in which, and the *persons* by whom, the school is to be conducted.

The notice may be given *by the pastor* of the church in which it is to be formed, who can take occasion to commend the effort to the patronage and prayers of his people; or *by the missionary;* or *by elders, deacons,* and *private Christians* who engage in the work, in the most advantageous manner that their circumstances may admit of.

The notice should be directed first of all, to *owners and managers* and their support entreated: next, to the *parents* of the children, and the Sabbath school commended as affording that religious instruction to their children which in a majority of instances they cannot furnish themselves, and which will contribute to the peace and order of their families and to the respectability and happiness of their children; and last of all, to the *children and youth themselves.* It will answer a good purpose to go into some detail with them, as to the manner in which the school will be conducted, and what will be taught, and for what end, and how much good the school will do them for time and eternity, the advantages yielded them by it, being suitably improved.

When the school is collected and opened, if *teachers* can be procured, interested in the work and disposed to be useful, then *divide the school into classes,* as in any other school, as nearly according to *age* and *sex,* as may be possible. Each teacher will then instruct his own class, and at the close of the school, let the superintendent take the book and question the school, class by class, and all together, applying the lesson with suitable remarks and giving the scholars praise for their punctuality, good order, and improvement.

Should it be impossible to obtain teachers, let the school be seated according to *size* and *sex,* the youngest nearest to the teacher, and then let the teacher whoever he may be, teach the *whole together, on the infant school plan.* I have known a minister including in a school of this character, his *entire* colored congregation — children and adult. His spacious church every Sabbath afternoon would be crowded with the young and old, manifesting the deepest interest and making commendable progress; and in his pastoral visitations, hailed by the people one very plantation as their friend and benefactor.

I would say something on *manuals* and *plans of instruction.*

In the *first part* of this work several *manuals of instruction* for colored persons were mentioned. They may be mentioned again in this place with advantage. There is the " *Short Catechism, for the use of colored members on trial of the Methodist Episcopal Church, in South Carolina,*" prepared by Dr. Capers, and used by the missionaries of that church in South Carolina and Georgia. There is " *the Catechism to be used by the teachers in the religious instruction of persons of color,*" etc., "prepared in conformity to a resolution of the Episcopal Convention of the diocese of South Carolina, under the direction of the bishop;" used by the Episcopaleans in South Carolina and Georgia. There is *Dr. Palmer's Catechism; Rev. John Mine's*; and there is the " *Catechism of Scripture Doctrine and Practice, designed for the oral instruction of colored persons ;*" prepared by myself.

Some persons use " *Scripture Cards,*" illustrating by a picture some event in our Saviour's life ; the passages of Scripture together with questions and answers, are printed on the cards. Entire portions are taught embracing parables and miracles, extracts from the book of Common Prayer are also used. Others take the Scriptures and select the more interesting events and histories — beginning with the creation, and continuing through the New Testament. They first read the passage and briefly explain it, and then take it, verse by verse, and ask questions, and repeat, until it is well committed to memory.

The " *Union Questions.*" prepared by the Sunday School Union, may be used by the teacher as a *guide* to his *subjects*, as well as *questions*. He must of course *select* the questions that are most suitable to his scholars. " *Brown's Catechism*," and " *Watts' first and second Catechism*," are also used. I have never heard of but one instance of the "*Assembly's Catechism*," in connection with " *Willison's*," being used in the oral instruction of the Negroes; that instance was reported to have been completely successful. I have no doubt but that the teacher might take *Willison's and Fisher's* catechisms and make a good use of them in the oral instruction of the Negroes. As much, it may with truth be said, depends upon the *teacher* as upon the *manual of instruction* used by him.

To give variety and interest to the exercises of the Sabbath school, it is proper to teach the scholars *hymns and psalms, and how to sing them.* They are extravagantly fond of music; and this taste may be turned to good account in their instruction. *Watts* will furnish a g eat number of suitable psalms and hymns, and they may be selected from various other authors. Some of the infant school and Sunday school hymns, written expressly for children, will answer well. As specimens of the kind of sacred poetry which the Negro children and youth readily learn, I would mention from Watts, "Lord in the morning thou shalt hear," "Behold the morning sun," "There is a God who reigns above," "When I can read my title clear," "Jesus with all thy saints above," "I'm not ashamed to own my Lord," "Salvation, O the joyful sound," "Now in the heat of youthful blood;" and from others, "Jesus thou heavenly stranger," "Blow ye the trumpet, blow," "There is a fountain filled with blood," "Come humble sinner in whose breast," "To whom my Saviour, shall I go," "Glory to thee my God this night."

The tunes should not be intricate but plain and awakening. One great advantage in teaching them good psalms and hymns, is that they are thereby induced to lay aside the extravagant and nonsensical chants, and catches and hallelujah songs of their own composing; and when they sing, which is very often while about their business or of an evening in their houses, they will have something profitable to sing.

In giving oral instruction *two plans* may be pursued. First, the teacher asking the question, and stating the answer and then requiring the *whole* school, or his whole class, to answer *together*. Second, the teacher requring the scholars in his class, or school to answer the questions, *one by one*, one after another, until it is apparent the whole know it. Let *both plans* be united.

The teacher must be regular and punctual in attending the school; expect and bear with *irregular attendance* on the part of his scholars, as they cannot always command their own time, and are subjected to a variety of interruptions; use his best efforts to win their esteem and confidence, and to interest them in their lessons and hymns; deal largely in encouragement, and let his manner be lively and spirited without irreverence, sober without austerity, and his language plain and intelligible without being foolish and inaccurate. To relieve the schol irs, he should vary their *posture*, sometimes let it be that of sitting and sometimes that of standing. The school should always be dismissed in an *orderly manner class by class*, and the children and youth, *warned* against noise and play on the holy Sabbath.

The *success* of Sabbath schools, under God, depends upon the zeal and fidelity of those who have the management of them. If superintendents and teachers are not of the right character, with the best materials at command, the schools will go down.

3. *Manner of conducting Plantation Meetings.*

No plantation meeting should be held except *with the knowledge and consent of the manager or owner,* The owner should have *timely notice* of the meeting, so that he may make whatever arrangements may be necessary for it. The pastor or missionary will find it proper to send a little note, at times, to this effect:

"DEAR SIR:—If it is agreeable and convenient, I will preach for your people on Wednesday evening next.

> Respectfully and truly,
> Your friend,
> C. C. J."

The invariable reply will be like the following:

"DEAR SIR:—It will be both agreeable and convenient for you to preach for us on Wednesday evening next. It will afford me pleasure to see you.

> Very respectfully yours,
> W. L."

The owner thus takes the meeting under his care and is responsible for the congregation and the order of it; and he may or may not, as he pleases confine the meeting to the people on his plantation. It is, however, *best and every way most desirable to have no people present but those belonging to the plantation upon which the meeting is held.* A collection of Negroes from several plantations around on one central to the whole, at night, to attend religious meetings ought not to be allowed. The evil in the long run will more than counterbalance the good.

The attendance of the planter and his family should be solicited, as it serves to encourage both the missionary and the people, and does themselves good also. In the majority of instances they need no solicitation, they cheerfully go of their own accord.

The people being assembled the exercises are precisely those of *an evening sermon or lecture.* They are opened with singing and prayer, reading the Scriptures, singing a second time, and then a sermon or expository lecture, *plain, pointed, short;* and the whole closed with prayer and singing.

With preaching to the adults the pastor or missionary may connect *a catechetical exercise with the children,* and also *a meeting for the enquirers,* should any be on the place; and these two services may be attended to either before or after the lecture for the people.

Now and then a planter will object to preaching, on his own plantation, from prejudice against the minister or missionary; or against such kind of meetings, because he has seen or heard of some irregularities connected with them; or from a hatred to the Gospel itself —not wishing its light to shine where he may more

directly feel its influence. And while he thus excludes
the Gospel from his plantation and forbids the people to
assemble for religious worship, he will allow them from
time to time to assemble and have dances and midnight
revels! All is peace and safety while Satan reigns:
God only is the author of all evil! There are now, as
there were in the Apostle's days, " unreasonable and
wicked men," and like him, we should pray to be delivered from them.

4. *Manner of treating opposition to the good work.*

As every work of benevolence has to encounter some
degree of opposition, so has that of the religious instruction of the Negroes. It is impossible in all cases to
discern the cause whence the opposition proceeds. The
causes are as various as are the interests, passions, and
prejudices of depraved men, and as hidden as are the
thoughts of the heart.

There being opposition it is to be met *according to
its nature and weight,* and much must be left to the
christian judgment and prudence of the minister of God.
Our Lord has promised to assist his ministers in a special
manner when exposed to opposition from men. The
following general rules I would suggest for consideration.

Let opposition be met *silently.*

As long as access is had to the field of labor, and
there are good friends, notice nothing said or done —
especially if said or done behind one's back. Go on as
though there were no opposition.

Let it be met *forbearinly.*

Be rather *driven* to extremities than *led* to them. Forbearance gives one's own mind time to settle down and
act discreetly, while it gives time to the understanding

and conscience of the enemy to work, and both probably will work right, and the enemy will thus vanquish himself and you be saved the trouble of encountering him. Forbearance, on the whole, conquers more than open resistance and defiance.

Let it be met *prudently*.

Speak and act so that they will have no evil thing to say of you. "Be swift to hear, slow to speak, slow to wrath : for the wrath of man worketh not the righteousness of God."

Let it be met *kindly*.

If you know a man is opposed to you and to your work, do not treat him so as to make him see that you know and feel it; on the contrary treat him openly, candidly, and kindly. Have *no quarrels* with men because they choose not to agree with you in your favorite plans and principles.

Should the opposition be open and direct, and there is no possibility of avoiding contact with it, then let it be met *openly, decidedly, and with Christian temper.* Let your object be not to overcome *men*, but their *errors ;* not to exalt *yourself*, but *the principles of the truth of God.* But to conclude : settle it in your mind that where there are one hundred cases which upon first sight appear to demand notice, *after reflection* will prompt you to pass over ninety-nine *in silence.* "The beginning of strife is as when one letteth out water; therefore leave off contention before it be meddled with." — *Prov.* 17 : 14.

5. *The manner of speaking and acting in relation to the Civil Condition of the Negroes.*

As ministers or missionaries to the Negroes, in the discharge of our official duty, and in our intercourse with the Negroes, *we should have nothing to do with their civil condition.* We are appointed of God to preach " the unsearchable riches of Christ " to our perishing fellow-men. We are to meditate upon the duties and responsibilities of our office; and to give ourselves *"wholly" to it.* We shall, by so doing, in the most effectual manner subserve the interests of masters and servants, for time and eternity. It is too much the fashion of late years, for ministers (I speak not of all,) to consider themselves, *ex-officio, the supervisors* of human affairs; the *conservators* of the theological, the civil and the political interests of society, and of course, as possessing wisdom, experience, and observation suffi-cient " to entitle them to be heard." Any subject, any object of pursuit, however, remotely touching upon the religion or morals of the people, is considered as legiti-mate "work" to which they may conscienciously devote all the powers which God has given them. The evil is increased by many who depart out of country places and villages, to sojourn where they may find a place, (in large cities if possible.) Some society or newspaper, the organ of some reform party, offers the Levite " ten shekels of silver by the year, and a suit of apparel and his victuals," and he is content to dwell there, and be a priest unto them.

The common reply is that it is an age of free inquiry and of discussion and of onward movement, and *ministers* above all others are bound to speak and " to give direc-tion to the public sentiment;" nor can they do their duty unless they "come out and give support to right principles, and decidedly condemn institutions and practices in society which they know to be wrong," and much of the same import. Thus societies and parties have already decided what is right and wrong, and what it is the duty of ministers to do and not to do, and so their right of private judgment and of independent action is taken quite away, and they become mere footballs to be struck in any direction at the will of those who have the privilege of playing upon them. The people have a great horror of being *priest-ridden;* I think the priests ought to have an equal horror of being *people-ridden.*

It is much easier for men to become public lecturers, or newspaper editors, and society agents, and pulpit declaimers against the sins of their neighbors, and against great evils, as they call them, in society, and be overwhelmed at *their* own responsibility for their existence, than to traverse obscure lanes and enter wretched and abandoned houses, or expose themselves to midnight airs and summer suns in unhealthy climates, to relieve the very people for whom they have so great a love, and for whom they feel so deep a sympathy, of some of their temporal sufferings, and to convey to them in their ignorance and spiritual ruin the glad tidings of salvation. To their own master they stand or fall.

On the civil condition of the Negroes, I here take occasion to say, that the Southern people are a far more reflecting and discerning people than is imagined by some. They are great lovers of their country and of the Union. No people understand their political rights better or have a more sacred regard to the happy constitution under which we live ; and no people are more independent, decided and fearless in maintaining both the one and the other. The degree of general intelligence among the middling and higher classes of society is not surpassed by the same classes of society in any part of the Union; and they are disposed to live on terms of perfect amity with their fellow citizens from every section of our great country. They expect to find the citizens of the free States, *at home* and when they come *South*, entertaining views different from their own. They would not take away the right of private judgment and opinion. They accord to others what they demand for themselves. But having had the institution of slavery entailed upon them, and its existence recognized, and its perfect control and management secured to them under the Constitution, they claim exemption from the dictation and interference of people no way responsible for, nor affected by, the institution; and the right to regulate it in such a manner as in their best judgment shall promote the best good of all concerned therein — the very right which has already been exercised by *eight* of the original "thirteen States," without any interference at all on the part of the remaining States. Hence, occupying this ground, they make no objection to merchants, lawyers, physicians, divines, teachers or mechanics, coming and settling among them from any part of the world. They are entitled to their own opinions, but they are neither to be expressed nor propagated so as to produce disturbance in society.

6. *The best form of Church Organization for the Negroes.*

In the free States it is judged most advisable both by whites and blacks, that the latter should have their own houses of public worship and church organizations independent of the former.

But in the slave States it is not advisable to separate the blacks from the whites. It is best that both classes worship in the same building ; that they be incorporated in the same church, under the same pastor, having access to the same ordinances, baptism and the Lord's supper, and at the same time ; and that they be subject to the same care and discipline ; the two classes forming one pastoral charge, one church, one congregation.

Should circumstances beyond control require the Negroes to meet in a separate building and have separate preaching, yet they should be considered part and parcel of the white church. Members should be admitted and excommunicated, and ordinances administered in the presence of the united congregations.

This mingling of the two classes in churches creates a greater bond of union between them, and kinder feelings ; tends to increase subordination ; and promotes in a higher degree the improvement of the Negroes, in piety and morality. The *reverse is*, in the general, true of *independent church organizations of the Negroes,* in the slave States.

The appointment of *colored preachers* and *watchmen* (the latter acting as a kind of *elders*,) *by the white churches, and under their particular supervision,* in many districts of country has been attended with happy effects, and such auxiliaries properly managed may be of great advantage.

Such are the means and plans for promoting and securing the religious instruction of the Negroes, in the United States, and of those in the Southern States in particular, which experience and observation have suggested to my own mind. And having brought this part of the subject to a close, I have reached, in the good providence of God, the end of my undertaking.

CONCLUSION.

After saying so much on the Religious Instruction of the Negroes, I feel that the *conclusion* need not be extended.

I would respectfully and earnestly commend the subject to the serious consideration of *Masters.*

You are commanded of God " to give unto your servants that which is just and equal; knowing that ye also have a master in heaven — neither is there respect of persons with him." The religious instruction of your people will promote your own interests for time and eternity, and will confer on them blessings infinitely valuable, even the redemption of the soul, which is precious. Your responsibilities in the word and providence of God are very great. If you neglect them, a fearful account awaits you at the judgement seat of Christ ! Contribute, therefore, according to your ability, of your property, your influence and personal efforts, to this good work ; and do it speedily.

I would commend the work also to *Ministers of the Gospel.*

Our Divine Lord, " though he was rich, yet for our sakes he became poor, that we, through his poverty, might be made rich." He was annointed of God " to preach the Gospel to the poor," and through him, while on earth, " the poor have the Gospel preached to them." In this he has left us an example that we should follow his steps ; for " the disciple must not be above his Lord," Like the Apostles of old, we should " be forward to remember the poor." It is disgrace and iniquity when we forget them ! God is judge ! On the ministers of the Gospel the religious instruction of the Negroes in the United States depends, more than upon all the other classes and professions of society put together. It is *their work.* They are to promote it — by conversation, by preaching, and above all, by example, in *personal labors.* They have it in their power, by their piety and zeal and efforts, to advance and sustain this work, or by their impiety and lethargy, and absolute inactivity, to retard and break it down, throughout the length and breadth of the land. There has been neglect — shall it be said, a *criminal* neglect? I feel it. Others feel it. The whole country sees it. Can there be no reformation? Shall the ministers of Jesus Christ never be moved with compassion on the multitudes who faint and are scattered abroad as sheep having no shepherd? Shall their hearts' desire and prayer to God never be that this people may be saved? Shall they never be attracted and drawn towards this people by their very spiritual destitution and miseries, and spend and be spent for them, constrained by the love of Christ, towards their own souls? Alas! it is the darkest feature in all this dark scene that the ministers of the Gospel, taken as a body, feel no more and do no more for the salvation of the Negroes in the United States! Let no one suppose that we wish the church thrown into a state of excitement on the subject; and the good that has been done, and now is doing, and the many able and efficient minis ters in this field to be overlooked and buried in oblivion. Let no one suppose that we wish this work to be repre- sented and urged before the country, *as the great work to be done,* to which all other works of benevolence are to contribute, and in comparison with which they are nothing worth. Let no one suppose that we desire ministers to form great societies and distribute agents

over the land, to arouse their brethren to their duty.
Far, very far from any thing of this kind are our views
of propriety and our impressions of duty. On the
contrary, there are organizations and associations enough
in existence through which every thing can be done,
necessary to be done by them in the religious instruction
of the Negroes. What is required is that every minister
do his own duty in his own sphere of ministerial action ;
let him begin *with himself first*, and then if opportunity
offers, let him seek to influence others, in some of the
ways already pointed out.

I would commend the work also to the *Members of
the Church of Christ.*

You are expected to be forward to every good word
and work. Here is an abundant opportunity for doing
good opened before you. Enter into it for the improvement of your own graces, as well as for the salvation of
souls. All your zeal for missions may find ample scope
for exercise here. Be forward to superintend schools,
to take classes, to act on committees of instruction, and
be not weary in well doing, for in due season you shall
reap if you faint not.

I would commend the work also to *every Lover of his
Country.*

The moral and religious improvement of *two millions
eight hundred thousand persons*, must be identified with
our individual peace and happiness, and with our national
prosperity and honor. "Righteousness exalteth a nation,
but sin is a reproach to any people."